SICILY

MELISSA MULLER

SICILY

the cookbook

RECIPES ROOTED in TRADITIONS

Photography by Sara Remington

RIZZOLI
NEW YORK

New York · Paris · London · Milan

*This book is dedicated to my grandmother
Francesca Fasulo; to my family, in honor of their
individual contributions helping me bring to
fruition this testament to my love of Sicily;
and above all, to Jesus.*

First published in the United States of America in 2017
by Rizzoli International Publications, Inc.
300 Park Avenue South
New York, NY 10010
www.rizzoliusa.com

© 2017 by Melissa Muller

All photography © 2017 by Sara Remington except on
pages 9, 10, 17, 30, 75, 86, 152, 212, 230, and 292 © 2017 by
Alfio Garozzo; page 35 © by Realy Easy Star/Salvatore Pipia/
Alamy Stock Photo; page 109 © by Chuck Haney/Design
Pics Inc/Alamy Stock Photo; and page 279 © 2017
by Fabio Sireci

Illustrations on pages 6 and 89 by Veronika Goba

Designed by Toni Tajima

2017 2018 2019 2020 / 10 9 8 7 6 5 4 3 2 1

Distributed in the U.S. trade by Random House, New York

Printed in Italy

ISBN-13: 978-0-8478-4865-2

Library of Congress Catalog Control Number: 2016952696

CONTENTS

SICILIA

Ustica

Stromboli

Filicudi · Panarea
Alicudi · Salina
· Lipari
AEOLIAN
ISLANDS · Vulcano

TYRRHENIAN SEA

Milazzo
San Vito Lo Capo   Terrasini   Monte Pellegrino   Capo D'Orlando Tindari   Messina
EGADI   Palermo   · Mirto
ISLANDS   Levanzo Erice   Riserva dello   Bagheria   Cefalù   Caprileone
Marettimo   Trapani   Zingaro   Piana degli Albanesi   Nebrodi Mountains   Le Gole dell'Alcantara   Taormina
    Favignana   Castelbuono   Linguaglossa
    Mozia   Salemi   Polizzi   Bronte
            Generosa
    Marsala   Madonie Mountains   Mt. Etna
        Valledolmo   Aci Trezza
Mazara   Monti Sicani   Feudo Montoni   Catania
del Vallo   Cammarata   Leonforte
    · Cattabellotta   Mussomeli   Enna
    Sant'Anna
    Sciacca   Caltanissetta
                        Piazza Armerina   IONIAN SEA
                Delia   Caltagirone
                Agrigento
MEDITERRANEAN SEA   Licata   Hyblean Mountains   Siracusa
                                        Ortigia
    Linosa   Noto
                Lampedusa   Ragusa
Pantelleria   Modica

N

ROOTED IN SICILY

AN IMMENSE AND UNIQUE TERRITORY, both spatially and culturally, where multiple ethnic traditions have amalgamated—Sicily requires meditation, time, and patience to understand. My own perception of the island is in continual flux, incessantly transforming into a new set of images and sensations.

I covet the reality of Sicily that is hidden in the core of the island, far from the tourist attractions and ancient ruins. My pathway to this appreciation of the country necessitated years of experiencing the place on many levels, not only with my own senses and heart, but with those of my grandmother Francesca. It was January of 1936 when my grandmother, then a thirteen-year-old, departed from Sicily to emigrate to America. Despite her move, Sicily never left her, remaining forever etched in the repository of her mind.

For Francesca, Sicily remained the sulfur-water fountain in her town, the water of which she used to clean her clothes and body, to boil pasta, and to quench her thirst. For her, it remained the sweetest water imaginable. Sicily was the piece of fruit that her grandfather would hide in his pocket every day upon return from his farm. Francesca would yell out in excitement, "*Nonno*, what did you bring me today?" He would open his eyes wide as he brought his stiff pointer finger up to his lips, for the fruit was a special treat only for her.

Sicily was the goat that nourished her with milk as a baby when her mother was indisposed. Sicily was the altar she decorated with ornate bread, spring flowers, and hand-crocheted tablecloths on Saint Joseph's Day. Sicily was the heat that scorched her arms as she stirred tomatoes in a gigantic copper cauldron placed over a wood fire in August. Sicily was the hand-rolled pasta, *busi*, which she learned to craft before she was old enough to go to school. My grandmother's Sicily was the inheritance she left me, the stones that I built my life upon, the most precious gift I ever received.

I first cultivated my love for the island in my youth, during the summers I spent in her village, Sant'Anna, a small mountain town of five hundred people. My first visit took place in 1980, just months after my second birthday. Year after year, as soon as summer recess began, my family and I returned to the village. During the school year, I used to count down the days, from September until June, longing to arrive in Sicily, feeling as if the land pulled me back, like a gravitational force, absorbing me into its mysterious essence.

During these wondrous summers, I felt liberated from the confinements of American city life. I breezed around the village, teaching friends how to do cartwheels and sitting on the steps of the piazza watching other children kick soccer balls into the wall of the church. The sound of their happiness was radiant. Their embraces were sincere.

When the southern *scirocco* winds arrived in the town, the sweet scent of jasmine flowers intermingled with those of sugar emanating from the pastry shop and with the scent of bread baking in wood-burning ovens of the *panificio*. Well-being dwelled inside me, and I felt a sense of belonging. This was the Sicily of my childhood, a place that held the key to my innocent youthful bliss.

When summers came to an end, I used to hide my passport from my parents, dreading our inevitable departure. My heart longed to live year-round in Sicily. When our flight took off from Palermo's airport, I used to stare out the window until I couldn't see even a small trace of the land beneath me. I remember feeling like a tree, whose roots where being yanked with force out of the soil.

Back in New York, as I grew older I discovered the key to keeping Sicily alive throughout the year. I began to cook, filling our home with the bold aromas of

ingredients such as anchovies, oregano, and eggplants. From the flavors and scents that exuded from the kitchen, my sensory memories were stimulated and I re-experienced Sicily in a personal way, albeit from four thousand miles away.

But despite my summers in Sant'Anna, I knew little about Sicily as a whole, neither about its history nor about the cultural and culinary nuances that characterize each area of the island. As a young adult, Sicily became my focus of study, first as a culinary student and, later, at the university. This is when I began to explore the interconnectedness between the past and the present, and the roots of today's traditional cuisine.

During those years of my life, I often thought about the centuries-old olive tree that stands tall on the outskirts of Sant'Anna. I wondered how many tongues it had heard spoken? How many stories would it have to tell of times bygone? Just as Sicily is home to a mosaic of architectural remains from the past, combining Greek temples and Roman mosaics with medieval Jewish bathhouses, Norman palaces, and ornate late-Baroque-era cathedrals, Sicilian cuisine is a patchwork of different cultures and time periods. Separated from mainland Italy by the Strait of Messina, Sicily is the largest island in the Mediterranean. Because of its strategic position between North Africa and Europe, and its highly fertile soil, it has long attracted visitors, from invaders to traders. Over time, Sicilians have embraced several food traditions brought to their shores, melding techniques, recipes, and ingredients from other ethnic groups with the pre-existing cuisine.

I developed a strong desire to bring a broader understanding of this cuisine's complexities to America. When I opened my Sicilian restaurant in Manhattan, I avoided the typical Italian-American "red sauce" dishes that New Yorkers had assumed to be Sicilian. Instead I offered dishes prepared with iconic Sicilian ingredients, from sardines to sea urchin, from goat meat to sheep's milk ricotta. That was the moment when Sicily became the subject of my professional realm.

I shared my love of Sicily with customers, telling them stories about the island. In doing so, I realized that the time had come for me to delve deeper, to learn even more about the cuisine firsthand. For five years, I ventured every few months from New York City to Sicily to fulfill this self-imposed assignment, discovering along the way that the island is host to *multiple* Sicilian cuisines, landscapes, dialects, and traditions. Every village seemed to have dishes that cannot be found anywhere else.

What's more, over the last twenty years, a new Sicilian cuisine has emerged, driven by skilled chefs around the island. As elsewhere in Italy, this young generation of chefs is revisiting old classics to create new versions. Some also invent their own unique dishes using Sicilian flavors combined with international techniques. Due to an alliance between chefs and the Slow Food organization (which aims to preserve traditional foodways), this new crop of Sicilian restaurants often relies on rare heirloom ingredients that are making a resurgence on the island. Sub-regional culinary variations are less noticeable in the realm of such restaurants, unlike in home kitchens.

As I gathered recipes and stories for this project, I fell in love with Sicily all over again, exploring its many facets and tasting new dishes and traditional foods each step of the way. I visited forests hosting a rare breed of black pig, an apiary run by a ninety-year-old beekeeper, the craters of Mount Etna, the stands

of Palermo's street food vendors, animal farms built inside the enclaves of rock mountains, Michelin-starred restaurants, prickly pear farms, and more. I encountered hundreds of dedicated individuals passionate about their crafts: winemakers, home cooks, bakers, cheesemakers, shepherds, farmers, and fishermen, in all corners of the island.

Whenever I thought that I had come to know Sicily, the next day new perfumes, new experiences, new territories, and new recipes presented themselves to me, because in Sicily, nothing is stagnant, and nothing is as it appears to the untrained eye. I came to the conclusion that I could continue my travels for decades and never know all of the nuances of the island's culinary landscape.

Toward the end of my last research trip for this book, in the spring of 2015, as I sat under an olive tree on a hillside in the interior of Sicily, staring out at the vineyards of Feudo Montoni's fourteenth-century

At Feudo Montoni, organic is not only about avoiding pesticides and chemicals, but rather encompasses an entire philosophy of life. Owner Fabio Sireci doesn't believe that we can recuperate the damages we've done to the Earth or stop the mechanism that humans have created in order to live and to do so in comfort, but at least we shouldn't contribute to its demise.

winery, I became overwhelmed with gloom. What would I do now that the book research was complete? How could I satisfy my heart's desire to return on a regular basis to Sicily? I yearned to experience Sicily day after day, not for mere two-week intervals. I desired to live in the midst of nature, to get my hands in the Sicilian earth, and to be more than a spectator. My soul needed that inner peace that I felt only in Sicily, which I couldn't connect to in Manhattan. The perfume of my Sicilian kitchen no longer satisfied my craving.

To my surprise, that inner torment led to the realization of my childhood dream of never having to leave Sicily. This book transformed into the catalyst for an unplanned, life-altering move, bringing me to the next chapter in my relationship with the island. Not even a half a year later, I left behind two successful restaurants and a so-called comfortable modern life in New York City, to create a new home base in both Palermo and in rural Sicily.

Upon arrival in Sicily, one of my first stops was to return to the Feudo Montoni winery, which was in the middle of the *vendemmia*, harvesting grapes. I lent a hand, helping in any way possible, destemming grapes arriving from the fields, and cleaning the floor of the *cantina*, while relishing the musty smell of the fermenting grape juice I was inhaling.

Feudo Montoni is a certified organic winery and farm owned by a third-generation winemaker, Fabio Sireci, whose love of Sicily, and respect for nature, exudes from his every pore. His winery was founded in 1469 A.D. by a noble Aragonese family. In the late 1800s, the history of the winery became intertwined with Fabio's family when his grandfather, Rosario, purchased the property, recognizing the unique microclimate of the land. In the heart of Sicily, where the provinces of Agrigento, Palermo, and Caltanissetta collide, his winery and farm consists of about seventy-five acres of vines as well as fruit tree groves and fields of wheat, beans, and olive trees.

From then on, I traveled from Palermo to the farm every weekend to take part in the wine tastings, but also found myself actively partaking in other agricultural duties, from picking olives to pruning fruit trees. I started observing the wild plants and flowers, and began to experiment in the kitchen with the plants I learned were edible. Soon after, I started planting seeds, and in addition to the vegetables that emerged from the land, my own life purpose began to sprout.

These days most of my time is spent participating in the daily country life of Sicily, bringing me full circle, back to the old-fashioned way my grandmother once lived. My encounters with the other world I once inhabited come in the form of leading guests on rural journeys into the core of Sicily, far from the typical tourist destinations, to a place where travelers can create their own bonds with the land. I offer farm-to-table experiences that last from one to five days, guiding guests on a journey into the organic fields, into the vineyards, into the fruit tree grove and into the bountiful vegetable gardens, before heading to the kitchen, where I intertwine history, agricultural culture, and food.

Today I view Sicily as the rhapsody created by the gushing wind as it weaves its way through the leaves of eucalyptus trees, emulating the sound of waves; as the clumps of oval-shaped green fava bean leaves as they surface from fields of cold rock-hard chocolate-colored earth; as the scent of smoke emanating from stacks of pruned olive branches, as they burn in the countryside; as the cluster of delicate bright-yellow flowers that emerge from wild broccoli plants all winter long, lining the edges of pathways and vineyards; as the fragrance of garlic, herbs, and onion that permeates my hands everyday; as the flock of sheep that graze on a carpet of fuchsia honeysuckle flowers, which emerge almost magically after spring rains; as the sweat that rolls under my straw hat when picking tomatoes, peppers, and eggplants under the heat of the August sun; as the sensation of eating eggs from my chickens, who in turn consume the vegetable scraps from my kitchen; of waking up to the sound of my rooster crowing.

I used to gaze at the Sicilian landscape and see what was obvious to the eye. Living here, I'm now seeing the fine details that were unapparent to me as a kid or during my whirlwind research trips as an adult. As I watch how the landscape transforms day after day, I'm learning about nature and its cycles, which ultimately teach me more about myself and my heritage. I used to enjoy Sicilian summers, but now I love every moment of the year for its uniqueness. More than just a physical move, my transfer from New York has allowed me to live from my heart. My roots are finally planted in the soil where they always desired to be, and as they grow deeper, I am certain that Sicily will continue to redefine itself and transform in ways still unknown to me.

AUTHENTICITY AND
THE IMPRINT OF THE FAMILY

This book contains a wide range of recipes but does not encompass the entirety of Sicilian cuisine, which is so vast it would take multiple lifetimes to catalog. My intention is to paint a picture of the types of food eaten in Sicily today and to introduce you to the culinary traditions, which I hope you also will be inspired to discover in person.

With the exception of a few dishes that are creations shared by chefs on the island, the recipes here were given to me by home cooks. From province to province, from town to town, and from family to family, the same dish is made in different styles. Take something as simple as tomato sauce, for example. So many variations exist and there is no one recipe. Which version is the most authentic? As my dear elderly aunt (and culinary mentor) Zia Franca puts it: "**Ogni ricetta ha l'impronta della famiglia**," or "**Every recipe contains the imprint of the family**." This vast range in the execution of so-called "traditional dishes" throughout Sicily cannot be underscored enough.

I have yet to meet a home cook on the island who can provide specific quantities of ingredients or exact cooking temperatures and times of these old family recipes. Such details are factors that need to be felt with the senses, with a sort of culinary intuition. Children grow up observing their elders in the kitchen and come to learn family recipes by osmosis. Although I provide measurements and directions, I urge you to cook the dishes in the book with the freedom to add your *own* family touches, and most importantly to impart your *own* culinary intuition. Sicilian food needs to be felt with all the senses: It's not a science, but an act of pure love, transmitted from the cook to the family.

MY ANCESTRAL VILLAGE, SANT'ANNA OF CALTABELLOTTA

My grandmother Francesca was born in a small village, Sant'Anna, which is part of the municipality of a larger town, Caltabellotta, situated on the southwestern corner of the island, in the province of Agrigento. Sant'Anna was founded in 1622. The mountainous rural territory where it is nestled has traces back to prehistoric times. A natural spring fountain (*bevatoio*) situated in front of a monastery, Santa Maria di Montevergine, was the only source of water in the village when my grandmother was a child. The spout carried from a mountaintop spring an endless stream of water, rich in sulphur, for the townspeople to use for drinking, cooking, and for bathing. A round receptacle in front of the fountain was also filled for animals. Francesca relished the taste of the water. Every time she passed the fountain, she would tilt her little head to the left and take a drink of its mineral-rich water.

On the day she emigrated to America in January of 1936, with her relatives and townspeople at her side, Francesca and her mother walked down the cobblestone roads of Sant'Anna and stopped to sip the sweet water one last time before proceeding by donkey to a nearby village where they boarded a train to Palermo.

As their journey unfolded, they passed their cousin the shepherd with his flock of sheep, and then mountain necropoli built thousands of years ago by the area's indigenous Sicans. Soon they came across Francesca's grandfather's farmland, which was filled with endless rows of olive trees and thin green grass sprouting from the limestone earth as that year's grain crop had been seeded a few weeks prior.

This farm area was located in Contrada Troccoli, which takes its name from the famed Greek settlement, Triokala, which in turn had been built on the ruins of a Sicanian stronghold from the Bronze Age. The *trio* in *Triokala* refers to the spots' three gifts of nature: its high-peaked cliff, providing the perfect defense for a fortress, the abundance of spring water, and its fertile lands. The Greeks used the land as a major urban and rural center, producing olive oil and honey as well as making wine in underground amphorae. During the first Punic war, the town was destroyed by the Romans but its inhabitants re-founded Trokalis (the New Triokala) in the area that is now Contrada Troccoli. When ancient Trokalis finally fell to the Romans in 99 B.C., it embarked on a long history that transformed the land into a cultural crossroads.

In the ninth century, Sicily was conquered by the Aghliabids, a Muslim dynasty that ruled part of North Africa. They gave the mountain where Sant'Anna is nestled its present-day name, Caltabellotta, from the Arabic *Qalat-al-Ballut*, meaning fortress among the oak trees. In the subsequent ages, Sicily would continue to be fought over, sacked, and dominated by other groups who believed it to be the ideal location for life and trade in the Mediterranean Sea. And as each invader would introduce new crops, Sicilian cuisine expanded and became more and more nuanced.

As Francesca rode her donkey to the train stop, she was unaware that the landscape in front of her was like a patchwork quilt, representing the fruits of centuries of inhabitants. She knew not of the Muslim inhabitants who lived side by side with the Greek Byzantines and the Jewish Sicilians. She knew only that her land was Sicily, which had been unified with Italy shortly before her grandparents were born.

When leaving, Francesca had no way of knowing that it would be forty years before she would return, nor that she would never touch the hands of her grandparents again. That day, as she put her lips to the running water, she said a prayer in her head, asking Jesus and Saint Michael to bless her journey. Decades later, just before she passed away, Grandma told me that if she had known that water so sweet couldn't be found elsewhere, she never would have left. Today, I can't help but think of her life, her sacrifices as an immigrant in a new land, and her deep-rooted love of Sicily every time I walk pass Sant'Anna's fountain.

Sicilian Winemaking Throughout the Ages

Bonu vino fa bonu sangu.
GOOD WINE MAKES GOOD BLOOD.

At my cousin Maria's house in Sant'Anna, there was always a bottle of homemade wine on the table, and I grew up drinking it with lunch, splashing a drop in a glass of sparkling water or Sprite. That wine, produced every year by her husband, Accursio, is very high in alcohol content and tends to be oxidized, but I find comfort in its perfume and taste, perhaps because of the childhood memories that it invokes. Many agricultural families in Sicily produce wine for their personal home consumption. Wine is elemental here, with a long and rich history.

ANCIENT ROOTS

With an ideal climate for winemaking, grapes have been cultivated in Sicily for millennia. Rainfall on the island is predominantly limited to the winter months. Sunlight and intense heat produce concentrated grapes that produce high-quality wines. Over time, the success of the commercial industry has fluctuated, depending on who ruled the island. Homer tells us that wild grape vines existed in prehistoric times, although the Greeks and Carthaginian settlers introduced wine production in the eighth century B.C.—and archaeological discoveries have supported these claims. Wine played a major role in the communal Greek society, such as during their ritual *symposium*, where cultural events and pleasures were intertwined with drunken revelry. Wine—both young and aged—not only was the centerpiece at such events, but became a recurring theme in the poetry of the time.

Under Roman rule, prized wine continued to be produced. Among the most famous Sicilian wines known in the Empire were the sweet Malvasia from the Aeolian Islands and the Mamertino from Messina, both of which are still produced today. In the early centuries of Christianity, most vineyards came under the control of the Church, which kept the winemaking tradition alive. With the Barbarian invasions, production slowed down, only to resurge again with renewed vigor during Byzantine rule in the sixth century, spurred by winemaking innovation and improvements.

During the Muslim period, there is evidence that winemaking continued, although to a lesser degree than before since alcohol consumption was forbidden by Islam. With the Normans came a revitalized winemaking industry, but two centuries later excessive taxation forced Sicilians to halt planting vines. Throughout the subsequent centuries, wine production continued to be subject to similar vast transformations. At times the industry flourished, at times it was confined to small territories.

UPS AND DOWNS

The Sicilian wine industry of today is a result of a combination of factors, including local ambition, the recognition of Sicily's ideal climate, Northern Italian influence, European wine laws, and the adoption of international winemaking techniques.

During the 19th century, the roots of today's quality wine renaissance took hold when the Duke of Salaparuta began bottling delicate wines in Bagheria, which were imported to the United States. Over the next few decades, quality winemaking was on the rise, and by 1880, the island possessed its highest ever amount acreage of vineyards. The booming industry, however, was tragically interrupted when most of the island's grape plants were destroyed by a microscopic louse known as *phylloxera*.

Until the mid-twentieth century, most vines were not replanted and vineyards were abandoned. Sicily had lost a major portion of its agricultural labor due to emigration abroad, and World War I suppressed the market for wine. During the Fascist period between the two World Wars, vineyards began to be replanted.

In post–World War II Sicily, wealthy landowners controlled vast estates of land that were farmed by local farmers. Masses emigrated to Northern Italy in search of more lucrative work, causing Sicily to lose manpower. When Italy was declared a republic, those peasants who remained gained plots of land, thanks to agrarian reforms that divided estates into smaller plots. Such farms were not large enough for individual families to produce their own products, and thus the Italian government funded the establishment of cooperatives.

Over the next few decades, trade agreements in the European Community continually allowed for the free flow of wine. The co-ops revived Sicily's wine industry, making it one of the largest bulk wine producers in Europe, where quantity, rather than quality, was of utmost importance. They produced cheap grape must and bulk wine, called *vino da taglio*, which was used as a filler in French and Northern Italian wines.

Up until this point, vines in Sicily were planted as free-standing bush trees—known as *alberello*—and planted in the midst of other crops. Such vines are not trained on trellises but rather pruned low to the ground. Grapes grown in this style tend to develop more intensity and make concentrated wines with high alcohol contents for two reasons: their yield is restricted and they absorb heat from the ground.

New vines were typically planted in trellised rows to allow for mechanical harvesting and irrigation. Such mechanization was often subsidized by European Union programs, and helped lower the costs of winemaking by reducing the need for manual labor. Alongside the cooperatives, a few Sicilian aristocratic families began to produce quality wine.

A RENAISSANCE BEGINS

By the 1980s, a turning point in Sicilian winemaking had occurred. The co-op structure began to collapse, as government subsidies dematerialized. A handful of Sicilian winemaking families seized the opportunity to begin producing high-quality wine. Such ambition, and belief in the richness of Sicily's fertile soil and climate, led to a true wine renaissance. By the nineties, new wineries—both family and corporately owned estates—were founded all over the island, with an emphasis on quality, rather than quantity.

In addition to large Sicilian family-owned estates, smaller family-operated niche wineries exist. Cooperatives still bottle wine as well. In addition,

individual non-Sicilian wine producers who believe in the potential for making great wines on the island have claimed their own stake here. Northern Italian wine conglomerates as well have invested in the island.

With their focus on quality, winemakers are looking at modern international winemaking techniques as well as to the past for inspiration. Several producers around the island have adopted the old technique of growing *alberello* style vines, which are more labor-intensive but produce superior juice. Indigenous grape varietals have also gained popularity. At the same time, grape quality is being improved by clonal selection. Cutting-edge grape harvesting, fermentation, and maturation techniques are used now. The amalgamation of old and new techniques is proving extremely successful, and holds promise for the future of winemaking in Sicily.

The popularity of Sicilian wines produced today mirrors the industry's ancient fame. Both then and now, the climate and splendor of Sicily's terroir are recognized and celebrated. Homer attested to its natural fertility in the *Odyssey*, and despite all the foreign domination, little has changed when it comes to the richness of the Sicilian earth.

GRAPE VARIETALS AND DENOMINATIONS

International varietals are popular in Sicily. Beginning in the 1980s, Sicily's Regional Institute for Vine and Wine studied the potential of international varietals, most importantly Chardonnay, Syrah, Cabernet Sauvignon, and Merlot. Such varietals were adopted by Sicilian wineries, in an effort to produce wines that could be marketed internationally and subsequently establish the island as a place where quality wines could be made. Other than Cabernet Sauvignon, which was planted once in Sicily in the nineteenth century, this was the first time international varietals were tested on Sicilian soil. (For more information I highly recommend the book *World of Sicilian Wine* by Bill Nesto and Frances Di Savino.)

For the last decade, interest in native Sicilian varietals, especially some that were nearing extinction, has overshadowed the trend of producing international varietals on the island. The following is a list of indigenous Sicilian grape varietals.

Carricante	Carricante has been cultivated for centuries on Mount Etna. The grape is known for its high acidity, which gives it long aging potential. The volcanic soil of Mount Etna provides strong mineral characteristics in wines produced with this grape.
Catarratto	Catarratto is the second most planted single variety in all of the Italian peninsula and is one of the grapes used in the production of Marsala. The high-yielding grapes make wines with an elevated acidity which positively influence the fresh aromatics and taste. On the nose, Catarratto is often characterized by white flowers. On the palate, it is sapid and dry.
Grillo	Most commonly cultivated on the western side of Sicily, Grillo has historically been the quintessential grape used in Marsala, but recently the grape has been transformed into sapid single-varietal and blended dry white wines. Its origins are uncertain, but some historians believe it was introduced into the island of Sicily from Puglia. It is genetically related to the Moscato grape and therefore is high in aromatics. In Sicilian, it is pronounced as *riddu*.
Inzolia (also known as Insolia or Ansonica)	A varietal confined mainly to Sicily although it is also found in Tuscany under the synonym Ansonica. Together with Grillo and Catarratto, Inzolia is part of the blend that goes into both sweet and dry versions of Marsala. Increasingly found as a table wine with floral notes and low acidity, Inzolia possesses undertones of bitter almonds; citrus fruits and fresh herbs are common. However, when grown at high altitudes, it possesses a low pH and high acidity.
Grecanico	Grecanico is similar in style (but not genetically) to a Sauvignon Blanc. Most often blended with other white grapes, this varietal has medium acidity and notes of crisp apple.
Malvasia	Malvasia is a group of wine grape varietals found in the Mediterranean lands. In Sicily, it is predominantly used to produce a sweet dessert wine on the Aeolian Islands, but is also found in the form of a dry white wine, with highly floral overtones on the nose.
Zibibbo (Moscato d'Alessandria)	Predominantly used to produce Moscato and Passito in Pantelleria. Donnafugata produces a dry white wine with Zibibbo. The name *Zibibbo* comes from the Arabic word for grape, *zibib*. The skin is thick and resilient. Therefore is dries well in the sun. The dessert wines are intense, with strong floral aromas and rich flavors of warm spices, citrus rind, and dried fruits.
Moscato Bianco	This muscat variety has been produced in the southeast corner of Sicily for several centuries. Naturally sweet, the grapes produce a wine rich in aromas of ripe stone fruit and honeysuckle. Unlike Zibibbo, the skins of this muscat are thin and do not dry well when exposed to the sun. Recently, certain producers have experimented by making Moscato Bianco into an orange wine, by fermenting the skins along with the juice of the grapes.
Nero d'Avola	Nero d'Avola is Sicily's most popular red grape and its growth on the island has been documented for centuries. Until the 1980s, commercial use of Nero d'Avola was dedicated almost exclusively to fortifying weaker reds in France and Northern Italy. It was also blended in Sicily with other varieties. In the past, Nero d'Avola, like other Sicilian reds, was often syrupy, as the high sugar content in the grapes baked under the Sicilian sun, making a wine with an alcohol content reaching 18%. In the 1980s the first 100% Nero d'Avola wines were bottled in Sicily. The aromas and flavors of this grape are primarily of maraschino cherry and blackberry with spicy notes. When grown at higher altitudes, Nero d'Avola tends to have more mineral personality, and a more pronounced acidity. Nero d'Avola can be aged in stainless steel vats and released young, but also has the potential for long aging and refining. Terroir and microclimate, which range significantly around Sicily, are the main determining factors of the wine's ultimate sensory profile.

Frappato	This varietal most likely has its origins in the Ragusa province of Sicily, where its cultivation has been recorded over two hundred years ago. Frappato produced in its pure form presents as a light, refreshing wine, with floral and spicy notes, a slight bitterness, a low tannin content, and notable acidity. It does not age well. Frappato is commonly blended with Nero d'Avola to produce Cerasuolo di Vittoria, Sicily's only DOCG. Nero d'Avola gives Cerasuolo its body and richness (appropriately enough, the word means "cherry-like"), while Frappato adds aromatics and acidity to the final blend. Generally, a Cerasuolo di Vittoria expresses ripe fruit, medium body on the palate, and a finish with moderate tannins and lively acidity. For years, while Cerasuolo was a DOC wine, the mix was almost always 60% Nero d'Avola and 40% Frappato. As of the 2005 vintage, the wine was recognized with DOCG status, a classification that allows more blending freedom for winemakers. Cerasuolo di Vittoria can be aged in various ways. Some producers use large oak casks, while others prefer oak barriques, small barrels, or even vessels made from terra cotta that are modeled after the same pots used by the Greeks more than two thousand years ago.
Perricone	Perricone is a less-cultivated red grape, also known as Guarnaccia, Pignatello, or Tuccarino, depending upon the area. Not very popular on an individual basis, this slightly bitter wine has strong tannins and is an important contributor to several DOC varietals from the western part of the island. It is highly resistant to disease and mildew, thus being known as the grape of the *contadini* or farmers. However, with its thick skin, large pit, and tendency to make a wine heavy in unripe tannin, it is challenging to work with in the cantina.
Nerello Mascalese	Pleasantly earthy and flowery, with hints of tobacco and notable tannin content, the Nerello Mascalese produces an elegant wine with much complexity. A major component of Etna Rosso DOC, the Nerello Mascalese lends itself well as an addition to aged varietals, adding a spicy, lively element. Nerello Mascalese grows throughout the island and is not exclusive to Mount Etna. Here at Feudo Montoni, it is made into a rosato wine, rich in notes of wild strawberries.
Nerello Cappuccio	Also known as Nerello Mantellato, this varietal is native to the Etna region. It produces a floral, light- to medium-bodied red wine with a delicate fruitiness. Most often blended with the more acidic and bold Nerello Mascalese to produce Etna DOC, a few producers on Mount Etna, spearheaded by Benanti, are now producing a single-varietal Nerello Cappuccio. Such wines are best consumed up to five years after bottling. The vines that grow on Mount Etna are rooted in soil of volcanic origin, which is rich in minerals, such as basalt, silica, magnesium, and iron, among other elements contained in the lava. Depending on the altitude of a vineyard, the volcanic soil ranges from brown and rocky to sandy and dark black.
Nocera	Nocera is a lesser known varietal that is blended in the production of Faro DOC and Mamertino DOC. In small quantities it is also cultivated in the provinces of Catania, Ragusa, and Siracusa. On the hills overlooking the Straight of Messina, Faro has been produced since antiquity. In addition to Nerello Mascalese, Faro is traditionally blended with Nerello Cappuccio and Nocera.
Corinto Nero	The Corinto Nero vine is believed to have arrived in Sicily from Greece, perhaps from Corinth as suggested by its name. Corinth was the source of many grape varieties in the Middle Ages, and gave its name to the dried "currant" we know today. The varietal is also known in Lipari as Passolina. Today it is mainly cultivated in the Aeolian Archipelago, mostly on the island of Salina. Typically the grapes are dried after harvest and added in small quantities to the sweet Malvasia. However, single varietals are commonly produced on Salina, and possess intense aromas, medium body, and a roundness.
Minnella Bianca, Albanello, Damaschino	Other very rare Sicilian varietals

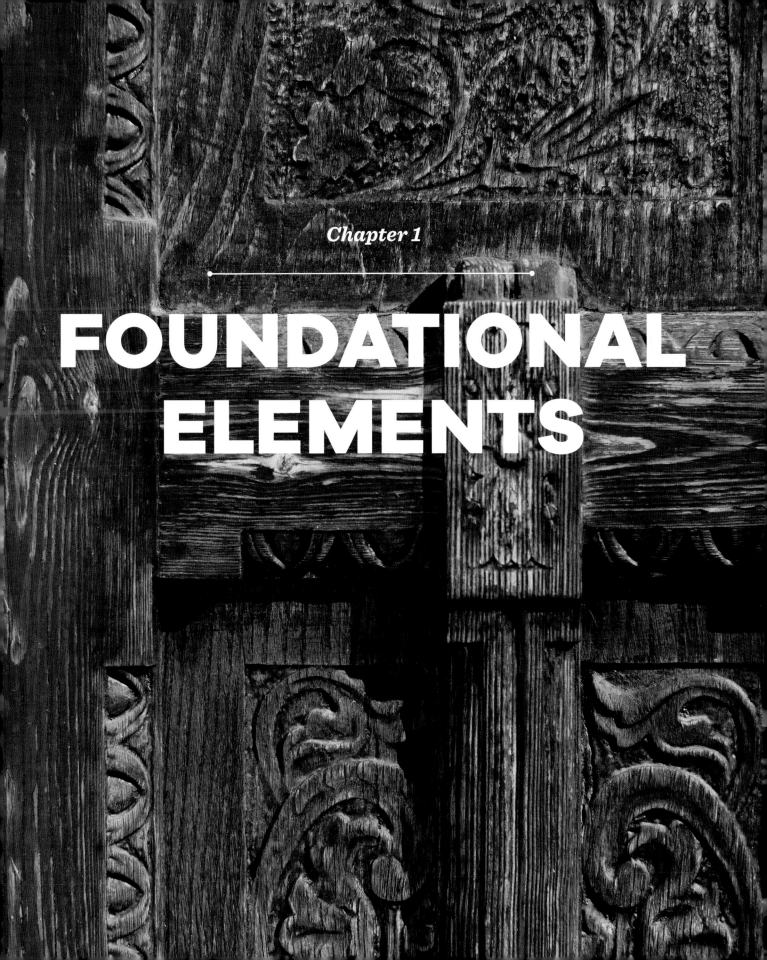

Chapter 1

FOUNDATIONAL ELEMENTS

SICILIAN CUISINE is composed of countless ingredients, most of which are available only seasonally. However, there are certain ingredients traditionally found year round in any Sicilian kitchen. I explain these in detail in this chapter so that you might have a greater understanding of their roles in the other dishes later in this book. I also give some essential basic recipes that are used over and over again in Sicilian cuisine.

Oli ed Ingredienti Acidi

The main fats used in traditional Sicilian cooking are olive oil and lard. The former is used for frying, sautéing, and as a condiment. The latter is used in baking and also for frying. Nowadays, vegetable oil has gained popularity as a fat for frying, but it is untraditional. Butter can be found in the Sicilian kitchen, but is more often used as a breakfast spread for toast. However, some pastry shops no longer use lard and have replaced it with butter. As in most cuisines, acidic ingredients like vinegar and wine play a complementary role to cooking fats, but in Sicily they are employed in unique ways.

LARD {*Strutto*} SAIMA

Lard is a common fat used in cooking, especially in savory and sweet doughs. It is also used often for frying. In pastries and bread, it produces a light, flaky crust. Produced from pork fat, lard can be purchased at a butcher shop or your local farmers' market. Ask for leaf lard, which has minimal pork flavor and is ideal for use in baking. This white mass of fat breaks down when melted in a stockpot over very low heat and is stored in jars; it looks similar to vegetable shortening. For those who avoid pork, or are looking for an alternative ingredient lower in saturated fats, butter (for baking) or vegetable oil (for frying) can be substituted in equal quantities.

OLIVE OIL {*Olio di Oliva*} OGGHIU R'ALÍVA

The different grades of olive oil—extra virgin, virgin, and pure—are categorized depending on the amount of acidity, or oleic acid, in the oil. Extra-virgin olive oil is made by the first cold press of high-quality olives and contains an acidity level of less than 0.8 percent. Cold pressing is a natural, heat-free extraction method, which retains the flavor and beneficial health properties of the olives. Like wine, the taste and aroma of olive oil vary based on the variety of olive, the pruning methods employed by the farmer, the type of soil the tree grew in, the harvest conditions, and the climate throughout the months leading up to the harvest.

Finer extra-virgin oils should be reserved for use as a condiment or as a finishing oil. For cooking, less expensive (and less flavorful) virgin and pure olive oils are best. For frying and deep-frying, high temperatures (those over 400°F) may burn the oil (depending on the level of acidity in the oil), causing a foul taste and destroying its nutritional qualities. Vegetable oil is best for deep-frying because it can hold up most dependably under higher temperatures. Nevertheless Sicilians value the taste of olive oil in fried foods. At Montoni, all of the olive oil is of the utmost quality, so for frying vegetables or meat, I use oil that is leftover from olive curing, which is rich with the flavors from the olives, garlic, and celery. When frying potatoes, for instance, I've discovered that this oil imparts a nuanced flavor.

VINEGAR {*Aceto*} ACITU

Vinegar can be found in the same colors as the wine it is made from: white, pink, and dark red. Cider or distilled vinegars are not found in Sicily. Some specialty producers on the island are producing balsamic-style aged vinegars. Vinegar is used to dress lettuce or potato salads, to prepare syrupy sauces, and to marinate meat, but its most ubiquitous form is in a sweet-and-sour sauce known as *agrodolce*, a mixture of vinegar and honey or sugar.

LIQUID GOLD

Olive oil extraction techniques were first introduced to Sicily in the eighth century B.C. by the Greeks, who invented a stone mill and press known as *u trappitu*. They considered the olive tree to be sacred and harshly penalized anyone found guilty of damaging one. For centuries, as a Greek colony, Sicily produced olive oil in abundance. Diodorus Siculus, a first-century historian, wrote about the opulent olive groves of Akragas (present-day Agrigento). The city financed the construction of their temples by exporting olive oil, as well as grain and wine.

Throughout the following centuries, olive oil production fluctuated in quantity, depending on the rulers of the island. During the Roman era, the olive tree was an artistic symbol of prosperity. Production was at a peak and exportation increased. During Arab rule, olive groves were overshadowed by the introduction of other fruit-bearing plants. At that time, most olive oil was imported to Sicily from North Africa, but resurged in production during Norman rule.

During the Kingdom of the Two Sicilies, oil was exported around the Mediterranean not only for consumption, but to illuminate ceramic lamps. More recently, in postwar Sicily, the Italian government provided incentives to farmers to plant olive trees, which resulted in the uprooting of many other types of trees. Today, the region is a forerunner in Italian olive oil production, falling third after Puglia and Calabria.

Olive trees require little care (other than pruning) throughout the year and can last for centuries. Production of oil generally commences at the beginning of October and lasts until late November. When first picked, freshly pressed oil is very low in acidity, possessing a pleasant peppery tang. In dialect, we say that the new oil, raw and strong, *ti pizzica la vucca*—"stings the mouth." On the other hand, overripe olives produce an oil that is higher in acidity, somewhat bland, and lacking in the level of spicy intensity.

The olive harvest is a highly anticipated time in Sant'Anna and Caltabellotta as most residents grow olive trees, some for commercial use and others for home use. My cousin Accursio grows two types of olives for oil production. The first, Nocellara del Belice, is predominantly green when ready to pick and produces a delicately flavored table olive, but an intense and full-bodied oil. The second variety is Biancolilla, which is recognizable from its white-and-magenta-colored skin and which has spicy notes of tomato, fresh grass, artichoke, and almond. Unlike Nocellara, Biancolilla olives produce a low amount of oil from their flesh. For optimal flavor, structure, and yield, Accursio makes his extra-virgin olive oil from a mix of both olive varieties.

Many olive varieties are grown on the island, each with its own taste profiles. In the Hyblean mountains of the Val di Noto, the Tonda Iblea variety is predominant. Nocellara olives come in different varieties, depending on where they are grown. In the forest-filled mountains of the Val Demone, the rare and ancient Minuta olive trees produce olives with a delicate flavor and are noted for their highly nutritious properties.

During the harvest, most commercial farmers use electric rakes to shake the olives from the branches. On smaller farms, hand-picking is often preferred. Underneath the trees, nets catch the olives as they fall. Some leaves fall into the pile, but are later removed at the olive press. For optimal oil quality, olives need to be pressed within one day of being picked.

At the *frantoio* (olive press), olives pass through a few machines before exuding their oil. The process used to be done with actual stone presses, but today is done by machine. First, olives are stemmed to remove all leaves and tiny branches, then are washed with water. Next, they are transferred into a machine that purees the flesh into a brown-colored pulp. Finally, that pulp is transferred into a three-phase centrifuge, which spins the pulp, separating it into oil, water, and solids. The pits and skin that remain are used for fertilizer or are sent to another olive press to be made into pomace oil.

WINE { *Vino* } VINU

Wine adds acidity and flavor to dishes. Red wine is commonly used to prepare a ragù, or a sauce, and to marinate or braise meats, but can also be found as an ingredient in desserts. White wine is more commonly used with seafood.

CITRUS { *Agrumi* } AGRUMI

Juice and rind—from all varieties of citrus fruit—are used in both savory and sweet recipes. Citrus juice is used to add acidity, marinate seafood, and accentuate other flavors in a dish. Rind is used fresh, dried, and candied. Dried zest is most often used in custards and other desserts, but fresh zest is grated into numerous savory dishes, used to dress raw seafood, and made into granita, liqueurs, or marmalades. Candied orange and citron rinds are a staple ingredient in desserts.

In addition to enhancing the taste of food, oranges, mandarins, clementines, citrons, and blood oranges are enjoyed at the table, usually after a meal during winter months. For more detail about citrus varieties see page 290.

Aromi Siciliani

The following list delineates the most important ingredients used to flavor Sicilian food. These plants and flowers actually impart a unique fragrance, more than a taste, to the food. When asked how Sicilian food differs from other Italian cuisines, I usually give a long and complex answer about the multiple ethnic groups who conquered the island, and how each invader introduced new ingredients and preparations. But beyond the history of Sicily's cuisine, the difference lies mainly in the scents that can be categorized as Sicilian. When the following ingredients are combined in the traditional ways described throughout this book, they create a unique perfume, which carries a Sicilian signature.

The Sicilian climate is ideal for the proliferation of herbaceous plants, and thus the cuisine is rich in both wild and cultivated herbs. The former grow in old stone walls, on hills, and in mountainous areas around villages, while the latter are commonly grown on terraces and in courtyards, in close proximity to kitchens so they can be picked fresh as they are needed. If you have space and sunlight, it's simple to grow herbs for culinary use. If space is limited, contain each plant in a separate planter, especially mint, which spreads quickly.

In addition to the ingredients and aromas listed below, gardens often include lemon balm, aloe, lavender, and pink peppercorn trees, the leaves, berries, or flowers of which can be used in cooking, but are ornamental in Sicily. Rose bushes are also very common and their petals are sometimes used to prepare rose water essence, which can be added to custards.

ANISEED ｛ *Anice* ｝ ÁNASU

Aniseed is sweet and aromatic. In Sicily, it is used in ritual breads and biscotti, but rarely in other types of dishes. A famous anise-flavored nonalcoholic beverage called *acqua zammù* used to be sold in street stalls in Palermo.

BASIL ｛ *Basilico* ｝ BASILICÒ

Basil is one of Sicily's most important herbs, used to flavor tomato-based sauces and to prepare pestos. For best results, plant sweet basil, Genovese, or fine-leaved bush basil, which are easy to grow and exude an intense aroma.

BAY LAUREL LEAVES ｛ *Alloro* ｝ ADDAURU

Bay leaves are used whole to flavor marinades, soups, liquors and liqueurs, braised meats, liver, seafood, and certain sweet-and-sour dishes. They are typically placed between foods—such as sardines—when grilling on skewers. There are several varieties of bay leaves in international cuisines, but in Sicilian cooking, the *Laurus nobilis* variety is used. Unlike other herbs, bay leaves grow on trees, which can reach up to thirty feet in height. Fresh leaves are mild in flavor, but gain a strong aroma when dried. Use whole leaves when cooking and remove and discard them before serving.

Dried bay leaves are also kept on hand in the Sicilian kitchen as a popular home remedy for stomach discomfort. Five or 6 dried leaves are boiled in 2 cups water with a piece of lemon rind. When the water turns light green, the tisane is ready to drink.

CELERY LEAVES ｛ *Sedano* ｝ ACCIA

For flavoring sauces and sweet-and-sour preparations, such as caponata, wild celery leaves have been a staple ingredient in Sicilian recipes for millennia. In your garden, instead of the more common "stalk celery," plant green leaf celery, which has a more concentrated flavor and resembles the parsley plant.

CHILE PEPPER ｛ *Peperoncino* ｝ PÍPI ARDÉNTI

The most common variety of spicy pepper found in Sicily is the *Capsicum annuum*. Chile peppers can be found dried, preserved in oil, and fresh. They can be an ingredient in bean soups, tomato-based sauces, stuffings, cured meats, sausages, and fish stews. Dried peppers are sold whole or in flaked form. Whole dried chile peppers are placed in jars with olive oil to make a spicy condiment for pizza, boiled vegetables, and pasta.

CINNAMON ｛ *Cannella* ｝ CANNÉDDA

In medieval recipes, cinnamon was an indispensable ingredient in meat and seafood dishes. In Sicily today, the bark is most commonly used in powder form in pastries. A typical dessert is cinnamon gelatin, which is often topped with crushed pistachios. The spice is also used to make a sweet liqueur. Even today, cinnamon sticks are used to flavor braising liquids and marinades for meat.

CLOVES ｛ *Chiodi di Garofano* ｝ GALÓFARU

Cloves are the dried red flower buds from a type of evergreen tree. They are used profusely on the island for broths, soups, boiled and braised meats, vegetables and mushrooms, and in numerous types of sweets.

ELDERBERRY FLOWERS { *Fiori di Sambuco* }
CIURI DI SAMBUCO

Elderberry is known as *sambuco* in Italian—not to be confused with anise, which is the main flavoring used in the Italian liqueur sambuca. Elderberry flowers have a delicate flavor and are used in certain local breads. On the Aeolian Islands, where they grow profusely, the flowers are made into a syrup and used in frozen desserts.

GARLIC { *Aglio* } ÀGGHIA

Garlic is a staple ingredient of the Sicilian pantry. The bulb is used as a flavor enhancer in all types of dishes. A popular Sicilian pasta is prepared with garlic, chile pepper, and olive oil. When sautéing garlic in oil, make sure not to brown it, which makes it bitter.

In Sicily, you can buy braids of garlic, most commonly red garlic bulbs from Nubia (*aglio rosso di Nubia*), an area of the town of Paceco in the province of Trapani. Cultivated in dry, dark clay soil, in rotation with melon, beans, and wheat, Nubian garlic is harvested fresh in the month of May or June, then dried in part on the fields. Harvesting takes place in the evening because it makes the leaves, being more moist, easier to braid. The Nubia red garlic flavor is very intense, thanks to its well above average allicin content.

JASMINE { *Gelsomino* } GERSUMÍNU

A highly fragrant flower introduced to Sicily during the Arab period, jasmine flavors a variety of Sicilian desserts, including custards, gelatins, granita, sorbet, and gelato. A popular use of the essence is to add a floral scent to watermelon custard. To prepare the essence, flowers are left overnight in water. In Modica, chocolate bars are prepared with jasmine flower.

NEPITELLA (CALAMINT) 〔 *Nepitella* 〕 NIPITÉDDA

Nepitella (*Calamintha nepeta*), which tastes somewhat like a cross between oregano and mint, grows in the wild, but is also cultivated for household use. Although not diffused in all parts of the island, this herb is used in many traditional dishes. The unique scent of nepitella has no substitute.

NUTMEG 〔 *Noce Moscata* 〕 NÚCI MUSCÁTA

The seed of an evergreen tree fruit, nutmeg grows in tropical environments. In Sicilian cuisine as in other European cuisines, it is used to flavor potatoes, ragù, hearty soups, cauliflower, stuffings, béchamel, and desserts. In order to retain nutmeg's characteristic aroma, it should be stored whole, not pregrated.

MARJORAM 〔 *Maggiorana* 〕 MAJURÁNA

From the same family as oregano, marjoram is used both fresh and dried in soups and ragù, and in wild game, peppers, beans, and eggplant dishes.

MINT 〔 *Menta* 〕 A MÉNTA

Several varieties of mint grow spontaneously in Sicily, but peppermint (*Menta piperita*) is the most commonly cultivated and used in cooking. It flavors salads and sauces, roasted eggplant, seafood and lamb dishes, and liqueurs and desserts.

ONION 〔 *Cipolla* 〕 CIPUDDA

Sicilian cuisine is rich in onions, the island being a producer of several varieties of the bulb. While yellow onions are the most common, specialty onions are also widespread. In the town of Giarratana, in the Hyblaean mountains of southeast Sicily, oversized sweet onions are similar to Georgia's Vidalia onions in color and taste. Another prized type is the red onion of Partanna, which has a sweet taste and aroma, and can weigh up to 1 kilogram (2.2 pounds) per bulb. Many traditional recipes also call for *cipollotti* or green "spring" onions.

ORANGE BLOSSOM 〔 *Fiori d'Arancio* 〕 ZAGARA

Another highly aromatic flower, orange blossom is a flavor typically associated with Sicily. Its essence (in liquid form) is an elegant ingredient in desserts, including custards and gelatins.

OREGANO 〔 *Origano* 〕 ARIANU

Oregano grows in Sicily's rocky calcium-rich soil, needing little irrigation. To dry the plant, stems are tied together in bunches and hung upside down during the summer months. The dried leaves are then removed from the stems before being added to countless Sicilian preparations. When purchasing dried oregano, look for the Sicilian variety, which has a unique, intense flavor. Other varieties tend to have a lemony flavor that is nonexistent in the Sicilian kind. Often the stems are sold intact and need to be removed by hand. To discard any remaining small twigs, place the oregano in a metal colander set over a bowl and gently rub the oregano with your hands until the leaves separate from the stems.

PARSLEY 〔 *Prezzemolo* 〕 PITRUSINU

In Sicily, to express ubiquity, one would say something is "present everywhere like parsley." This proverb points to the fact that parsley is indeed used as a staple ingredient in many recipes, including vegetable, seafood, poultry, and meat dishes.

ROSEMARY 〔 *Rosmarino* 〕 ROSMARÍNU

A hardy plant with thick stems, rosemary can be used fresh or dry. Popular in baked and grilled chicken, fish and meat dishes, it is also used to flavor beans and soups. When using in baked dishes, I suggest placing several rosemary stems (as opposed to leaves) in between the main ingredients. When the dish is cooked, the flavor will be diffused throughout, but the stems can be removed easily.

SAFFRON { *Zafferano* } ZAFFERANU

Once called the "red gold of Sicily," saffron—the crimson stigmas of the crocus flower—was introduced to the island by medieval Arab inhabitants. Although production has diminished over the last century, saffron has retained its popularity in Sicilian cuisine, and is now in resurgence on the agricultural landscape. Saffron is famously used to flavor *arancine* (page 165).

SAGE { *Salvia* } SÁRVIA

Several varieties of sage are cultivated in Sicily, common sage being the most popular. Sage is often used in stews and to flavor meat.

THYME { *Timo* } RIANEDDU

An aromatic plant with stunning violet flowers, thyme grows in the wild in both mountainous and seaside areas. It's popular in seafood dishes.

WILD FENNEL { *Finocchietto Selvatico* }
FINOCCHIU RI MUNTAGNA

Of all of Sicily's wild plants, *finocchietto selvatico* is most important to the island's cuisine and can be found in traditional dishes, from sausage to cookies. All around Sicily, fennel grows in abundance in the wild. The thin stalks and leaves of the whole plant are used fresh (available from mid-fall to mid-spring) and the seeds are typically used dried (available in the summer, shown at left). At Montoni, I chop up and blanch large quantities of wild fennel in salted water, and store it in freezer bags for use in the summer.

Most famously, the fennel is used in Pasta with Sardines (page 179), but one of my favorite recipes simply calls for the fennel to be blanched, chopped up, battered, and fried.

Since wild fennel is not readily available in North America (although it does grow in California and I've seen it at farmers' markets around the U.S.), I suggest purchasing seeds (see Sources, page 326) and growing your own, since there is really no substitute for its flavor. However, a combination of fennel fronds and dill can somewhat mimic its taste and aroma.

Elementi Salati

More than just a flavor enhancer, salt has been used over the centuries and to the present day most importantly as a key ingredient to conserve perishable foods for long preservation. In Sicilian cuisine, salt is used to preserve food for later use, such as curing olives, aging cheese and *salumi*, and canning or drying fish (see page 54).

Sea salt results from a simple process: ocean water in tubs is evaporated, leaving behind crystallized salt. Four natural elements are needed for its production: seawater, wind, the heat of the sun, and a lack of rainfall. Harvested from July to September, Sicilian sea salt, compared to other cooking salts, contains more potassium and magnesium and a smaller amount of sodium chloride.

Via del Sale

Around the cities of Trapani and Marsala on the western coast of Sicily, salt has been harvested from the sea since the eighth century B.C., when Carthaginian colonists first settled there. The salt trade, for which they had a monopoly in ancient Sicily, was a key component of their economy. For centuries, production flourished and spread to other coastal areas of the island, while the harvesting techniques remained nearly unchanged.

Today, amid dilapidated windmills—which were once used in salt production to pump water and grind salt —flamingos and hawks soar over sectioned-off bodies of seawater that bask under hot sun rays. In between the marshes, multiple rows of salt pyramids rise up in summer months, resembling miniature snow-covered mountains.

In Nubia, home of the Natural Reserve of Trapani, a museum housed in a three-hundred-year-old structure displays old extraction tools used in the production of salt. Explanatory panels and images allow the visitor to glimpse into the past. To arrive at the museum, visitors pass through the salt marshes, which are inside a designated rare bird sanctuary—a landscape to enjoy preferably at sunset. Annually at the end of August, the museum hosts a three-day food festival, to celebrate Nubia's salt and red garlic harvest.

SALTED ANCHOVIES

Rich in omega-3 fatty acids, iron, calcium, and protein, fresh and preserved anchovies are main ingredients in countless Sicilian recipes. Preserved anchovies are used in sauces for pasta and seafood, to dress pizza, as a condiment, in breadcrumb stuffings for fish dishes, and to stuff fried vegetables and breads. When purchasing anchovies for your pantry, look for cans of salted whole anchovies or jars or cans of salted anchovy fillets preserved in olive oil, as opposed to marinated anchovy fillets, which are preserved in a vinegar brine. When adding to a sauce, first crush the preserved anchovies with the back of a fork to make a paste. Do not add too much additional salt when cooking with preserved anchovies.

Another product made from salted anchovies is *colatura di alici*, a salty, amber-colored fermented liquid. Although colatura is more popularly consumed in Campania and Calabria, it is also produced in Sicily, and used as a fish-flavor enhancer.

Reading Italian Product Labels

Throughout Italy, products may be labeled "DOP," short for *Denominazione di Origine Protetta* ("protected designation of origin"). This certification ensures that products are locally grown and packaged, and guarantees that the food was made by local farmers and artisans using traditional methods. Not all local Italian specialties are recognized as DOP. For example, if a farmer produces olive oil outside of a designated area, his product will not be certified, even if it is of utmost quality.

You may also find products with the designation "IGP," *Indicazione Geografica*

Protetta ("indication of geographical protection"). This less strict certification traces food specialties back to their geographical origin but does not ensure that the product was produced following traditional methods or by locals.

The Slow Food organization, founded in Italy in 1986, also categorizes certain artisanal foods, animal breeds, and local ingredients that are risking extinction. Such foods protected by Slow Food are part of their Presidium, or *Presidio*. Farmers receive donations from the Slow Food organization to promote the continuation of these foods.

OLIVES 〔 *Olive* 〕 ALIVI

Olives are an essential ingredient in countless savory preparations, from caponata (page 74) to meat and seafood dishes. Green, unripe olives—like those used in olive oil making—are brined in salted water to remove their bitterness and render them edible. Black olives, which are picked when fully mature, are left in the sun to dry before they are cured in buckets with sea salt. The latter are known as *passuluna* in dialect, and are often served warm directly out of a sauté pan, where they are heated with some garlic, orange rind, and dried spicy pepper (page 121).

When purchasing green olives for cooking in the United States, look for those labeled "cracked Sicilian olives." Sometimes, labels will also call them "Castelvetrano" olives, but this is not an actual Sicilian designation. For online sources for olives, see page 326.

When purchasing black olives, Sicilian varieties are difficult to find and can be substituted with Moroccan olives, which are wrinkled and black. Such olives are very salty and should be rinsed multiple times before use in cooking.

CAPERS AND CAPER BERRIES
{ *Capperi e Cucunci* } CHIÀPPARI E CUCUNCI

The caper plant is a sun-loving perennial evergreen shrub of tropical origin. Its delicate white flowers contain a purple stamen with hints of fuchsia. In the wild, the plant flourishes on steep walls, emerging from crevices between old stones and in hard-to-reach areas. The plants grow all over Sicily but are cultivated on the islands of Salina—one of the Aeolian Islands—and Pantelleria, where they are integral parts of the landscape. The plant has been domesticated for centuries. Capers have been known since antiquity as a flavoring agent, as well as an aphrodisiac. Romans used them in their *garum*, which is a paste made from tuna parts, herbs, and capers that is once again being produced in Sicily.

Capers are flower buds, while caper berries, known as *cucunci*, are the fruit of the plant, emerging from the center of the flowers after they bloom. Straight off the shrub, both the bud and berry are highly bitter in taste. They are preserved in salt, and occasionally in vinegar, but I prefer those preserved in salt alone, as they seem to retain the purest flavor.

The harvest unfolds in the summer, from May to August. The caper farmers start picking at dawn in order to avoid the hot sun. Initially, capers are left to dry in the sun to prevent the buds from opening. Later in the day they are separated according to their size and packed in coarse sea salt in large wooden barrels. After the initial salting, the capers are transferred more than once to new barrels with more salt. After a few months, the buds are ready to use and can be preserved for up to two years.

Capers are not only incorporated into countless Sicilian recipes, but are also used to flavor sheep's milk cheese and even chocolate. Caper berries are often included in preserved vegetable antipasti or in pasta dishes. When cooking with capers or caper berries, make sure to rinse off the salt before use. As in any recipe that uses a salted ingredient, taste the food before adding additional salt.

Frutta Secca

In Italian, nuts are categorized as a dried fruit. In fact, there is no direct translation for the English word *nuts*. Almonds, hazelnuts, pistachios, and so on are all considered *frutta secca* ("dried fruit"). I include sesame seeds in this category, as they are used in a similar fashion, and honey, which is often combined with nuts. In Sicilian cuisine (unlike other Italian cuisines), dried fruits play a major role in both sweet and savory preparations.

ALMONDS { *Mandorle* } MENNULE

Introduced during the Muslim rule, almonds are widespread throughout Sicilian cuisine and the main protagonist of Sicilian pastry. Sweets are prepared with whole and ground almonds, as well as with their flour. Creams, marzipan, gelato, granita, and custards are also prepared with the nuts. On the savory side, almonds are a component in countless sauces, pestos, and meat dishes.

Almond production is a tedious process; hence, many farmers on the island have stopped producing them and uprooted their trees. Harvests occur manually in the heat of August and September. Husks that cover the shell are first removed and the almonds are laid in a single layer on large jute sheets and dried in the sun for nearly two weeks. During this time, they need to be covered or removed during rain showers. Once dry, they are stored for several months in burlap sacks, but need to be cracked open one by one in order to extract the sweet meat inside.

Several varieties of almonds exist in Sicily, comprising two main categories: sweet and bitter. Nowadays, the latter is less popular, as fewer trees remain on the island, but they are mixed into some cookies to add a bitter undertone.

The almonds of Noto, in the southeastern corner of the island, are most prized due to their high content of essential oil. Because of their diminishing production quantities, Noto almonds have been included in Slow Food's Presidium, in order to spur their production and establish a better market.

CAROB { *Carruba* } CARRÚBBA

Carob has long been considered the poor man's chocolate due to its similar taste and color, although the tree arrived in Sicily centuries before cocoa and grows well on the island. Carob beans grow to about 8 inches in length. The pulp of the fruit is the part predominately used for cooking. Sweet and savory recipes, including candies, are prepared with flour or syrup made from the dried carob pulp. Occasionally, flour from the seeds is also used in recipes.

CHESTNUTS { *Castagne* } CASTÁGNI

Chestnut trees (the *Castanea sativa* variety) in Sicily grow most typically in the woods of mountainous areas, such as in the Nebrodi and Madonie mountains and on Etna. The nuts are sold fresh during the autumn, or dried and peeled all year round. Dry chestnuts are most typically used in soups, while fresh chestnuts are roasted or boiled.

COCOA { *Cacao* } CACÁU

Brought to Sicily from the New World during Spanish domination, cocoa plays an important role in Sicilian cuisine. In addition to its use in chocolate and desserts, the beans are a traditional ingredient in savory dishes in certain pockets of the island. Cocoa is used to flavor meat and wild game dishes, as well as in some sweet and sour preparations. See page 276 for a pork dish prepared with a cocoa sauce. Recently, some chefs are flavoring fresh pasta dough with bitter cacao (see page 193) for use with meat ragùs.

HAZELNUTS { *Nocciole* } NUCÍDDI

Although hazelnuts are eaten at the table in Sicily, in cooking they are exclusively used in desserts. Gelato flavored with hazelnut puree is very popular in Sicily, although usually prepared with a packaged hazelnut base. Along with walnuts, hazelnuts commonly appear in Christmas desserts, such as in the *buccellato* (page 308), a cake stuffed with a paste made from dried figs, raisins, candied fruit, spices, and nuts. Hazelnut *torrone* and cookies are also popular.

HONEY { *Miele* } MELI

Sugarcane was introduced as a crop to Sicily during the tenth century. Before it was available, honey was the sweetener used in all Sicilian dessert making. Today, there are still several traditional desserts made exclusively with honey, such as *cubbaita* (page 297), a nut bar classically cooked with honey. In addition, honey is added, along with vinegar, to sweet-and-sour preparations.

In Sicily, multiple types of honey are produced from individual flowers, each with its own nutritive values, sweetness, aromas, and consistency. Some of the most popular monofloral honeys are those made from the nectar of cardoon, French honeysuckle (known as *sulla*), orange, lemon, prickly pear, thyme, eucalyptus, and chestnut blossoms. The latter two have strong flavors and are best enjoyed with cheeses or simply spread on toast.

For millennia, Sicily was home to the black bees, known as *api nere*. In the 1970s, when beekeepers around the island disposed of their traditional beehives made from dried fennel stalks, they imported a bee species from Northern Italy, pushing the black bees to near extinction. Recently, however, with the help of Slow Food, the Sicilian black bee population is back on the rise.

When in Sicily, you can taste the different flavors of honey in many gourmet shops or directly on farms that produce honey. In addition, hotels usually offer various types of honey with their morning breakfast spreads. In cooking, use Sicilian orange blossom honey, which is delicate in flavor, or substitute wildflower honey from your local farmers' market.

PINE NUTS ❴ *Pinoli* ❵ PIGNÚLI

Pine nuts are the seeds from pinecones that grow on tall trees found in many areas around the Mediterranean Sea. In Sicily, although pine nuts can be found in some cookies and desserts, they are more commonly used in savory dishes, from pestos to meat, vegetable, and fish sauces. Pinecones are also a symbol of fertility and are represented ubiquitously in ceramics, adorning terraces and entrances to homes.

PISTACHIOS ❴ *Pistacchio* ❵ FASTUCHI

Pistachios have a unique flavor that pairs well with many Sicilian preparations. Whole nuts are used in pastries and to make nut bars. Ground pistachio nuts are used to make cookies, cannoli, and cakes as well as pesto, and as a crust for meat and seafood dishes. Pistachio puree is used as a base in gelato and cakes, and in pistachio marzipan. Flour from the nut is used to prepare desserts as well as pasta dough.

RAISINS ❴ *Uva Passa* ❵ PASSULINA

Raisins are used more often in Sicilian savory preparations rather than in desserts. Used in stuffings and in sweet-and-sour preparations, raisins are best when first soaked in water or wine. The most popular type to use in cooking is the *uva sultanina*, a white seedless grape cultivated in Sicily. When dried, they are amber in color.

SESAME SEEDS ❴ *Sesamo* ❵ GIUGGIULÉNA

Sesame seeds are used in dessert making and to add texture to the crust of bread. Famous sweets made with sesame include sesame cookies, known as *biscotti reginelle* (see page 301), and *cubbaita* (page 297), a type of nut bar prepared by cooking sesame and almonds with honey and nuts.

WALNUTS ❴ *Noci* ❵ NÚCI

Predominantly used in desserts, walnuts are also commonly consumed during the winter on their own. Cookies prepared with walnuts are traditional, although not as popular as those made with almonds or pistachios. Savory recipes using the nuts include pesto, bread, and rabbit dishes. Avoid roasting walnuts, as the heat turns them bitter.

THE SAP OF THE ASH TREE

Several years back, in the middle of August, a childhood friend from Sant'Anna invited me on a visit to a manna farm. To arrive at the farm, we parked on a mountain road and trekked a few kilometers by foot to the uncontaminated land where Giulio Gelardi, a manna producer, awaited us. Gelardi not only cultivates the ash tree sap, but is an expert on its health benefits and historical origins.

Produced in the Madonie mountains, between the towns of Castelbuono and Pollina, manna is a natural sweetener, a resinous substance extracted from the bark of ash trees, which hardens when exposed to the sun. Deep incisions are made into the trees with curved knives by skilled farmers, who collect the sweet sap (referred to as *sangu*, or "blood") during July and August. The manna (considered as such only after the sap hardens) is collected on wire or nylon string that hangs from the tree trunk. Shards of pottery, agave, and prickly pear leaves (without their thorns) are used to collect additional drippings.

The centuries-old collection techniques—passed down from generation to generation—have survived only in this corner of the island. In Sicilian dialect, sap collectors are known as *mannaluòru* ("those who produce manna") or *'ntaccaluòru* ("those who make the *'ntacche*," the incisions in the bark). To be a successful manna farmer, one must possess a synergistic relationship with the trees and with the environment. The bark must be handled with the utmost care and must be cut with surgical precision at the right moment in order to produce manna. The expert *mannaluòru* collect the sap during the hottest hours of the day. The heat promotes the detachment of the manna from the bark and prevents loss of the resin to condensation. Throughout the harvest months, the farmers (traditionally with the aid of their families) must be careful observers of the sky and continually monitor atmospheric changes, often anticipating the harvest night or day to avoid exposure to humidity, fog, or rainfall.

Manna has multiple uses. It is used as a natural sweetener, having a low glucose and fructose content, putting it low on the glycemic index. Composed predominately of mannitol, it can be consumed safely by diabetics and babies. A significant portion of manna is sold to pharmaceutical companies for its numerous health benefits, in particular its effectiveness as a diuretic and gentle laxative. In Sicilian food, manna is an ingredient in meat dishes, as well as an addition to chocolate bars, marmalades, and most famously as a glaze topping a holiday panettone produced in Castelbuono by Fiasconaro.

Different grades of manna are sold. The sap that is collected on strings, without ever touching the trees or the ground, and is crystallized into sticks, is known as *manna cannolo*. Small chunks of manna that have fallen off the string or solidified against the bark are known as *manna rottame* and sell for a lower price, as they often contain impurities.

Since the 1950s, when mannitol began to be produced from other products, production of manna diminished. Today, collectors of manna belong to a consortium, which is part of a Slow Food Presidium supported by the region of Sicily, in an effort to support and rebuild the industry. In the Piazza Duomo of Pollina, a museum dedicated to manna displays tools and historical references to this rare, prized sap.

During my visit, I quickly became fascinated by this product, as it was a food I had never heard of until that day. Giulio gifted me a map of Sicily produced by Slow Food, containing all the animal species, ingredients—such as manna—and traditional recipes the organization is helping to preserve from extinction. After studying the map, I realized just how many other foods existed in Sicily that I had never heard of. This is when I set my initial challenge to visit farms from which each of these items hailed, giving birth to this book project—true manna from the heavens.

GRAPE REDUCTION

{ Vino Cotto }

VINU COTTU

Vino cotto*, which translates to "cooked wine," is actually prepared by cooking grape must, the fresh juice extracted during the pressing of grapes for wine. In Sicily,* vino cotto *is used as an ingredient in cookies and other sweets, as well as in meat and game preparations. Old recipes add wood ash with the grape must during the cooking process, which adds a light smokiness to the liquid. If you choose to do so, add only 1 tablespoon wood ash for every quart of grape must.*

To obtain grape must, you can purchase some freshly pressed, unpasteurized, unsweetened grape juice at a farmers' market, or use a juicer to extract the juice from fresh grapes. Depending on the type of grapes and their water content, you will need 4 to 5 pounds of grapes to obtain 2 quarts of juice.

As a substitute for homemade vino cotto *in a recipe, look for a product called* saba, *a Northern Italian grape must reduction (see Sources, page 326).*

Makes 2 cups

2 quarts freshly pressed white or red grape must

1 cinnamon stick

2 whole cloves

Dried peel from ½ orange

Fresh peel from ½ lemon

1 bay leaf

1 Strain the grape must through a fine-mesh strainer to remove any skin or seeds.

2 In a medium saucepan, bring the must to a boil. Reduce the heat and simmer until the liquid has reduced by half, about 30 minutes. Add the spices and aromatics and cook over medium heat, until the liquid has reduced by half again and become syrupy, about 30 minutes. Let cool.

3 Pour the *vino cotto* into an airtight container and store in the refrigerator, or place in a sterilized bottle and conserve in a dark pantry. The vino cotto will keep for several months.

TRAPANESE PESTO

{ Pesto alla Trapanese }

PESTU ALA TRAPANISI

The style of pesto commonly served outside of Italy is typical of Genova, a city in Northern Italy. But in Sicily, Pesto alla Trapanese is an old recipe that originated in the ports of Trapani, where Genovese sailors first introduced basil pesto to Sicilians, who then modified the recipe with local ingredients, specifically almonds and tomatoes.

Traditionally, all the ingredients for pesto should be pounded in a mortar, but in the absence of one, a food processor or blender also works well; the resulting pesto will be less chunky and more emulsified. Make sure not to overmix the ingredients, which can produce a brown paste.

In Sicilian dialect, this dish is also called 'agghiata, meaning that it is a garlic-based sauce. Use it to dress pasta, in pasta salads, layered inside vegetable-based baked pastas, spread on grilled bread, and even as a condiment for fish dishes. My cousin Maria typically prepares spaghetti, tossing it with the following pesto, as a midnight snack in the summer, although her version omits the almonds. Instead of adding salt, she adds salted pasta water, serving the dish with some broth.

In Favignana, a small island off the coast of Trapani, walnuts, pine nuts, and parsley are added to their version of this pesto.

Makes about 2 cups

20 peeled almonds

1 garlic clove

50 fresh sweet basil leaves, or leaves from 5 sprigs of bush basil

3 fresh ripe or canned plum tomatoes, peeled, seeded, and diced

1 cup grated pecorino cheese

1 cup extra-virgin olive oil

2 teaspoons sea salt

Black pepper

1 In a mortar, crush the almonds with a pestle. Add the garlic and continue to crush the mixture. Add the basil leaves and crush until the basil has been broken down into small bits. Finally, add the tomatoes and pecorino and crush without the letting the tomatoes turn into a sauce.

2 Transfer the mixture to a glass bowl and, using a fork, whisk the pesto while streaming in the olive oil. Season with the salt and pepper to taste. This will keep in an airtight container in the refrigerator for up to 3 days.

GARLIC PASTE

{ *Aglio* }

ÀGGHIA

Makes about 1 tablespoon

6 garlic cloves

1 teaspoon medium-coarse sea salt

Extra-virgin olive oil (optional)

1 With a large chef's knife, finely chop the garlic on a cutting board and sprinkle with the salt. Making sure that the edge of the knife is facing away from you, press the flat side of the knife against the garlic with the palm of your opposite hand and crush the garlic. The graininess of the salt will help to release the liquids in the garlic and turn it into a paste.

2 If you need to hold the garlic paste for a few hours before using it, mix it with some olive oil. However, make sure to store the garlic paste in an airtight container in the refrigerator to avoid the growth of bacteria. It will keep for up to 2 days.

FLAVOR BASE SOFFRITTO

{ *Soffritto* }

SOFFRITU

This mixture of sautéed onion, carrot, and celery is the base of most ragùs, soups, and braises. It can be stored in the refrigerator for up to three days or frozen for up to a month, although it is best made the day of use. Many Sicilians add garlic to their soffritto, but if preparing it in advance, I suggest omitting the garlic.

Makes 1 cup

½ cup ¼-inch-diced onion

½ cup ⅛-inch-diced carrot

½ cup ⅛-inch-diced celery

1 tablespoon olive oil

1 Place the onion, carrot, celery, and 1 cup water in a saucepan. Bring the mixture to a simmer over medium heat.

2 As soon as the water has evaporated and the mixture dries out, add the olive oil. Sauté, stirring occasionally, without browning, for 3 to 5 minutes, until the onion is translucent.

ONION MARMALADE

{ Marmellata di Cipolla }

MARMELLATA RI CIPUDDA

This savory marmalade pairs well with aged Sicilian cheese, Tuna Sausages (page 242), or roasted game. Variations use red onions and/or red wine, or omit the raisins and/or the orange juice and zest.

Makes 2 cups

4 large white onions, finely chopped	1 teaspoon grated organic orange zest
1/4 cup olive oil	1/2 cup fresh orange juice
3 bay leaves	1/2 cup honey
1 cup white wine	2 tablespoons raisins

1 Place the onions, olive oil, bay leaves, and 2 cups water in a heavy-bottomed saucepan. Cook over medium heat until the water has evaporated. Reduce the heat, add the wine, orange zest, orange juice, honey, and raisins and cook until the liquid has reduced and the marmalade has a thick consistency, about 30 minutes.

2 Let cool and remove the bay leaves before serving the marmalade. Use immediately or store in an airtight container in the refrigerator for up to 5 days.

LEMON-OREGANO OIL

{ Il Salmoriglio }

U SAMMURIGGHIU

The term sammurigghiu *derives from a fusion of three words: salt, oil, and oregano, the three main ingredients in this easy-to-prepare sauce. Drizzle it over grilled fish, vegetables, or meat. While the garlic is optional, it is a delicious addition, especially with barbecued meat.*

Makes 1 cup

Salt to taste	1 teaspoon Garlic Paste (page 40)
Juice of 2 lemons	3/4 cup extra-virgin olive oil
1/2 teaspoon cracked black pepper	
1 1/2 teaspoons dried Sicilian oregano	

In a small bowl, dissolve the salt in the lemon juice. Add the remaining ingredients and mix well. This condiment is best when used immediately but can be stored in an airtight container in the refrigerator for up to 2 days.

BREADCRUMBS

{ *La Mollica* }

À MUDDICA

Breadcrumbs are made from a toasted mixture of bread, herbs, garlic, and cheese. In Sicilian cuisine, they are used as a coating for fried foods, as a stuffing for vegetables such as artichokes and peppers, and as a filling for rolled meats or fish.

They are also sprinkled over pasta. This tradition began as an alternative to grated cheese, which was not readily available in peasant households in the past. Not only does a breadcrumb mixture add flavor to a pasta, it provides a pleasant crunchiness.

Two main textures of breadcrumbs are typically prepared, depending on their use: fine or coarse. Traditionally, before the widespread use of food processors, toasted or stale bread was hand grated into breadcrumbs.

No need to throw away odds and ends of bread that dry up before you can use them fresh; keep them in a paper bag until you have enough to make this recipe.

Some recipes, such as the pasta with sardine recipe (page 179), call for sweetened breadcrumbs. In this case, the breadcrumbs are toasted with sugar instead of the savory ingredients here.

Makes about 4 cups

1 pound stale rustic bread (white or whole wheat)

1 tablespoon Garlic Paste (page 40)

1 cup grated caciocavallo or aged Sicilian sheep's milk cheese

¼ cup extra-virgin olive oil

1 tablespoon dried Sicilian oregano

Sea salt

1 Preheat the oven to 400°F. Break the bread into small pieces (the size of an olive) and place on a baking sheet. Toast in the oven for about 15 minutes, until golden brown. Pay careful attention so as not to burn the bread pieces. To test if the bread is sufficiently toasted, grab a cool piece between your fingers and squeeze. If the bread feels at all sticky or moist in the middle, return the pan to the oven. Ideally, the pieces of bread should be thoroughly toasted and dried out. Let cool.

2 Transfer the bread to a food processor and process until the bread breaks into very small clumps. Add the garlic paste, cheese, olive oil, oregano, and salt. For coarse or medium breadcrumbs, pulse the food processor five to ten times, until the bread breaks down to the desired crumb size. For fine breadcrumbs, continue pulsing until the bread is broken into pieces slightly larger than grains of sand.

3 Using a rubber spatula, scrape the breadcrumbs from the food processor and transfer to a sauté pan. Over medium heat, toast the breadcrumb mixture until dark brown, stirring continuously with a wooden spoon. Let cool before storing in an airtight container for later use. The breadcrumbs will keep in the refrigerator for 2 to 3 days. Warm them in a sauté pan before using.

PARSLEY-MINT OIL

{ *Condimento con Menta e Prezzemolo* }

'NZOGGHIU

Similar to the Lemon-Oregano Oil (page 41), this combination of parsley, mint, garlic, and vinegar is bold and refreshing. I like to use it to dress grilled meat, especially lamb chops.

Makes 2 cups

1 bunch fresh parsley, tough long stems removed

20 fresh mint leaves

2 teaspoons Garlic Paste (page 40)

1/2 cup white wine vinegar

1 teaspoon salt

1 cup extra-virgin olive oil

1/2 teaspoon cracked black pepper

1 In a food processor, combine all the ingredients and process until fully incorporated, but not pureed.

2 Remove the top of the food processor. Using a rubber spatula, push down any pieces that were not fully chopped, and pulse for an additional 2 to 3 seconds. The oil will keep in an airtight container in the refrigerator for up to 2 days.

CAPER PESTO

{ Pesto di Capperi }

PESTO RI CHIÀPPARI

Spread this caper pesto on bruschetta, use it as a pasta sauce, mix it into a potato salad, or use it on grilled fish.

Makes about 1 cup

$1/3$ cup salted capers, well rinsed

2 garlic cloves

1 chile pepper (either dried, fresh, or preserved in olive oil)

Handful of celery leaves (or a combination of celery leaves and parsley)

$1/3$ cup extra-virgin olive oil

1 In a food processor, combine all the ingredients and process until fully incorporated, but not pureed.

2 Remove the top of the food processor. Using a rubber spatula, push down any pieces that were not fully chopped and pulse to combine. Store in the refrigerator in an airtight container for up to 3 days.

PARSLEY-CAPER SAUCE

{ Salsa Verde }

SARSA VIRDI

This sauce makes an excellent accompaniment to grilled fish.

Makes 2 cups

1 bunch fresh parsley, tough long stems removed

1 tablespoon salted capers, well rinsed

1 hard-boiled egg

1 garlic clove

2 tablespoons red wine vinegar

$1/2$ teaspoon salt

$1/2$ teaspoon cracked black pepper

1 cup extra-virgin olive oil

1 In a food processor, combine all the ingredients and process until fully incorporated, but not pureed.

2 Remove the top of the food processor. Using a rubber spatula, push down any pieces that were not fully chopped and pulse to combine. Store in an airtight container in the refrigerator for up to 3 days.

ANCHOVY SAUCE

{ Salsa di Acciughe }

SARSA RI ANCIOVE

This sauce can be tossed with spaghetti and topped with breadcrumbs, or used as a condiment on freshly baked bread.

Makes about 1 cup

8 whole salted anchovies

²/₃ cup extra-virgin olive oil

2 tablespoons pine nuts, slightly crushed

1 teaspoon dried Sicilian oregano

With the back side of a fork, crush the anchovies in a bowl until they turn into a rough paste. In a saucepan, warm the olive oil over medium heat. Add the anchovy paste, pine nuts, and oregano. When the pine nuts turn light brown in color, remove the pan from the heat. Use immediately or store in an airtight container in the refrigerator for up to 5 days.

ALMOND, COCOA, *and* ANCHOVY SAUCE

{ Salsa con Mandorle, Cacao, ed Acciughe }

SARSA SAN BERNARDO

This combination makes a surprisingly delicious sauce, which is traditionally used as an accompaniment to boiled meats and artichokes.

Makes generous 1 cup

1 cup day-old stale bread, crusts removed, cut into small chunks

4 tablespoons olive oil

½ cup blanched almonds, lightly toasted

2 salted anchovies, rinsed and mashed into a paste with the back of a fork

1 tablespoon honey

1 tablespoon red wine vinegar

1 ounce dark chocolate, melted

1 Preheat the oven to 350°F. On a baking sheet, toss the bread and 1 tablespoon of the oil. Bake for 10 to 15 minutes, until the bread starts to brown. Let it cool, then transfer it to a food processor and add the almonds. Process until the mixture has the consistency of thick sand.

2 In a saucepan, combine the crumb-almond mixture, remaining 3 tablespoons olive oil, and the mashed anchovies and heat over low heat, stirring with a wooden spoon to incorporate.

3 In a small bowl, whisk together the honey and the vinegar until the honey has dissolved. Add the honey-vinegar mixture to the saucepan and continue stirring the ingredients for a few minutes. Finally, add the melted chocolate and mix well. The condiment will appear paste-like in consistency. Use immediately or store in an airtight container in the refrigerator for up to 1 week. Warm in a saucepan over low heat, stirring continuously as to not burn the sauce, before using.

SWEET-AND-SOUR SAUCE

{ *Agrodolce* }

AGRU E DUCI

This recipe is at the base of most sweet-and-sour vegetable, meat, and seafood preparations, including caponata (page 74).

Makes 1¹/₂ cups

1 cup red wine vinegar

³/₄ cup sugar

In a saucepan, whisk together the vinegar and sugar and bring the mixture to a boil over medium heat. Remove from the heat and let cool to room temperature before using in recipes. Store at room temperature in a glass jar for up to 1 month.

PISTACHIO PESTO

{ *Pesto di Pistacchio* }

PISTU RI FASTUCHI

You will find this pesto used in various savory recipes in Sicily. It is often tossed with pasta or used as a sauce for grilled meat. The predominant taste of this sauce is not that of basil or garlic, but rather of the pistachios, which have a distinctive flavor and aroma.

Makes 1¹/₂ cups

¹/₂ cup raw pistachios

Handful of fresh basil leaves

¹/₄ cup extra-virgin olive oil

¹/₂ cup grated Parmesan cheese

2 garlic cloves

1 teaspoon grated organic lemon zest

Sea salt

1 In a food processor, combine all the ingredients with salt to taste and process until fully incorporated but not pureed.

2 Remove the top of the food processor. Using a rubber spatula, push down any pieces that were not fully chopped, and pulse once or twice to combine.

3 Store in the refrigerator in an airtight container for up to 3 days.

Chapter 2

PRESERVED FOODS

HISTORICALLY, before the introduction of refrigeration and modern technology, Mother Nature provided us with raw elements to keep food from spoiling: sun, salt, air, ice, wind. Today, this reliance on nature is still a major part of Sicilian cuisine. Food preservation is an important way to keep typical Sicilian flavors and aromas alive at all times throughout the year. Eggplants, for instance, grow in abundance in summer months and are cooked into luscious caponata (page 74), a quintessential Sicilian dish to be enjoyed in every month. Many fruit and vegetable seasons are extremely brief; preserving them allows us to extend their seasons. Preservation methods are also especially useful during an abundant harvest, when a family has more than can be eaten fresh.

In Sicily, there are two main ways to preserve food. The first is to cook and can fruits, vegetables, and seafood. The second type of preservation is based on salt; this is traditionally used for proteins—fish, meat, and dairy products—to transform them into salted fish, salumi, and cheese.

PRESERVED FRUIT

Even though I've been cooking since childhood, until I moved to Sicily, I never prepared fruit preserves. I always used to bring either homemade or artisanal Sicilian marmalade back to New York. With the abundance of fruit trees in the garden at Feudo Montoni, I finally took up the craft of marmalade making, at first out of necessity, so that I wouldn't waste fruit, and now out of joy. There's something ever so satisfying about tasting summer fruits—cherries, peaches, and apricot—in the winter months. The same goes for cold-weather fruits—citrus, persimmon, and pumpkin—in the summer.

CLOCKWISE FROM TOP LEFT: Pecorino nero stagionato, *Girgentana goat cheeses (robiola-style, top right, and with a Nero d'Avola rind, center right)*, provola delle Madonie, caci figurati

PRESERVED VEGETABLES

All throughout Italy, seasonal vegetables are preserved for enjoying at other times of the year. Chunks or slices of vegetables are cooked and conserved in olive oil (known as *sott'olio*, or "under oil") with added ingredients such as vinegar and herbs. Vegetables are also preserved by turning them into pastes, known as *pâté*, which are spread on toasted bread or tossed with pasta. In Sicily, in addition to preserving typical vegetables in the two styles mentioned above, vegetables are also preserved with a mixture of vinegar and sugar, such as for caponata (page 74).

PRESERVED FISH

Salt was introduced to Sicily during Phoenician times, and since Norman times has been used to preserve seafood. Although the island is surrounded by the sea, historically, the interior of the island did not have access to fish. My grandmother grew up in Sant'Anna, a mountain village just ten minutes by car from beaches and a thriving port city, but a century ago, when she was a child, the only way to arrive was by donkey.

In her times and for centuries prior, in order to disperse the abundance of fish throughout the island, before modern transport and refrigeration, seafood had to be preserved in order to arrive in the hundreds of mountain villages around Sicily. Today, not only is preserved seafood (including tuna packed in oil and salted anchovies and sardines) popular among Sicilians, it is a staple of Sicily's export economy.

TUNA

Several varieties of tuna swim in the waters of the Mediterranean, the most common being the bluefin. Tuna has long been considered the pig of the sea, in that all parts of the fish, including the heart, intestines, male and female reproductive organs, stomach, and liver are used in cooking. Only the blood is discarded. Innards are used in some traditional dishes and are prepared into a paste known as a *garum*. Heads and tails are used to prepare a ragù, by slow cooking these parts in a tomato-based sauce. The heart is salted, pressed, and dried. The male sperm sack, known as *lattume*, is a rare and highly prized gastronomic specialty, which can be preserved with salt or used fresh in pastas or in fried fritters. Below are the four most common preserved tuna parts to look out for when in Sicily.

Tuna Salame (Ficazza)	On the western side of Sicily, tuna salame (or salami), known as *ficazza*, is prepared with the organs, scraps, and muscular parts that remain around the backbone of the fish in the late spring, when tuna are caught in abundance around Trapani. Like sausage, the meat and tuna parts are minced and seasoned with salt and pepper, stuffed into casings, and then covered in salt and pressed for nearly a month, at which point the dark brown salame can be consumed or preserved for over a year in the refrigerator. When in Sicily, try the *ficazza* sliced and garnished with lemon and olive oil, as an antipasto.
Dried Tuna Loin (Mosciame)	*Mosciame* is dried tuna, from the lean loin. The word comes from the Arabic *musama*, meaning "dry," although the delicacy originally came from the Carthaginians, who dried tuna in salt so they could trade it around the Mediterranean. To prepare *mosciame*, the tuna pieces are salt-cured for a few days before being rinsed and laid out to dry in the sun for up to twenty days. The end result is a product that resembles a beef bresaola. It is usually served, as a delicacy before a meal, in very thin slices and dressed with olive oil and lemon or as an accompaniment to fresh figs and melon.
Salted Tuna Eggs (Bottarga)	Bottarga is the salted, pressed, and dried egg sack of a female fish, traditionally tuna. Production begins when eggs are available in the late spring. Its flavor is intense and bold. Produced in port cities where tuna is prevalent, most commonly on the western side of Sicily, bottarga is expensive. Therefore, it's common that chefs prepare their own bottarga when they happen to find an egg sack while filleting a fish. Recently, in restaurants, I've tasted swordfish and amberjack bottarga. In Sardinia, mullet bottarga is prevalent and is sometimes found in Sicily as well. In the States, bottarga can be found in gourmet and Italian specialty stores (see Sources, page 326). Prepare a shaved fennel salad with citrus segments and grated bottarga or simply shave slices of bottarga on top of grilled bread topped with fresh tomatoes. Toss bottarga shavings with spaghetti, garlic, and olive oil or place a chunk of the delicacy in a food processor with breadcrumbs to make a topping for pasta dressed with extra-virgin olive oil.
Preserved Tuna and Mackerel (Tonno e Sgombro sott'Olio)	Oily seafood, such as tuna and mackerel, is poached, packed in oil, and bottled. The best part to preserve is the belly or *ventresca*, which makes a tender chunk of fish, due to the fat content, when slow cooked during the preservation process. Preserved fish can be prepared at home, although bottled Sicilian bluefin tuna and mackerel ventresca, known in Sicilian dialect as *surra*, is available in specialty stores (see Sources, page 326). When not labeled as *ventresca*, the preserved tuna comes from the leaner loin, which is equally delicious, just slightly less tender. Look for fish preserved in extra-virgin olive oil, not in lower-grade olive oil. Consume on its own as an antipasto, in salads, or in a sauce for pasta, such as in the recipe on page 175.

SALTED AND MARINATED ANCHOVIES AND SARDINES

At fish-salting factories in Sicily, heaps of freshly caught sardines and anchovies arrive straight from the port. The fish are gutted and cleaned and their heads removed, a process undertaken completely by hand. The fillets are then placed in cans layered with coarse sea salt and weights are placed on top of them (which protrude from the cans) so that the water and oil will be expelled from the fish. Over the course of two weeks, the fillets reduce in size as they lose their moisture. The cans are then cleaned and sealed.

Anchovies are also marinated and then preserved in vinegar instead of salt. While salted anchovies are best when used as an ingredient in sauces and to top pizza, the marinated anchovies are normally eaten as an antipasto, direct from the marinade.

DRIED CODFISH

To preserve them, codfish fillets can be air-dried, known as *stoccafisso*, or salt-cured and dried, known as *baccalà*. In both versions the fish are first gutted and their backbones removed. *Baccalà* and *stoccafisso* are most commonly used during the winter season in Sicily.

For a long time, one of the only types of fish available in Sicily was *baccalà*, imported from the far Nordic seas, a product which is believed to have arrived for the first time on the island along with the Normans in the eleventh century. Its inexpensive price and ease of transport without spoiling contributed to its ubiquity on the tables of Sicilians, who welcomed the dried fish due to their religious obligation to shun meat on Fridays. *Stoccafisso*, however, is produced in Sicily.

Unlike the preserved sardines and anchovies, which are not dried and retain some moisture, these preserved fish need to be soaked in water before they can be used. While *baccalà* takes about three days to reconstitute, *stoccafisso* takes much longer, and since it is not salted, it is much firmer and has a more assertive smell than *baccalà*.

To rehydrate *baccalà*, first wash the fish thoroughly. Submerge the fillets in a large basin filled with cold water. Soak for at least three days, replacing the water with fresh cold water at least every eight hours. This can be done in the sink, but it is important that the temperature of the room is not too hot. After about three days, peel any skin off the fillets and use fish pliers to remove any bones that remain. The reconstituted fish is now ready to use in cooking. To rehydrate *stoccafisso*, follow the same instructions for the *baccalà*, but continue for another two days.

CURED MEAT

All throughout the island, cured meat delicacies such as prosciutto, guanciale, and pancetta are found in abundance. Pigs are ubiquitous in Sicily, to be found not only on farms where animals are raised for their meat, but also at cheesemakers' workshops, as the pigs consume the leftover whey. All parts of the pig are used in their entirety. Due to regulations, these cured meats are forbidden from being imported by the United States. So if you are a cured-meat lover, when in Sicily, go out of your way to taste these delicacies.

SICILY'S BLACK PIGS

I'll never forget the day I visited the Agostino farm on the outskirts of Mirto to see their black pigs. To call it a farm is a bit confusing, since here the pigs live in a natural forest. I really felt I was an intruder on their private territory, a sloping hillside of chestnut trees. As they sniffed out mushrooms and nuts through the underbrush and eyed me warily, I realized for the first time the difference between domesticated pigs and this heritage breed, which thrives in a wild environment.

Raised outdoors in the forests of the Nebrodi and Madonie mountains, this small, black-skinned breed of pig is famous for its high-quality meat. The black pig is disease resistant and able to survive in adverse climate conditions. The breeding of this pig has ancient origins, as fossil remains and documents testify to the presence of these animals during the Greek period. In the beginning of the twentieth century, black pigs flourished, but as forests diminished, so did the pigs. Twelve years ago, the pigs of the Nebrodi mountains were nearing extinction, but due to the efforts of Slow Food, their population has increased significantly.

The meat has a unique flavor and a high percentage of fat. Unlike preserved pork products from Northern Italy, such as San Daniele prosciutto made from the black pigs of Friuli, cured meats from Sicilian black pigs have yet to be exported to the United States.

Pork dishes prepared with meat from the black pig abound in restaurants in towns of the Nebrodi or Madonie mountains. Pork ragù (page 202) for pasta is common, as well as main courses prepared with pork chops and loin. At the restaurants Antica Filanda in Capri Leone and Nangalaruni in Castelbuono, appetizers are prepared with thin cold slices of black pig cured *porchetta* (page 268). Depending on the season, the sliced meat is topped with other local specialties such as *vino cotto* (page 37), citrus segments, slivered raw artichoke hearts, or ovoli mushrooms. Cured porchetta can be purchased at your local Italian market (see page 326 for sources) and prepared as an appetizer in this fashion.

CLOCKWISE FROM TOP RIGHT: *Sopressata, lardo, prosciutto, salame, capocollo, salame al pistacchio, pancetta, guanciale*

In Sicily, animals have the right-of-way. One of my favorite sensory experiences in Sicily is the sound of a sheep herd parading though the streets, their hooves tapping the ground and their bells ringing.

CHEESE

Sicily boasts an ancient tradition of sheep's milk cheeses. In the fifth century B.C., the many Greek colonies that dotted the island made Sicilian cheese famous abroad. Later, the Roman writer Pliny categorized cheeses, calling Sicilian pecorino one of the best of his time. In addition to sheep's milk, cow's and goat's milk are also used in classic Sicilian cheesemaking. (See a description of Sicilian goats on page 62.)

On the vast pastures of the province of Ragusa and beyond, the Modicana cow, a breed with a characteristic red coat, has found a home for centuries. While all cows on the island are grass-fed, as opposed to grain-fed, not all are pasture raised like the Modicana cow. The breed is able to withstand the tough summer heat, requiring little supplemental food. Its low yield in milk has led to its major decline, although the milk is still used traditionally in *ragusano* cheese. The pasture breeding ensures the highest quality milk, which is rich in flavor.

There are two main styles of Sicilian cheesemaking. Curd can be placed in hot water and stretched and pulled before being formed into specific shapes. This process, known as *pasta filata*, which literally translates to "spun paste," creates a cheese that melts and stretches easily. Mozzarella is made in this style, although it is not specific to Sicily. Alternatively, cheese is produced by placing curd into baskets full of holes, where it is left to drain on sloping boards for several hours until the whey drains off. Then the aging process begins. Both types of cheese can either be placed in a salt brine to age, or salted and left in aging rooms, such as aged black peppercorn pecorino cheese.

Other Milks in Sicily

Buffalo milk is produced in Sicily, but in very small quantities in the southeastern corner of the island. This is an artisanal production, on a much different scale than the buffalo-milk-mozzarella industry in the region of Campania.

There is one other type of milk consumed in Sicily, although it is not used to make cheese. Donkey milk, from the *asino ragusano*, is rare but highly prized, considered as close to human milk as possible. In the past, as well as today, babies were fed donkey milk for nourishment, when not able to consume the milk of their mothers. My grandmother, in fact, recalled being fed donkey milk straight from the animal, when her mother was indisposed.

CLOCKWISE FROM TOP RIGHT:
Primo sale, caciotta, *ricotta salata*,
piacentino ennese, vastedda,
ricotta, tuma persa, pecorino
pepato, caciocavallo ragusano

Girgentana Goats

One November, on the outskirts of Sciacca at the Bellitti animal farm, I stretched my arm underneath a mothergoat while Leonardo Bellitti pulled on the animal's nipple, releasing milk into a small plastic cup I was holding. As I stood among the flock of friendly Girgentana goats (known in Italian as Capre Girgentante), who were rubbing against my legs, I sipped the raw milk with caution, assuming that the gaminess would be overwhelming. To my great surprise, the flavor of the liquid was sweet, and I devoured it instantly. Nearby, another mother goat was giving birth in the open, while others were locking their unmistakable tall spiral horns for play.

Since then, when in the Sciacca area, I've yet to miss a visit to the Bellitti farm. Girgentana goats are an old Sicilian breed, possibly having originated in Tibet. The animals are raised on a pasture rich in a wide variety of wild herbs and plants, which impart a complex flavor to their milk. There's something very welcoming about the Girgentana goats; they are alert yet trusting, as if they can feel one's good intentions.

Giacomo Gatì prepares an assemblage of Girgentana goat cheeses in his caseificio *in Campobello di Licata. This soft cheese is not only wrapped in a fig leaf, but is prepared with a rennet he extracts from the stems of the fig tree's leaves.*

SICILY'S RENOWNED CHEESES

Cheese	Description	Provenance
Caci Figurati e Ainuzzi	A soft, sweet cow's milk *provola* (a light, unaged cheese that is brined) produced from a pulled curd, this cheese is formed into decorative animal shapes before it is salted in brine.	**Caci:** Province of Palermo, in the town of Contessa Entellina. Province of Messina **Ainuzzi:** Province of Agrigento, specifically in the towns of Cammarata and San Giovanni Gemini
Caciocavallo Palermitano	This cow's milk cheese is excellent when lightly pan-seared and drizzled with *agrodolce*.	Province of Palermo
Il Formaggio di Santo Stefano di Quisquina	Aged for a minimum of six months, this cylindrical cheese—produced from a combination of sheep's and cow's milk—has a soft light yellow rind. The flavor reflects the rich pastures where the animals graze.	Province of Agrigento and Palermo, specifically the town of Santo Stefano di Quisquina
Maiorchino	Predominantly a sheep's milk cheese. Goat's and cow's milk are often added in small quantities. The cheese is formed into large wheels and aged for three months with salt, then rubbed with olive oil and aged for at least one month more or up to two years. The flavor is sharp, especially when aged.	Province of Messina
Pecorino Primo Sale	A soft sheep's milk cheese that is salted once. Melts well. Can also be found flavored with black peppercorn or capers, pistachio, wild fennel, sun-dried tomatoes, and more.	All over Sicily
Pecorino Rosso	A pulled-curd cheese that is rubbed with olive oil or tomato paste after three months of aging.	All over Sicily
Pecorino Secondo Sale	Sheep's milk cheese that is salted twice. Firmer and saltier in taste than a *primo sale*.	All over Sicily
Pecorino Stagionato	Sheep's milk cheese that is aged for up to eighteen months. Salty, sharp, and crumbly. Good for grating or to be enjoyed on its own with drizzled honey.	All over Sicily
Piacentino Ennese	A bright yellow aged pecorino flavored with saffron and black peppercorn.	Province of Enna
Provola dei Nebrodi e delle Madonie	Also pulled-curd cheeses, produced from cow's milk and salted in baths of whey. They differ in size. Can be smoked.	Madonie e Nebrodi Mountains
Ragusano DOP	Historically known as *caciocavallo ragusano*, this cheese is one of Sicily's oldest, an item of trade outside of the island since the fourteenth century. Shaped as a large brick and produced exclusively with milk from the *razza modicana* cow breed. The taste is aromatic and ranges from sweet to spicy, depending on its age. Melts well when young. Excellent as a grated cheese when aged.	Province of Ragusa and Siracusa
Tuma Persa and Canestrato	Tuma Persa has a sweet, spicy, not salty, long aftertaste. *Persa* means "forgotten" and probably derives from the fact that the cheese is left to age for up to ten days before it is salted. Its rind is rubbed with olive oil and ground peppercorn. *Canestrato* is made in the same style, but does not get rubbed with olive oil.	Monte Sicani, Castronovo di Sicilia, Campofiorito
Vastedda del Belice DOP	A soft, round, flat cheese prepared with a pulled curd. Only prepared in artisanal methods. Melts well.	Province of Agrigento

MANDARIN MARMALADE

{ *Marmellata di Mandarino* }

MARMILLATA RI MANNARINU

Most Sicilian fruits, from strawberries to peaches to lemons, are transformed into marmalades and fruit preserves. I always keep Sicilian citrus marmalades— especially those with minimal sugar—in my pantry, adding a touch to marinades, sauces, and desserts. Although not traditionally used in this manner in Sicilian cuisine, I find that mandarin marmalade adds the essence of Sicily to simple meals, from barbecued chicken to fruit salads.

The amount of sugar here can vary, although the 1 cup here is the minimum, as some sugar is needed to thicken the marmalade. Taste the marmalade while it's cooking, keeping in mind that it will sweeten as it reduces, and add more sugar if you please. You can substitute lemon, orange, citron, or any other variety of citrus for the mandarin, but there's no fruit in my mind that exudes the flavor of Sicily as the mandarin does.

Makes two 12-ounce jars

1 pound organic mandarins
1 cup sugar, or more to taste

1 Bring a large pot of water to a boil. Add the mandarins, reduce the heat to low, and cook for about 20 minutes. Remove the mandarins with a slotted spoon and place them on a rack or dishtowel to dry off and cool down.

2 Halve and seed the mandarins. Place them in a food processor, skins and all, and pulse until they break down into a chunky pulp.

3 Transfer the pulp to a heavy-bottomed pot and add the sugar. Set the pot over medium heat and bring the pulp to a boil. Reduce the heat to low and cook, stirring frequently, for about 45 minutes. Meanwhile, place a small plate in the freezer. To check if the marmalade is finished cooking, place a spoonful on the chilled plate; if liquid separates from the pulp, continue to cook until it thickens up.

4 Spoon the marmalade into sterilized jars (see page 70). If you would like to can the marmalade, proceed according to the jar manufacturer's instructions. Otherwise, the marmalade will keep in the refrigerator for at least 2 months.

QUINCE PASTE

{ *Cotognata* }

À CUTUGNATA

Quince are used in Sicilian cuisine to make marmalade and cotognata, *a stiff paste that is traditionally dried in the sun under a sheet of cheesecloth. The alluring taste of these treats is a bit hard to describe— somewhere between the flavors of an apple pie and stewed pears. In Sicily, the paste is poured into little ceramic molds, which hold about 1 cup and are adorned with decorations. You will need about ten of these unique containers, but in their absence, you can use muffin tins.*

The amount of sugar needed varies depending on the amount of puree; the sugar and quince should be used in equal quantities.

Cotognata *is eaten on warm bread or toast for breakfast or as a snack. It also pairs well with a wide range of aged Sicilian cheeses, as its sweetness complements the saltiness and pungency of the cheese.*

Makes 10 to 16 pieces

5 ripe quinces, peeled, cored, and quartered

3 to 4 cups sugar, or as needed

1/4 teaspoon ground cinnamon

1/4 teaspoon ground cloves

Grated zest and juice of 1 organic lemon

Grated zest of 1/2 organic orange

Grapeseed oil, for greasing the pan

1 Place the quinces in a stainless steel pot and add cold water to cover. Bring to a boil over high heat. Reduce the heat to low and cook for 20 minutes, until the fruit is soft and a paring knife slides smoothly into the flesh. Remove the pot from the heat and let the quince cool in the cooking water.

2 Drain the quince chunks and pass them through a food mill into a bowl or puree in a food processor.

3 Measure the puree, then measure out the same amount of sugar. Combine both in a clean saucepan and bring to a boil. Lower the heat and cook, stirring continuously, for 20 minutes. To determine if the puree is done, gather some on the wooden spoon. Turn the spoon vertically: if the puree remains on the spoon, remove the pan from the heat. Otherwise, continue cooking until the puree stays on the spoon. Add the cinnamon, cloves, lemon zest, lemon juice, and orange zest.

4 Slightly moisten the inside of your molds or muffin tin(s) with water. While the cooked quince paste is still hot, pour it into the molds and let it set overnight at room temperature. Cover with a lightweight clean kitchen towel.

5 The next day, preheat the oven to 120°F. Use the oil to lightly grease a baking sheet. Turn the paste out of the molds onto a the baking sheet; if the quince paste does not slip out easily, use a knife to loosen the edges. Place the baking sheet in the oven for about 1 hour and 10 minutes, until the surface of the paste is no longer tacky to the touch. Loosely wrap the quince paste in waxed paper and store in an airtight container. The quince paste will keep in this manner, at room temperature, for up to several months.

PRESERVED ARTICHOKE HEARTS

{ *Carciofi sott'Olio* }

CACOCCIULI SOTT'OGGHIU

These preserved artichoke chunks are delicious on their own or as an antipasti, but they also make great additions to salads and pasta dishes. In addition, they can be chopped up or ground in a food processor for use as a spread. I particularly enjoy making them into a paste by pureeing them in a food processor with a few sun-dried tomatoes (page 73), some high-quality extra-virgin olive oil, salted capers, and olives. This makes for a wonderful snack when spread on warm bread. The oil leftover in the jar is a tasty bonus; use it on salads or anytime you want the flavor of artichoke. Preferably choose small artichokes, which are more tender than large varieties.

Makes two ¹/₂-pint jars

Juice of ¹/₂ lemon

1 tablespoon salt

2 pounds small (or baby) artichokes

2 cups white wine vinegar

2 bay leaves

1¹/₂ cups olive oil, plus more if needed

1 tablespoon dried Sicilian oregano

¹/₂ teaspoon dried chile pieces or red pepper flakes

1 Fill a bowl with cold water and add the lemon juice and salt. Clean each artichoke by removing two layers of the outer leaves. Trim the stem to a 1-inch stub. Remove about 1 inch off the tops of the artichoke leaves using a sharp serrated knife. You will be left with the inner heart and some of the more tender leaves of the artichoke. (Small artichokes should not have a tough inner choke that needs to be removed.) As each piece is cut, place it the lemon water so it does not turn brown.

2 In a large pot, combine the vinegar, 2 cups water, and bay leaves and bring to a boil. Remove the artichokes from the lemon water and add them to the pot. Cook for about 12 minutes, until the inner hearts are soft to the touch. Make sure not to let the hearts overcook. Drain in a colander, then place upside down on a clean dishtowel to drain for about 2 hours.

3 Sterilize two ¹/₂-pint canning jars and tops (see page 70).

4 Pack the artichoke hearts as tightly as possible into the sterilized jars, leaving about ³/₄ inch of space at the top. Mix the olive oil with the oregano and chile and pour it over the artichoke hearts to fill the jars, leaving about ¹/₂ inch of head space. Top with more olive oil if any pieces of the artichokes remain above the surface. Place the tops on the jars. If desired, can the jars following the jar manufacturer's instructions. The sealed jars will keep in your pantry for up to 6 months. Otherwise, the artichokes will keep in the refrigerator for up to a few months, as long as they remain submerged in the oil. In any case, let the artichokes marinate in the mixture for at least 10 days before tasting them.

PRESERVED EGGPLANTS *with* CAPER BERRIES

{ *Melanzane sott'Olio con Cucunci* }

MILINCIANI SOTT'OGGHIU CU CUCUNCI

This type of preserved eggplant is popular all throughout Southern Italy. They are also referred to as melanzane a funghetto, *in other words eggplants disguised as mushrooms. Indeed, these eggplant strips are so savory, meaty, and delicious that they can be easily mistaken for preserved mushrooms.*

Makes two ¹/₂-pint jars

2 eggplants, cut into 1-inch cubes

Coarse sea salt

2 cups white wine vinegar

3 cups olive oil, plus more if needed

10 caper berries

3 garlic cloves, left whole

1 teaspoon dried chile pieces or red pepper flakes

2 tablespoons dried Sicilian oregano

1 Place the eggplant cubes in a strainer and sprinkle generously with coarse sea salt. Set the strainer in the sink and let sit for about 30 minutes. The salt will draw the bitter liquid from the eggplants.

2 In a large pot, bring 1 gallon water and the vinegar to a boil. Squeeze about one-third of the eggplant cubes in your hands to release any water and drop them into the poaching liquid. Cook for about 2 minutes, until the eggplant starts to soften. Using a slotted spoon, remove the eggplant from the liquid and place in a clean strainer. Repeat with the remaining eggplant. Let cool.

3 In a large bowl, mix the olive oil, caper berries, garlic, chile, and oregano. Add the eggplant pieces and toss to coat.

4 Sterilize two ¹/₂-pint canning jars and tops (see page 70).

5 With a small ladle, transfer the eggplant pieces and oil mixture to the jars, leaving space at the top of the jars in case you need to add more oil. Let the pieces settle in the jars. Add more olive oil if the eggplant pieces are not fully submerged. Place the lids on the jars.

5 If desired, can the jars following the jar manufacturer's instructions. The sealed jars will keep in your pantry for up to 1 year. Otherwise, the eggplant will keep in the refrigerator for up to a few months, as long as it remains submerged in the oil. In any case, let the eggplant marinate in the mixture for at least 10 days before tasting.

FROM LEFT TO RIGHT: *Sweet-and-Sour Winter Squash (page 77); Eggplant Caponata (page 74); Preserved Eggplants with Caper Berries (this page); Preserved Artichoke Hearts (page 67); Dried Tomatoes (page 73) in olive oil; Warm and Spicy Black Olives (page 121) in olive oil*

HOMEMADE TOMATO PULP

{ *La Salsa di Pomodoro in Bottiglia* }

'A SARSA

Throughout the month of August, in front of village homes and in the countryside, townspeople can be found preparing tomato pulp, or la sarsa di pommurola. *Making pulp for the entire year is an undertaking that requires multiple hands, and is usually a family activity. Not only is it a time-consuming process, but, as it requires standing over boiling liquid under the scorching summer sun, it is an arduous one as well.*

Many varieties of tomatoes exist, but the best types for pulping are cherry, plum, and costoluto *(pictured on page 220). The yield of the pulp depends on the variety and climate. Tomatoes should be very ripe and juicy.*

Once bottled, the unseasoned plain pulp can be held for months in jar. When used in a recipe, it is cooked with aromatic herbs, garlic, or onion. In Sicily, there's no one recipe for cooking tomato pulp into a sauce. In every home and town, it is prepared in a different manner. Some cooks add lightly sautéed garlic, while others use onion. Many add a pinch of sugar and/or baking soda to their sauce to balance out acidity.

Makes 4 to 6 pints tomato pulp

15 pounds tomatoes, stemmed and cleaned thoroughly

5 fresh basil leaves

6 tablespoons fresh lemon juice, or 2 teaspoons powdered citric acid (optional)

Note: If you do not plan on canning the pulp, then you may omit the lemon juice or citric acid. While my cousins skip this step, the additional acidity from the lemon juice or citric acid helps to reduce the possibility of spoilage.

1 Bring about 1 gallon water to a rolling boil in a large stockpot. Place the tomatoes in the water and let the water return to a boil. When the tomatoes split open, use a strainer or slotted spoon to transfer them to a bowl. Let cool slightly.

2 Set a food mill over a clean pot and run the tomatoes through the mill to crush them into pulp.

3 Place the pot over medium heat and bring the pulp to a boil. Reduce the heat and simmer, stirring often and making sure the sauce does not stick to the bottom of the pot, until the sauce has reduced by about one-quarter, about 20 minutes.

4 Remove the sauce from the stove and add the basil leaves. The pulp is now ready to be used immediately or can be preserved for later use. To freeze the tomato pulp, first let it cool completely, then divide it among freezer bags and seal the bags, pressing out any excess air. The pulp will keep for many months in the freezer.

5 TO CAN THE SAUCE IN JARS: Before preparing the pulp, in a large pot, sterilize the jars: Immerse them in water to cover, bring to a boil, and boil for 10 minutes. Use jar tongs to retrieve the jars from the water and set them upside down on clean dishtowels to dry. Place the lids in a large heatproof bowl and cover with very hot water to let the rubber seals soften.

6 When the tomato pulp is ready, stir in the lemon juice. Use a funnel or ladle to fill each jar to 1/2 inch from the top of the jar.

7 Place the lids on top of the jars, with the rubber binder side of the lid facing down. Place the ring around the jar top and screw on to just finger tight.

continued ↓

8 To ensure that the jars are sealed correctly and to avoid the growth of bacteria, the jars must now be boiled in a water bath or pressure canner on your stovetop. The amount of water you place in the canner will depend on the exact type you purchase. Each type of canner comes with different instructions. Make sure to follow the directions that come with yours, not only for the amount of water used, but also for the amount of time that the jars need to stay in the water.

9 After carefully removing the jars from the canner with the jar tongs, let the jars cool on a clean dishtowel for several hours without letting them touch one another.

10 Before storing, loosen halfway the screw-on rings (leaving the lids in place). This is to make sure that there is no residual moisture that has collected under the rings, which would cause the metal to rust. Then check that the lids have sealed completely by pressing with one finger on the center of the lid. If the lid

makes a popping sound, it is not sealed. Either store the unsealed jar in the refrigerator and use within a few days, or repeat the canning process with the unsealed jar(s).

Sun-Dried Tomato Paste

On the hottest and most arid days of summer, sun-dried tomato paste, known as *astrattu*, is made by hand by spreading tomato pulp on wood boards to dry under the sun. After the moisture from the pulp concentrates, the paste that remains is extremely thick, with a concentrated flavor of tomato. Not to be confused with canned tomato paste, *astrattu* is an artisan product used in sauces and ragùs or simply enjoyed with fresh bread and a drizzle of olive oil. (See Sources, page 326 for where to purchase *astrattu* in the United States.)

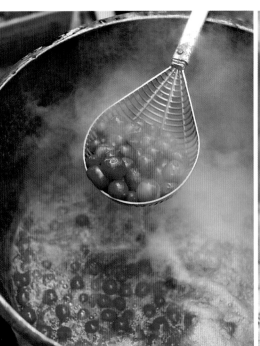

DRIED TOMATOES

{ Pomodori Secchi }

PUMADORA SICCHI

Most commercially produced tomatoes labeled as "sun-dried" were in fact dried in ovens, not in the sun. However, along with most Sicilians, I create a genuine product by dusting cut tomatoes with sea salt and laying them out to dry on racks under the sun for about ten days. During the summer, to prepare sun-dried tomatoes at home, all you need is a spot in your garden or on your terrace that receives direct sunlight.

In Sicily, sun-drying tomatoes takes place in summer months thanks to very arid weather and little to no rainfall. If it does rain, showers usually come only in short bursts. After the rain when the sun reappears, the salt is replaced on the tomatoes and the drying continues. A motion detector that plays the recorded screech of an eagle when it senses movement keeps animals away.

In the southeast corner of Sicily, cherry tomatoes are grown in abundance. They are called pomodorini pachino, *as this variety originated from the town of Pachino, on the Aeolian Islands. On the balconies of homes there, you will spot whole cherry tomato clusters hung up on strings; this is a particularly Aeolian custom.*

Dried tomatoes can be dressed with olive oil (as well as some dried Sicilian oregano and black pepper, if you like) and served as a cold antipasto. I like to turn them into a paste in the food processor, then spread the paste on grilled slices of bread or mix it into pasta dough to create a sun-dried tomato fresh pasta.

All types of tomatoes, not just cherry tomatoes, can be dried. But the best are those with more flesh and less inner pulp, such as cherry tomatoes, grape tomatoes, and plum tomatoes. The exact yield will vary depending on the water content in the type of tomato you use.

Makes about 1 pound dried tomatoes

2 to 3 pounds plum, grape, or cherry tomatoes, halved lengthwise

2 tablespoons semi-coarse sea salt

1 In a large bowl, toss the tomatoes with the salt.

2 Line a baking sheet with a metal rack. (This will allow air to circulate between the tomatoes and the baking sheet.) Place tomatoes cut-side up on the rack. Make sure to leave space between each tomato piece to allow the air to circulate sufficiently.

3 TO DRY TOMATOES IN THE SUN: You should attempt to dry your tomatoes in the sun only on the hottest and most arid days of summer when the temperature is above 90°F and the humidity is below 60 percent. If you live in an area that gets frequent summer rain, or if you don't have access to direct sun for at least 8 hours a day, dry your tomatoes in the oven following the instructions below.

Place a piece of cheesecloth on top of the tomatoes to protect them from insects and dust. Place the baking sheet in direct sunlight and leave the tomatoes to dry for up to 2 weeks, until the tomatoes are shriveled but still soft to the bite. Bring them indoors in the evening to avoid attracting animals and prevent exposure to nighttime humidity. Also, bring them indoors when it rains or when the humidity exceeds 60 percent.

TO DRY TOMATOES IN THE OVEN: Preheat the oven to 150°F. Dry the tomatoes in the oven for 3 hours, then turn the tomato pieces over and dry for another 3 to 4 hours, until the moisture has fully evaporated from the tomato pieces.

4 Since traces of moisture will remain in the dried tomatoes, they are best stored in jars or in airtight plastic bags in the refrigerator or freezer. Alternatively, sun-dried tomatoes can be placed in sterilized jars, covered with olive oil, and stored in a dark pantry for up to 6 months.

EGGPLANT CAPONATA

{ *Caponata di Melanzane* }

CAPUNATA RI MILINCIANI

Some assert that the word caponata *is a derivative of* capone, *the name of the mahimahi fish once prepared in a similar style to today's caponata. According to the late Sicilian food chronicler Giuseppe Coria, in aristocratic kitchens of the past, the dish was prepared predominantly with seafood, usually octopus, and mixed with eggplant, artichokes, and other vegetables, pine nuts, and raisins. Peasants copied the dish, omitting the fish.*

Of all the recipes in this book, caponata is the one that varies most in preparation. The word itself now loosely denotes a form of preparing any cold appetizer or side dish with chunks of fried vegetables or seafood that have been tossed with olive oil and sweet-and-sour agrodolce *(page 46). Although the caponata classically highlights eggplant, on menus around Sicily the dish can be found prepared with apples, squash, artichokes, tuna, or swordfish as the primary ingredient instead of eggplant. Most versions contain celery, onion, and tomato sauce; some also contain peeled tomato. Some cooks use capers and olives to add salty notes, while others use raisins to add an additional sweetness instead. Carrots, garlic, potatoes, pine nuts, and/ or almonds are also popular additions, but are not required. In Siracusa, bitter cocoa is mixed into the caponata before serving and some towns top the caponata with toasted breadcrumbs (see the variation on the next page). Peppers are optional, but when used are often added in abundance. One of my favorite bottled versions of caponata is prepared with peppers, not eggplant; it's made by Fratelli Burgio and sold at their flagship store in the Siracusa market.*

Caponata can be eaten with bread or directly as an appetizer.

Serves 6 as an appetizer

1 cup olive oil

2 medium eggplants, cut into 1-inch cubes

1 large onion, cut into 1-inch pieces

3 celery stalks, cut on an angle into 1-inch pieces

$1/2$ cup *agrodolce* (page 46), prepared with white wine vinegar

$1/2$ cup pitted green Sicilian olives

$1/4$ cup rinsed capers

2 tablespoons tomato paste, dissolved in 1 cup water

Salt

1 In a sauté pan, heat $1/2$ cup of the olive oil over medium heat. Add the eggplant and fry, stirring occasionally, until golden brown, about 5 minutes. Remove from the oil using a slotted spoon and transfer to paper towels to drain excess oil. Fry the onion and celery in separate batches using additional olive oil as needed, until soft to the touch. (It is best to cook the vegetables separately because they have different cooking times.)

2 Meanwhile, in a small saucepan, heat the *agrodolce* over medium heat. Transfer the cooked vegetables to a large sauté pan and add the olives and capers. Cook over medium heat until well heated, about 5 minutes. Add the tomato paste mixture and the *agrodolce*. Cook for 10 minutes more, until the ingredients are well incorporated and the eggplants have soaked up the sauce. Taste and season: about 1 teaspoon salt is usually sufficient. The caponata should be delicately sweet and sour, but you should still taste the vegetables. Let cool to room temperature and hold in the refrigerator until ready to serve, up to 1 week. Alternatively, the caponata can be canned following the jar manufacturer's instructions, and held in the pantry for up to 1 year.

* EGGPLANT CAPONATA WITH COCOA AND BREADCRUMBS *

Before serving the caponata, stir in 1 tablespoon cocoa powder and top with 2 tablespoons toasted breadcrumbs (page 42) and 2 tablespoons crushed blanched almonds.

* GREEN APPLE CAPONATA *

This can be served as an appetizer, but it also makes a great side dish with roasted or grilled pork chops. In place of the eggplant, substitute 4 unpeeled green apples, cored and chopped. When sautéing the apple, be careful to remove the pan from the heat before the apple breaks down. Continue with the recipe, but use only 1 tablespoon tomato paste.

* TUNA CAPONATA *

Instead of eggplant, use ½ pound tuna belly. Poach the tuna in olive oil as in the recipe on page 258. Continue with the caponata recipe as directed. Store in the refrigerator.

* ARTICHOKE CAPONATA *

Instead of the eggplant, use the hearts from 2 pounds fresh artichokes (clean the artichokes as directed on page 67). Quarter the artichoke hearts and remove the inner hairs (the choke) with a paring knife. (Place the artichoke hearts in lemon water as you are cutting them.) Cook the hearts in salted boiling water with a few pieces of lemon until they are soft to the touch, but not mushy, about 10 minutes. Drain, discarding the lemon pieces. Continue with the caponata recipe as directed.

CHRISTMAS CAPONATA

{ *Caponata Natalizie* }

CUNIGGHIU POLIZZANO

The name of this hearty caponata, cunigghiu, *translates as "rabbit." In the past, during the Christmas season in Polizzi Generosa, a hilltop town in the Madonie mountains, rabbit was baked with vegetables, olives, and capers in aristocratic homes. Peasants reinvented the dish with the more affordable and accessible salted fish. Today, it is traditionally served on Christmas Eve. It's to be expected that there are several local variations. Some cooks replace the potatoes with beans from Polizzi, known as badda beans, while others add tuna intestines or tuna belly to the recipe.*

Juice of 1 lemon,
plus more as needed

Salt

3 artichokes

$^1/_2$ head cauliflower,
cut into bite-size pieces

1 head fennel, cut into
bite-size pieces, green
fronds reserved

2 cardoon stalks, cut into
bite-size pieces (optional)

$^1/_2$ pound potatoes, peeled
and cut into bite-size pieces

About 2 cups olive oil,
for frying

1 pound salt-cured codfish,
rehydrated (see page 54)

2 cups Soffritto (page 40)

$^1/_2$ cup green olives,
pitted and halved

1 tablespoon salted capers,
rinsed well

$^1/_2$ cup *agrodolce* (page 46)

1 Fill a bowl with cold water and add the lemon juice and some salt. Clean each artichoke by removing two layers of the outer leaves. Trim the stem to a 1-inch stub. Remove about 1 inch off the tops of the remaining artichoke leaves using a sharp serrated knife. You will be left with the inner heart and some of the more tender leaves of the artichoke. Cut the artichokes in half and clean out the choke. As each piece is cut, place it the lemon water so it does not turn brown.

2 Bring a large pot of water to a boil. Working with each vegetable separately, blanch the cauliflower, fennel, cardoon, potatoes, and artichokes in the boiling water until each vegetable can be easily pierced with a knife, adding lemon juice to the water for the cardoons and artichokes in order to retain their color. The cauliflower, fennel, cardoon, and artichokes should be cooked through in about 5 minutes; the potatoes should be done in 8 minutes. As the vegetables are cooked, transfer them to a strainer to drain. Let the vegetables dry off for about 30 minutes before moving to the next step.

3 Heat about 2 inches of olive oil in a large sauté pan over medium to high heat. Fry the vegetables in batches until they are soft to the touch.

4 Meanwhile, heat 2 tablespoons olive oil in a separate sauté pan over high heat. Add the codfish and sear until the fish flakes apart easily with a knife, 6 to 8 minutes.

5 In a large pot over medium heat, add the soffritto and cook until heated through. Add all the vegetables, the codfish, olives, and capers and heat through. Add the *agrodolce* and toss to combine. Cook for no more than 5 minutes, just to let the flavors combine. Serve hot or cold. Store in the refrigerator for up to 10 days.

WINTER SQUASH CAPONATA

{ Caponata di Zucca Rossa }

CAPUNATA RI CUCUZZA RUSSA

In winter months, caponata can be prepared with vegetables typical of the season. I've tried many seasonal versions of caponata, and this recipe is one that I prepared often in my own New York City restaurants when eggplant was out of season. Sometimes I added cauliflower florets, celery root, or other vegetables available at my local farmers' market to the mixture.

Serves 6 as an appetizer

About ¾ cup olive oil

1 pound butternut squash, peeled and cut into ¾-inch cubes

2 onions, cut into ½-inch pieces

3 celery stalks, cut on an angle into 1-inch pieces

1 cup pitted green Sicilian olives

2 tablespoons golden raisins, soaked for 1 hour in water and drained

2 tablespoons pine nuts

¼ cup *agrodolce* (page 46)

Salt

1 In a sauté pan, heat ½ cup of the olive oil over medium heat. Add the squash and sauté, tossing occasionally, until softened but not mushy, about 4 minutes. Remove from the oil using a slotted spoon and transfer to paper towels to drain excess oil. Fry the onions and celery in separate batches, using additional oil as needed, until the onions are golden brown and the celery is soft. Make sure not to crowd the sauté pan or overcook the vegetables.

2 Toss all the vegetables together in a large bowl and add the olives, raisins, and pine nuts. Gently fold in the *agrodolce*, a little at a time, making sure not to break up the squash. You might not need to use all of the *agrodolce*, if you feel that the vegetables are getting either too sweet or sour. Taste and season with salt.

SWEET-AND-SOUR WINTER SQUASH

{ Zucca all'Agrodolce }

CUCCUZZA RUSSA ALL'AGRA E DUCI

In this recipe, the sweetness of winter squash is augmented with the sugar in the agrodolce, *but is balanced by the acidity of the vinegar. The dish is rounded out with garlic and mint. Serve cold as an appetizer, along with other preserved vegetables.*

Serves 4

Olive oil, for frying

1 pound pumpkin or butternut squash, peeled and cut into ½-inch-thick slices

½ cup *agrodolce* (page 46)

1 teaspoon Garlic Paste (page 40)

¼ cup finely chopped fresh mint

1 teaspoon salt, or to taste

½ teaspoon cracked black peppercorns

1 In a heavy-bottomed pan, heat about ½ inch of olive oil over medium heat. When hot, place a single layer of the pumpkin or butternut squash slices in the pan. Working in batches, fry the slices, turning them occasionally, until the edges turn light brown, about 5 minutes. Using tongs, remove them from the oil and transfer to paper towel–lined plates to drain any excess oil.

2 In a bowl, mix the *agrodolce*, garlic paste, mint, about 1 teaspoon salt, and some cracked pepper.

3 Heat a clean heavy-bottomed pan over medium heat. Add the fried squash and the *agrodolce* mixture. Cook until the liquid has been absorbed by the squash, about 3 minutes. Let cool before serving. The squash will keep in the refrigerator in an airtight container for up to 1 week.

VISITING A CHEESEMAKER

A few years ago, my chef friend Roberto proclaimed to me that he'd discovered the best pecorino of his life. I was intrigued, and on my next trip to Sicily, we set out to visit the man responsible for this cheese, Antonino Merandino. His farm is located in a secluded rural area in the outskirts of the village of Carlentini. The hills in this area of Sicily, part of the Hyblean mountains, were full of abandoned trellises from the preindustrial days, when trees were planted on the sides of steep cliffs. The limestone-rich territory was divided by rock walls into plots farmed by peasants under the former *latifundia* system, when it was controlled by wealthy absentee barons prior to Italian land reforms in 1950.

Upon arriving at Antonino's property, I was struck by its beauty: Cows grazed in deep valleys where ancient caves—built by indigenous populations during the Bronze Age—were nestled into the contours of the rocky mountains. Sicily was the land of the monstrous Cyclops, visited by Odysseus in Homer's *Odyssey*. The mythical Cyclops was a man-eater—but also a cheesemaker who kept both sheep and goats and collected their milk to make ancient variations of some of Sicily's current-day cheeses. Legend says he stored his cheeses in mountainous caves.

Antonino began our tour in a hundred-square-foot space called a *salatura*, where wheels of cheese are salted and aged. Roberto followed and pointed out one of the older cheeses on the shelf. He looked at me without saying a word and waved his right hand in circles while staring directly in my eyes. His gestures indicated that this was the cheese he had tasted and loved. He then said, "Pecorino like this is hard to find. Everyone makes it, but sincerely it has been more than twenty years since I have tasted such an old-fashioned style of cheese." He explained that other aged dairy products on the market taste chalky because they use milk powder as opposed to fresh milk to produce cheese.

The sheep's milk cheese was present in four stages: fresh (*tuma fresca*), first salting (*primo sale*), second salting (*secondo sale*), and aged (*stagionato*). The longer it is aged, the less moisture the cheese contains, and the harder and saltier in taste it gets. The first cheese we tried was the *primo sale*. It was aged about ten days and only lightly salty. As I bit into it, I noticed little holes throughout. It crumbled in my fingers, unlike the waxy types of young sheep's milk Sicilian cheeses I had previously experienced. Next we tried the *tuma fresca*, which is sheep's milk cheese before it has been salted, followed by a salted ricotta made from goat's and sheep's milk. Finally, we arrived at the wheel Roberto had claimed was the best of his life, the one I had waited over a month to try. Antonino offered us two versions of the *pecorino stagionato*, one of which had peppercorns in it. Both were saltier than anything we had tried so far, but not overly salty as many pecorinos I've tasted in the past had been. These pecorinos were nuttier, with multiple layers of flavor and a lingering grassy finish. I admired the sharpness of the one spiked with black peppercorns, which were soft enough to chew as a result of their long rest inside the moist cheese. I wanted to compliment his products, so I said to Antonino, "This cheese tastes so different from anything I've ever tasted." My friend Roberto abruptly corrected me, saying, "This cheese is made in the old-fashioned way, like my grandfather used to make. It is the other cheese that is different from this real cheese, and not the other way around."

While the cheeses we sampled were mouthwatering, Antonino claimed that his fresh ricotta was actually the driving force keeping him afloat. Throughout Italy, most commercial ricotta is made from a mixture of milk and milk powder, which contains flour and is dangerous for those with gluten intolerances. Labels fail to indicate this ingredient. "My pockets are empty," says Antonino, implying that they would be full of money if he added milk powder to the 300 liters of milk his animals produce each day. He claims he could double his production and reduce costs, but he is adamant that he will never sell anything but the genuine product. "I prefer to make real ricotta and cheese that are rare in the marketplace, than make money selling a bad product, even if I don't become rich from it," said Antonino.

RICOTTA GRIDDLE CAKES

{ Frittelle di Ricotta }

FRITTEDDI RI RICOTTA

Cheesemaker Antonino Merandino shared with me this recipe for cooking ricotta, not with pasta or a dessert as is typical, but in a way that highlighted the taste of the original product. This afternoon snack must be made with artisanal ricotta—even better if it's homemade (page 80). If it comes in a basket, you're in luck: it's already strained. If the ricotta you buy is not strained (this is the case if it comes in a tub and feels very wet to the touch), put 4 cups ricotta in a colander lined with a cheesecloth and twist the cheesecloth tightly to squeeze out the excess liquid. The trickiest part of making these griddle cakes is flipping them over without breaking them. I suggest a gentle turn in the pan with the help of a rubber spatula for best results.

Serves 8

3 cups strained fresh ricotta (preferably sheep's milk ricotta)

2 large eggs

8 slices toasted bread

Orange flower honey, for drizzling

1 In a bowl, beat the ricotta and eggs until smooth.

2 Heat a nonstick or well-seasoned skillet over medium heat. Working in batches, use a tablespoon to form the ricotta into balls. Press the balls into the pan, forming 2-inch patties. You will make about 20 patties.

3 Cook the patties, turning them once with a rubber spatula, until both sides are golden brown, about 3 to 4 minutes per side. Remove the griddle cakes from the pan and place two cakes over each slice of toast. Drizzle with honey and serve warm.

HOMEMADE TUMA *and* RICOTTA

{ *Tuma e Ricotta* }

Tuma is a Sicilian cheese produced from curd without any salt. Cheese cannot be preserved without salt, and thus tuma must always be eaten fresh. While tuma is delicious plain, it is also used in recipes. It possesses a moist and elastic consistency that slides against the teeth when bitten into. Due to its uncomplicated flavor profile, tuma pairs well with a wide range of ingredients, both savory and sweet. It can be seared in a nonstick pan before being drizzled with olive oil and vinegar, and sprinkled with salt, pepper, and oregano, a dish known as tuma all'argentiera. *In addition, the fresh cheese can be breaded and fried. A popular recipe known as a* cannolo di tuma *is prepared by rolling the fresh cheese with a meat and pea ragù (page 167) into the shape of a tube, which is then dipped in egg and breadcrumbs and deep-fried.*

Like tuma, fresh ricotta (literally "recooked") does not end up in the salting room. Ricotta is made from whey left over from the production of cheese, and therefore is not even technically a cheese. In Sicilian cuisine, ricotta is used in countless ways. It can be baked into pasta dishes, used as a stuffing for ravioli (page 204) or a binder, stirred into sauce, or lightly sweetened for desserts such as cannoli (page 305) and cassata.

Although ricotta can be produced with cow's, sheep's, or goat's milk, in Sicily it is most commonly prepared with sheep's milk. Ricotta is produced most of the year, although it is popular in the spring, when the grass is green and the milk used to make it is full of flavor.

When preparing ricotta at home, you will need rennet to coagulate the milk. Rennet is available in many forms: liquid, powder, or tablets. While calf rennet is considered the best for aged cheeses, vegetable-based rennet can be used to prepare tuma or ricotta (see Sources, page 326). If you have excess ricotta, a good way to save it from spoilage is by whipping it and sweetening it with confectioners' sugar. Store it in an airtight container in the freezer for up to 1 month.

When preparing desserts with the frozen ricotta, let it thaw overnight in the refrigerator.

Makes about 1 pound tuma and 1 pound ricotta

2 gallons whole sheep's, goat's, or cow's milk	**1 teaspoon rennet**

1 Place 1¼ gallons (20 cups) of the milk in a large pot and clip a candy thermometer to the side of the pot. Heat the milk over medium heat until it reaches 97°F, then take the pot off the heat and stir in the rennet.

2 Let the mixture sit at room temperature for 30 minutes. The curd will slowly accumulate at the top.

3 Using a rubber spatula or wooden spoon, gently break apart the curd (the *cagliata*) into small pieces. Using a slotted spoon, transfer the curd pieces to a large sieve lined with several layers of cheesecloth set over a bowl. Let the curd drain off excess moisture for 3 to 4 hours. Now you have tuma, which will keep in the refrigerator for up to 5 days.

4 To continue the process and make ricotta, combine the whey, the liquid that drained from the curds, with the remaining 12 cups milk in a large pot. Clip the candy thermometer to the side and heat the milk over medium heat until it registers 172°F.

5 Remove the pot from the heat. The curdled whey will float to the top. Skim these curds off using a slotted spoon and place them in a clean sieve lined with several layers of cheesecloth set over a bowl. Let the curds drain for 3 to 4 hours. Now you have ricotta, which is best used within 24 hours, but can keep in the refrigerator for up to 5 days.

BAKED RICOTTA

{ Ricotta Infornata }

RICOTTA 'NFUNATA

Ricotta is not only consumed fresh but is also commonly baked, a process that imparts a dark brown crust and a more concentrated, slightly caramelized flavor. Baked ricotta is also used in cooking, such as in the recipe for Pasta alla Norma (page 173). Cheesemakers sell rounds of baked ricotta, but you can easily prepare it at home with some leftover ricotta. All you'll need is cheesecloth and some aluminum foil.

Makes ½ pound

½ pound ricotta

1 Wrap the ricotta with cheesecloth and place it in a strainer set over a bowl. Refrigerate the ricotta overnight to drain.

2 Preheat the oven to 375°F.

3 Remove the ricotta from the cheesecloth and form it into a ball, then press it into a disc. Place the disc on a piece of aluminum foil and bring the edges up to wrap completely.

4 Bake the ricotta disc for about 30 minutes, until it turns golden on top. Remove the foil from the top of the ricotta. Bake until the ricotta is browned on the top, 10 minutes more. Let cool to room temperature before storing in the refrigerator, where it will keep for up to 5 days.

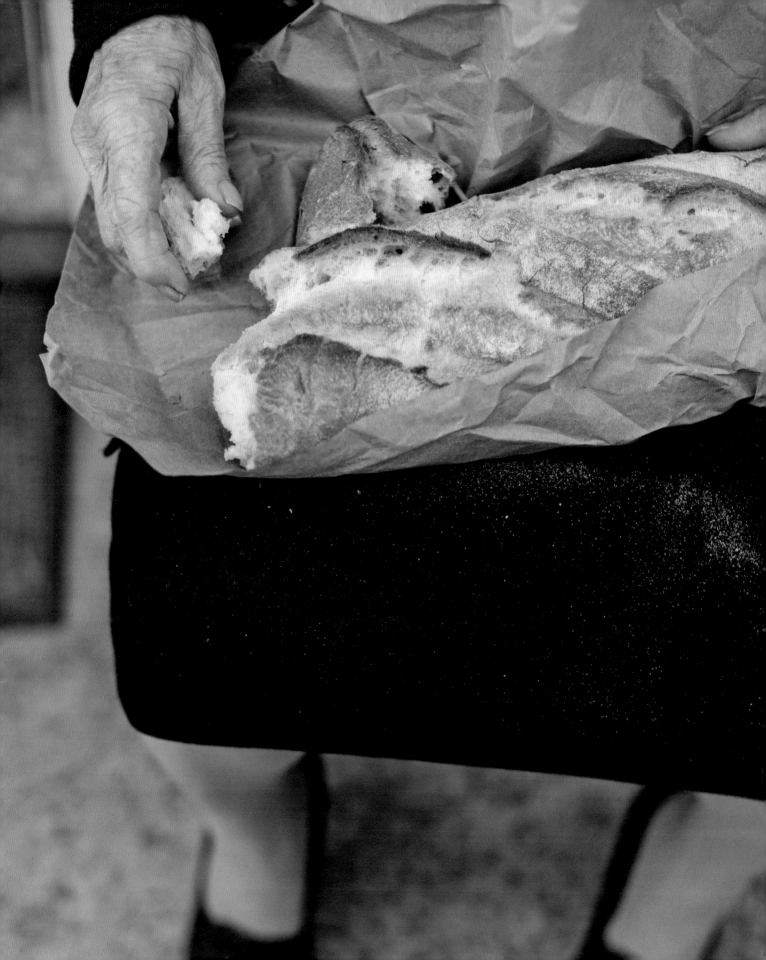

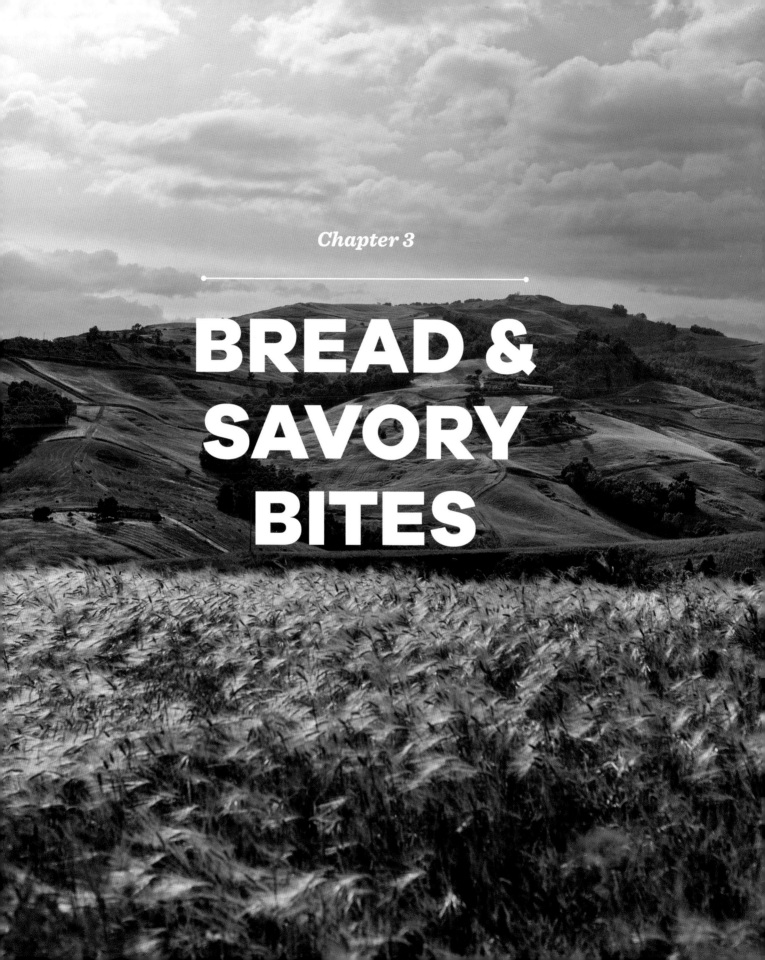

Chapter 3

BREAD & SAVORY BITES

O FTEN CALLED the granary of the Roman Empire, Sicily has cultivated wheat for nearly three millennia, and bread making was well established by the Greek colonizers. Wheat is more than a food in Sicily; a symbol of the fortitude of the land, it adorns the regional flag. Treated like the living organism that it is, wheat is celebrated and considered sacred.

For centuries, wheat also served as currency. The grain was measured not by weight, but by its volume, in receptacles known in Sicilian dialect as *tumuli*. Throughout the year, agricultural families would pay the barber or the butcher in *tumoli*. After the harvest, debts were paid and the grain left over would feed the family. This practice lasted until shortly after World War II.

During my childhood summers in Sant'Anna, I would wake up to the toasty scent of semolina bread baking in the wood-burning oven of the *panificio* permeating the narrow village streets. Straight out of bed, I ventured to the bread store to pick up a few loaves, ripping off and devouring the crusty ends before leaving the shop.

It's impossible for me to imagine a Sicilian meal without the presence of a loaf of crusty bread. In my home, as in most family environments, bread becomes an extension of the hand during meals. Chunks of bread are essential for soaking up sauces on the plate. My mother dips her piece of bread into a glass of red wine—just like her Sicilian grandfather.

I first learned bread making from my mother and grandmother. In our home kitchen in New York, baking was a ritual on weekends. They experimented with doughs and yeasts to try to reproduce a Sicilian-style bread. My grandmother used to place a pot of water in our oven to add moisture to the loaf as it baked. I loved to make bread as a teenager, so much so that when studying abroad in Japan during high school, I taught my family's bread recipes to my host family who owned a bakery and in turn successfully sold this Sicilian-style bread to their customers. It was my first experience as a consulting chef!

I learned the most important lesson about bread making from my mother: Bread is alive. Some say that kneading dough is a good time to get your anger and frustrations out. My mother, however, made sure that I treated the bread with love and care, since we would be consuming it. Perhaps that's why bread in our home always tasted so delicious.

As a general rule: The less yeast used in a bread recipe, the longer the bread needs to ferment and the stronger the flavor of the cooked dough. The more yeast used, the quicker the fermentation time needed and the less complex flavor in the final product.

Three main types of starters (which help dough to rise) are used in Sicilian bread making. The first type is mother yeast, or *lievito madre*, which is also referred to as a sourdough starter.

The next type of starter is known as a *biga*, which is prepared with packaged yeast, either dry or fresh. Such starters can be made in advance and can even be frozen, but would need to defrost for a few hours at room temperature before use.

My cousin Maria always reserves a piece of dough after making bread or pizza (see page 105) and uses it as a starter—a third option.

When preparing a *biga* or if adding packaged yeast directly to flour, I suggest using fresh yeast, which has a pleasant natural taste. Fresh yeast is usually sold at health food stores in blocks that you can store in the refrigerator or freeze. When adding it to flour, make sure that you first break the chunk of yeast into small pieces to avoid pieces of yeast in your dough. The more common dry yeast is sold in packets in supermarkets. Fresh yeast is called for in the recipes in this chapter, but you can substitute dry yeast; just use half the quantity of dried yeast to fresh.

When baking bread, I strongly recommend using a scale to follow the weight measurements provided. (Volume conversions are imprecise because different brands of flour vary in weight, and humidity and storage can also affect volume.)

VARIETIES OF WHEAT AND FLOUR

Two main types of wheat—soft and hard—are used in Sicilian cuisine. Soft wheat (*triticum vulgare*) makes powdery white flour. Durum wheat (*triticum durum*), on the other hand, produces a coarser flour with an amber color. Heritage varieties of durum wheat are gaining popularity in Sicily these days. They vary slightly in color. For instance, tumminia, the flour used traditionally in Black Bread (page 92) is tan in color—and darkens more during baking as compared to contemporary varieties of durum wheat. Both soft and durum wheats are used in bread baking in Sicily. Durum wheat is the flour of choice in pasta making, while soft wheat flour is used in pastries, cakes, cookies, and brioches.

Durum wheat flour absorbs less water than soft wheat flour. There are three types of durum wheat flours produced: hard wheat whole flour, semolina, and semola. Whole flour is gritty in texture, as it contains the bran and it is classically milled by stone. Semolina is coarse and slightly gritty. Semola, which is semolina milled a second time, is softer and more refined.

In Italy, five different types of soft wheat flours are produced: type 00, type 0, type 1, type 2, and whole wheat flour. Type 00, the finest of all, is a highly refined flour that undergoes multiple grindings. Type 0 is richer in gluten and makes dough more elastic and firm in consistency. The rising time for dough made with type 0 is longer. While the type 00 is used for pastries, the 0 works best in baking bread. Type 1 and 2 are even less refined. Whole wheat contains the bran, which is removed in the other flours.

"SNAKE" BREAD

MAFALDA

Bread made from remilled semola flour, also called semola rimacinata, is extremely popular throughout Sicily. The loaves can be found in many shapes. Most commonly, the bread is crusty and baked in a wood-burning oven. The recipe below, found all over Sicily, makes a firm loaf, with a tight dough structure, that is perfect for slicing.

Mafalda refers to the shape, which resembles a snake. Other popular Sicilian bread shapes appear opposite.

Makes 1 large or 8 small loaves

Dough
———

1 pound farina type 0 flour or all-purpose flour

3¹/₃ pounds remilled hard wheat semola flour

1 pound Starter Dough (below)

¹/₂ teaspoon wildflower honey

1 tablespoon fine salt

¹/₂ cup warm purified water

2 tablespoons extra-virgin olive oil

¹/₄ cup sesame seeds

1 Combine the two types of flour. In a stand mixer with a dough paddle, combine the starter, honey, salt, water, and half of the flour mixture. Mix on a low speed. Slowly add the remaining flour and mix well. The dough will be sticky at this stage.

2 Grease a large mixing bowl with olive oil, add the dough, turning to coat it with the oil and rolling it into a ball. Cover the bowl with a clean kitchen towel and let sit in a warm area of the kitchen for 1 hour or until doubled in size.

3 Punch down the dough and transfer it to a floured work surface. Knead the dough for about 10 minutes, until it is soft and smooth. Roll into a 3-foot-long log. To create the shape of a snake, twist the log into the form of a backwards *S* three times and use the end of the *S* to cover the dough on top in the middle of the loaf. Or, to make 8 small loaves, cut the dough into 8 pieces, roll each into a 12-inch-long log, and form into the snake shape.

4 Line a baking sheet with parchment paper. Transfer the dough shape(s) to the sheet. Using a kitchen brush, wet the top of each loaf with water and cover the tops with the sesame seeds. Cover with a clean kitchen towel and place each loaf in a warm part of the kitchen to let rise for about 1 hour, until nearly doubled in size.

5 Preheat the oven to 400°F. Bake the loaf for 30 minutes, or about 20 minutes if you have made 8 small loaves. The bread is ready when you knock the bottom of the loaf and hear a hollow sound. Let cool on a rack for at least 20 minutes before cutting.

Starter Dough
BIGA
———

Yields 1 pound

0.35 ounce (about 1 tablespoon plus ¹/₂ teaspoon) fresh yeast

1 pound bread flour (or substitute type of flour you will use in your bread making)

1 cup warm water

1 In a stand mixer with a dough paddle, combine the yeast, flour, and warm water on slow speed. When the elements have combined, mix for an additional 4 minutes on high speed, until bubbles begin to form on the surface of the water, indicating that the yeast is activating.

2 Remove the bowl from the mixer and cover it with plastic wrap. Let sit overnight on the counter or up to 2 days in the refrigerator.

CLASSIC BREAD SHAPES

Ciambella—round with a hole in the middle, like a doughnut

Filone, filoncino, quartino—long loaves in different weights/sizes

Gadduzzu—shaped like a crescent moon (typical of the area around Caltanissetta)

Miliddi di San Biagio—small rebaked chunks of bread served to celebrate the Feast of Saint Biagio

Minne—small rolls shaped like breasts—for Saint Agatha

Occhi di Santa Lucia—shape of an S representing the eyes of Saint Lucia

Panini di San Antonio—small braided rolls for the saint's day on June 13

Pesce—a long loaf with incisions on the side so that the bread resembles a fish

Stella—shaped like a star or a flower

Treccia—braid

Vastedda—round, flat, large loaf

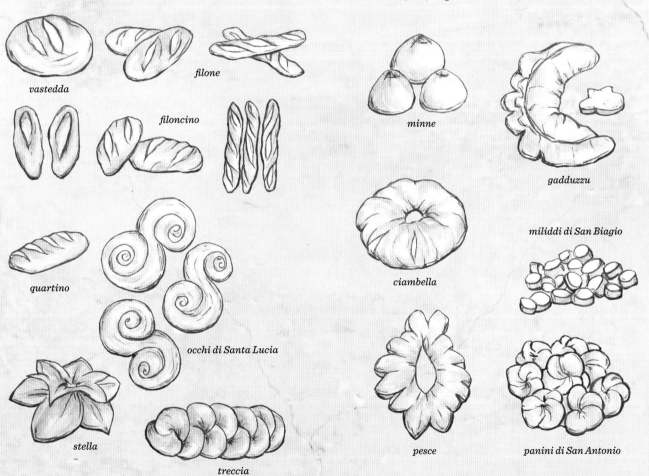

vastedda

filone

filoncino

minne

gadduzzu

quartino

occhi di Santa Lucia

ciambella

miliddi di San Biagio

stella

treccia

pesce

panini di San Antonio

SOFT ROLLS

MUFFULETTA

Muffuletta is a soft, small, round loaf of bread that is made all over Sicily. There are many different uses for the bread, as well as various ways the dough can be prepared. Sometimes the rolls are prepared in flat shapes with little crumb, while at other times they are puffed up with a moist crumb. The common denominator in the production of muffuletta *is that the dough always contains a greater percentage of water than regular bread.*

The muffuletta *is a classic bread of the winter holidays and is often enjoyed straight from the oven, served with ricotta and lard or with olive oil, pepper, anchovies, and cheese. In Palermo, the rolls served stuffed with* milza, *or spleen, are a common street food. Some towns consume* muffuletta *on November 2 for the Day of the Dead, while others eat it on November 11, for the Feast of Saint Martin, accompanied by a glass of new wine. The holiday is always the first day that new wine is tasted in Sicily.*

Makes 12 small rolls

1 pound bread flour	2 tablespoons wildflower honey
1 pound remilled hard wheat semola flour	2 cups warm purified water
0.3 ounce (1 teaspoon) dry malt	0.5 ounce (2^1/$_2$ teaspoons) salt
0.5 ounce (about 1^1/$_2$ tablespoons) fresh yeast, broken up into small chunks	^{1}/$_3$ cup extra-virgin olive oil, plus more for greasing
	^{1}/$_4$ cup sesame seeds

1 In a stand mixer with a hook attachment, combine the bread flour and remilled semolina flour, the malt, yeast, and honey. With the mixer moving on the slowest possible speed, pour in the warm water, little by little, until all of the ingredients incorporate. Add the salt and mix well. Slowly pour in the olive oil until it is fully absorbed by the dough. Place the dough on a floured work surface and form into a round ball.

2 Grease a large bowl with olive oil. Add the dough, turning to coat it with the oil, and make a cross on the top of the dough ball with a sharp knife. Cover the bowl with a dishtowel and leave in a warm area of the kitchen for about 2 hours, until doubled in size.

3 Transfer the dough to a floured work surface and cut into about 4 pieces, around 8 ounces each. You can use a scale to weigh the dough balls, if precision is important and you want to make sure all of the loaves are the same weight.

4 Line a baking sheet with parchment paper. Place the sesame seeds on a plate. Brush the top of the dough rolls with water and press the tops into the sesame seeds. Then place, sesame side up, on the baking sheet. Cover with a kitchen towel and place in a warm area of the kitchen to rise again for 30 minutes.

5 Preheat the oven to 400°F. Bake the rolls for 10 to 15 minutes. The rolls are done when the tops have turned golden brown.

DRESSED BREAD

{ *Pane Condito con Olio d'Oliva* }

PANI CUNZATO

Bread in Sicily is not only used as an addition to a meal or as a vehicle for sandwich fillings; often it is topped with condiments and served as an easy snack or a meal in itself. Following are two types of toppings for warm bread, straight from the oven. Pane cunzato, *which translates simply as "bread with a condiment," is found throughout Sicily in bars and other food shops, with toppings that vary from place to place. Quantities will, of course, vary, based on taste and the amount of bread. There's no exact recipe. Use the quantities that fit your taste.*

Makes 1 loaf

Garlic Paste (page 40)	Tomato slices
Extra-virgin olive oil	Caciocavallo or *provola* cheese, shaved with a cheese knife
Warm loaf of bread (preferably made from semolina flour), sliced open lengthwise	Salted anchovy fillets

1 Mix the garlic paste and extra-virgin olive oil in a bowl. Spread on the cut side of the bread.

2 Add the tomato slices, caciocavallo cheese, and anchovies.

3 You can serve as such, which is the common way in Sicily to serve *pane cunzato*, but I like to wrap the loaf in aluminum foil and place it in a 350°F oven for 5 to 8 minutes so that the garlic cooks and soaks into the bread and the cheese melts.

TOMATO *and* HERB PESTO *for* BREAD

{ *Pane Condito con Pomodoro* }

MATAROCCO

Matarocco *is the name of a condiment commonly made in the area of Trapani and Marsala, on the western coast of Sicily. In addition to this use, it's delicious tossed with spaghetti.*

Serves 2 to 4 as a condiment for bread

4 ripe plum tomatoes	1 fresh peperoncino (optional)
10 sprigs fresh parsley, tough parts of stems removed	1 tablespoon Garlic Paste (page 40)
20 fresh basil leaves	¼ cup extra-virgin olive oil
10 celery leaves	Sea salt
¼ cup pine nuts (optional)	Warm semolina bread, sliced

1 Cut a cross in the bottom of the tomatoes and remove the stem area. In a pot of salted boiling water, blanch the tomatoes for about 1 minute. Remove from the boiling water and place in an ice bath. When cool, using the tip of a paring knife, remove the skins. Cut each tomato in half and scoop out the seeds with a teaspoon. Chop the tomato into rough cubes.

2 In a mortar with a pestle, crush the parsley, basil, and celery leaves until broken down. Add the pine nuts and peperoncino, if using, and continue to crush the mixture with the pestle. Add the garlic paste and tomato cubes and crush until a rough paste is formed.

3 Transfer to a mixing bowl and add a steady stream of olive oil, while mixing the tomato and herb mixture with a fork. The resulting mixture will be soft and creamy. Add fine sea salt to taste (you will not need much salt, since the garlic paste already contains salt) and mix well. Spread the *matarocco* on warm bread and enjoy.

BLACK BREAD

{ *Pane Nero di Tumminia* }

PANI NIVURU RI TUMMINIA

A few years ago, I learned about a famed bread, known as pane nero, *at a bakery in Castelvetrano.* Pane nero *remains fresh for an unusually long time. The natural mother yeasts—as opposed to beer yeasts—used in* pane nero *do not continue their fermentation process once the bread is baked. (Bread becomes stale as the yeasts ferment.)*

Pane nero is commonly baked in traditional stone ovens heated by burning olive tree branches. The bread is placed on the floor of the piping hot oven and is cooked by the time the oven cools off.

Made from durum wheat flour and tumminia (see page 86), a heritage Sicilian grain, pane nero *has a thick, espresso-colored crust dusted with sesame seeds. Its soft interior is yellow-brown. In reality, the bread is not black, but this misnomer is probably due to the fact that the color is much darker than typical Sicilian bread prepared entirely from modern durum wheat flours that are lighter in color. The heritage wheat and natural yeasts impart a unique toasty aroma to the bread.*

While commonly associated with Castelvetrano, this bread is produced around the island, by home cooks, bakers, and chefs alike. Using 100% tumminia flour results in a dark brown bread that is thick in texture but very delicious.

Makes two 10-inch round loaves

²/₃ pound Mother Yeast (opposite)

0.35 ounce (1 teaspoon) dry malt

2¹/₂ cups warm purified water

1¹/₂ pounds tumminia whole wheat flour (see Sources, page 326)

²/₃ pound remilled hard wheat semola flour

1 tablespoon salt

About 1 cup sesame seeds, for topping the dough

1 In a stand mixer with a hook attachment, combine the mother yeast, malt, and warm water. Mix on a very slow speed for a few minutes. Turn off the mixer and add the two flours. Incorporate the ingredients on a slow speed, while slowly adding the salt. Mix well, until the dough forms a ball around the mixer's hook.

2 Remove the dough from the mixer and form into a ball with your hands. Cover the dough ball with some flour and place in a bowl. Cover with a kitchen towel and let rise at warm room temperature for nearly 5 hours, or until it doubles in volume.

3 Place the dough on a work surface dusted with flour and divide it into two pieces. Separately knead each ball of dough with the palms of your hands until it turns soft and smooth. The main object of this step is to remove air pockets from the dough.

4 Roll the dough pieces into balls and flatten the tops slightly to form the traditional *vastedda* shape (see page 89), about 8 inches in diameter. Sprinkle a handful of sesame seeds on a clean work surface and dip each piece of dough in the seeds to cover the top. Turn the loaf over, sesame seeds facing up, and place on a baking sheet lined with parchment paper. Cover with a kitchen towel and let the loaves rise for about 2 hours, until doubled in size.

5 Preheat the oven to 475°F. Bake the bread for 15 minutes. Lower the oven temperature to 400°F and bake for another 15 minutes. To check that the bread is ready, wearing a kitchen mitt, place a loaf in one hand and turn it upside down. Using the fist of your opposite hand, knock the bottom of the loaf. If it sounds hollow, it is ready. Otherwise bake for another 5 minutes and test again.

MOTHER YEAST

{ Lievito Madre }

Ù CRISCENTI

Mother yeast is a natural everlasting yeast (meaning it can remain alive indefinitely if used on a regular basis) made by a simple but long process of harvesting yeast from airborne sources and lactic acid. Before fresh and dry yeast was marketed, this was the only way to leaven bread.

There are a few methods of making this natural yeast. Some bakers ferment grape skins to add wild yeasts to the mixture, while others simply harvest the yeast from the air in a mixture of flour, water, and honey. Of the multiple recipes available, I like to use yogurt mixed with flour to start the process. Such yeasts create a deep nutty flavor in bread and a crunchy crust. They are everlasting if refreshed with flour and water on a regular basis.

For those intending to bake gluten-free bread, substitute the bread flour with rice or corn flour. The process to create the mother yeast takes a few extra days when using flour without gluten.

2 tablespoons plain yogurt

Bread flour or a high-gluten flour (quantity depends on how long you feed the starter)

Purified water

1 tablespoon wildflower honey

Extra-virgin olive oil

PHASE 1 In a glass bowl, combine the yogurt and 1 tablespoon flour and mix well. On a cutting board, form into a smooth ball. Place in a clean glass bowl and, with a paring knife, cut a cross in the dough ball. Cover the bowl with plastic wrap. Using a toothpick, make some small holes in the plastic so that air can pass through. This step is important so that microorganisms can develop and make the dough ferment. Leave the covered bowl at room temperature (78° to 82°F) for 48 hours.

PHASE 2 After sitting for 2 days, the dough needs to be refreshed on a daily basis. To do so, stir in about 1 tablespoon each of flour and water. The dough should be soft; if it seems too dry, add a touch more water. Store the dough in a glass jar in the refrigerator with a closed lid during this phase. Repeat every day for 14 days.

PHASE 3 On the 15th day, in addition to adding the flour and water, add the tablespoon of honey, which will help activate the natural yeasts. Rub the inside of a clean glass jar lightly with extra-virgin olive oil and transfer the dough to the jar. Cover and continue to store in the refrigerator.

PHASE 4 The next day, refresh the dough by adding 1 tablespoon each flour and water, as before. Repeat for the next 4 days. At this stage, the mother yeast should be ready. To test it, put the mother yeast in a clean glass jar and leave it for 3 to 4 hours at room temperature. The dough should double in volume.

PHASE 5 After using this mother yeast in your bread making, leave some of it in a clean covered jar in the refrigerator, refreshing it with more flour and water every 5 days.

FINDING THE FUTURE IN THE PAST

Nowadays, in an effort to save Sicilian heritage grains from extinction, many wheat farmers are growing varieties such as tumminia, *rusello*, and *perciasacchi*. Such heritage or so-called "ancient" grains were cataloged in the 1930s by a Sicilian agronomist, Ugo Di Cillis, and predate the Green Revolution, when high-yielding dwarf varieties of wheat were specially bred and began to be grown all over the world. Craft beer makers, bread makers, and pasta makers in Sicily are now using heritage grains in their products. The trend has also spread to the restaurants of the island, where it's popular to find a selection of housemade breads prepared with heritage grain flour.

Such grains contain an abundance of fiber, vitamins, and minerals not usually found in the wheat that is mass produced and most commonly eaten. This is because the heritage grains have undergone little to no hybridization over the centuries, unlike modern commercial wheat, which has been subjected to a great deal of genetic manipulation to increase its shelf life and suitability for mass-scale milling—often at the cost of nutrition and taste. On the other hand, heritage grains naturally contain a lower amount of gluten when mixed with water, making them easier to digest. However, unlike modern durum wheat with high levels of gluten, heritage wheat flour creates pasta and bread that contains less elasticity.

The best types of heritage grains are milled in antique stone mills, which are run by water power. Such stones mill the grain without heating it, thus keeping more of its nutritional value intact. The stones are able to obtain a meal of excellent quality and preserve all the best features of the grain, including the bran and germ, which is rich in essential fatty acids and vitamins.

Perhaps the most characteristically Sicilian heritage grain is tumminia, which also goes by the name *marzuolo*, as it is seeded in March. Its short vegetation cycle means tumminia is harvested in June. Yield is low of this grain, which has a tan color that the stone-grinding mechanism preserves. Other heritage durum wheat varieties include *perciasacchi* (Khorasan wheat, trademarked by farmers in Montana as Kamut), *bidì*, *biancolilla*, *russello*, and *majorca*. Heritage soft wheat flour is also produced in Sicily in smaller quantities. On my organic farmland in Sicily, I've been experimenting with small patches of each type of heritage grain, which I then use to make pasta and bake bread. Each wheat creates a completely different taste profile. Interestingly, even though I have an intolerance to gluten, I feel no ill effects after eating these heritage grains. How wonderful it is to have found the future of food tucked away in the past.

SQUID-INK BREAD

{ Pane al Nero di Seppia }

PANI A LU NIURU RI SICCIA

This bread is also black, but not due to the type of flour used. Rather, black squid ink gives this bread its signature color. The squid ink imparts a delicate fish aroma to the bread, but generally the loaves do not taste overly fishy. The squid ink can be purchased at most fishmongers.

Over the past decade, Sicilian chefs have started experimenting with their bread, just as they do with other types of food. I've seen versions of squid-ink bread on tables all over the island. And while it is not a traditional Sicilian bread, its ubiquitous nature has made it a new tradition. We make the bread in my own restaurants, and sometimes toast it to use as a seafood bruschetta. It is also delicious when Sicilian olives are added to the dough, but the olives are optional.

Makes 2 round loaves

2 tablespoons black squid ink

1½ cups purified water

1 pound bread flour

1 ounce (3 tablespoons) fresh yeast

1 teaspoon salt

¼ cup olive oil, plus more for greasing

Cracked Sicilian green olives (optional)

1 Mix the black squid ink with the water and stir to incorporate.

2 In a stand mixer with a hook attachment, combine the flour and yeast. With the mixer moving on the slowest possible speed, pour in the squid-ink mixture little by little. As soon as the ingredients are fully incorporated (the entire dough should be dark gray in color), add the salt and mix well. Slowly pour in the olive oil until it is fully absorbed by the dough.

3 Grease a large bowl with olive oil. Place the dough on a floured work surface and form it into a round ball. Place in the bowl and make a cross on the top of the dough ball with a knife. Cover the bowl with a dishtowel and let it rise in a warm area of the kitchen for about 2 hours, until doubled in size.

4 Transfer the dough to a floured work surface. Using a knife, cut the dough in half. Knead each half for about 10 minutes, until the dough is soft and smooth, then form into round loaves. Place the two loaves on a baking sheet lined with parchment paper. Cover with a dishtowel and place in a warm area of the kitchen for 30 minutes, until the loaves rise slightly.

5 Preheat the oven to 400°F. Bake the loaves for about 20 minutes. The bread is ready when you knock the bottom of the loaf and hear a hollow sound. Let cool on a rack for at least 20 minutes before slicing.

CLOCKWISE FROM TOP RIGHT: *Fennel-Sesame Breadsticks (page 108); Stuffed Focaccia with Potato, Cheese, and Onion Filling (page 102); Paper-Thin Flatbread (page 107); Squid-Ink Bread (page 95); Baked Chickpea Chips (page 109); Tomato and Herb Pesto (page 91) on Focaccia (page 102); Dressed Bread (page 91); Crispy Pockets Stuffed with Escarole and Anchovy (page 114); Stuffed Focaccia with Tomato and Onion Filling (page 102)*

STUFFED *and* ROLLED BREAD

{ *Pane Arrotolato* }

'MBRIULATA

On holidays, my grandmother used to make a rolled bread, stuffed with fennel sausage and braised Swiss chard. She sliced it into narrow pieces, making the rolled nature apparent and showing off the filling. It was delicious hot out of the oven, but I preferred it cold the next day as a snack, when all of the elements had solidified.

For dinner one night in Linguaglossa, on Mount Etna, I relished a rolled bread stuffed with eggplant, tomato, and basil, which was served alongside another bread rolled with black olives, caramelized onion, wild fennel, and sun-dried tomato.

Although the following recipe outlines how to make rolled bread with eggplant filling, I suggest rolling up the dough with other fillings of your choice. (My grandmother's fennel sausage–stuffed rolled bread was divine.) Just make sure the filling is not overly moist. Too much liquid in the filling can ruin the consistency of the bread. For example, if you use braised greens in your filling, put them in a cheesecloth and squeeze out a good portion of the water.

Makes 1 loaf

Filling

1 large eggplant

2 tablespoons olive oil

1 pint cherry or grape tomatoes, cut in half

Pinch of sugar

¹/₂ teaspoon sea salt, or more as needed

1 teaspoon Garlic Paste (page 40)

1 tablespoon dried Sicilian oregano

10 fresh basil leaves, finely sliced in a chiffonade

Dough

1¹/₂ pounds bread flour

1 ounce (3 tablespoons) fresh yeast

1 cup water

1 teaspoon salt

¹/₄ cup olive oil, plus more for greasing

1 FOR THE FILLING: Preheat the oven to 400°F. Place the whole eggplant (skin and stem intact) on a baking sheet and roast for about 45 minutes, until the eggplant deflates (to nearly half its original size) and softens significantly. Let it cool, then cut it in half. Using a spoon, scoop out the roasted eggplant pulp, discarding any large pockets of seeds. (Not all seeds need to be removed, only those that clump together and form a mass.) Using a fork, break down the eggplant pulp into a rough mash. Mix in 1 tablespoon of the olive oil.

2 Meanwhile, in a small baking pan, toss the tomatoes with the remaining olive oil, pinch of sugar, and the salt. Spread out on a baking sheet and roast alongside the eggplant for 15 minutes, until the tomatoes look shriveled.

3 Add the tomatoes, garlic paste, oregano, and basil to the eggplant pulp and mix them together. Taste for salt and add some if necessary.

4 FOR THE DOUGH: In a stand mixer with a hook attachment, combine the flour and yeast. With the mixer moving on the slowest possible speed, pour in the water little by little. As soon as the ingredients are fully incorporated, add the salt and mix well. Slowly pour in the olive oil, mixing until it is fully absorbed by the dough.

5 Grease a large bowl with olive oil. Place the dough on a floured work surface and form it into a round ball. Place in the bowl and make a cross on the top of the dough ball with a sharp knife. Cover the bowl with a kitchen towel and let the dough rise in a warm area of the kitchen for about 1 hour, until it doubles in size.

6 Transfer the dough to a floured work surface. With a rolling pin, roll out the dough until it forms a thin 18 by 10-inch rectangle of even thickness. Spread the filling in a thin layer on the dough, leaving a 3-inch border around the sides of the rectangle. Next, roll up the dough, starting from a short side. Grease a 12 by 20-inch bread pan with olive oil. Add the loaf, cover with a kitchen towel, and leave in a warm area of the kitchen for 30 minutes, until it rises by one-fourth.

7 Preheat the oven to 400°F. Bake the loaf for about 30 minutes. The bread is ready when the top is golden brown. Let it cool on a rack for at least 20 minutes before slicing.

SAINT JOSEPH'S BREAD

{ *Pane di San Giuseppe* }

PANI RI SAN GIUSEPPI

This recipe is for decorative bread that isn't intended to be consumed, although it would do no harm to eat it. Natural yeast should be used since it does not continue to ferment after baking, if you plan on conserving the bread as an ornament. (The loaves can last for years as decoration). In the absence of mother yeast, substitute a biga (page 88).

Makes 1 decorative loaf

2.2 pounds remilled hard wheat semola flour	2 cups warm water
	Olive oil, for greasing
4 ounces natural Mother Yeast (page 93)	1 large egg, beaten
	2 tablespoons lemon juice

1 In a stand mixer with a hook attachment, combine the flour and mother yeast. With the mixer moving on the slowest possible speed, pour in the water little by little until incorporated. Grease a large bowl with olive oil. Place the dough on a floured work surface and form it into a round ball. Place in the bowl and make a cross on the top of the dough ball with a knife. Cover the bowl with a dishtowel and let the dough rise in a warm area of the kitchen for about 1 hour, until it doubles in size.

2 Transfer the dough to a lightly floured work surface. Form the dough into decorative shapes of your choice (see the photos on pages 100 and 101 for ideas). An easy shape to prepare is a crown: Roll out the dough into a long rod and then form the rod into the shape of a doughnut. Tuck the two ends together so that a seam is not visible. Using a knife, cut slits around the exterior edge of the ring. Place the loaf on a baking sheet lined with parchment paper. Leave the unbaked dough in a warm area of the kitchen, covered with a kitchen towel for 30 minutes, until it rises slightly.

3 Preheat the oven to 400°F. Mix together the beaten egg and lemon juice. Using a brush, lightly brush the egg mixture on the top of the dough. Bake for about 20 minutes. The bread is ready when it turns golden yellow in color. Let cool on a rack for at least 20 minutes.

SYMBOLS WROUGHT FROM DOUGH

In Sicily, bread is not just a staple food but an art form that expresses devotion to the saints. Bread making, an ancient ritual craft stemming from the Hellenistic period, is closely related to the celebration of the agrarian deity Demeter, who, according to mythology, taught humans the art of bread making. Bread shapes relate to stories and legends and are deeply imbued with symbolism. Through ritual bread making, the stories of the venerated are kept alive, in the church and at the Sicilian table.

Unique ritual breads are not only prepared for major Catholic holidays such as Easter and Christmas, but for the Day of the Dead (November 2) and on saints' days, such as Saint Martin's Day (November 11). One of the most beautiful Italian ritual breads comes from the town of Salemi, on the western side of Sicily. Legend says that in 1542 the countryside of Salemi was threatened by a swarm of locusts, so farmers turned their prayers to Saint Biagio. When the locusts fled, the community dedicated small loaves of whole wheat flour, called *cuddureddi* (crowns) or *cavadduzzi* (horses) to the patron saint.

Each November 17, the same town, Salemi, celebrates Saint Elizabeth's (Queen of Hungary) Day. Legend says that she often left court to feed the poor until the king forbid her to do so. Her charity work continued despite the king's threats, and she began to make loaves of bread in the shape of flowers, so that the bread did not resemble food. The shape is still prepared today in Salemi in her honor and to celebrate her perseverance in feeding the poor.

The most famous saint day in all of Sicily for ritual bread making is without a doubt Saint Joseph's Day on March 19. Decorative breads are widespread on this feast day, though they differ from town to town and range from the simple to the ornate.

Every March in Sant'Anna, ladies work for days preparing bread in the shape of fish, crucifixes, and hearts for the feast of Saint Joseph's Day. Sicily's patron saint, Joseph, known in Italian as San Giuseppe, is said to have prevented a famine in Sicily during medieval times. According to popular belief, Sicilians prayed to Saint Joseph to bring them rain during a drought, promising to honor him with a feast. Three main forms of bread are baked on this feast day, one for Mother Mary, one for Baby Jesus, and one for Saint Joseph. Each is adorned with different items that symbolize their role in Christianity. For instance, jasmine flowers symbolize how Baby Jesus perfumes the world with his presence, ladders denote a quick route to heaven, and grapes represent wine, which denotes Christianity.

The tradition of the holiday is to offer food on an altar to the poor, known as the *tavolate di San Giuseppe*. Cookies and the elaborately decorated breads are prepared in abundance and put on display on the altar. Traditionally foods served on that day use breadcrumbs to represent sawdust, because Saint Joseph was a carpenter. In addition to venerating Saint Joseph on his feast day, the holiday is also Father's Day in Italy.

STUFFED FOCACCIA

{ *Focaccia Imbottita* }

SCACCIA

Typically, stuffed focaccia are found in rosticcerie *all around Sicily (see page 105), but they are also made at home. Like most Sicilian recipes, each town or area has its own specific recipe, according to local tradition. The term* focaccia ripiena, *"stuffed focaccia," is rarely used for this delicacy; instead every area seems to have its own way to refer to this hearty bread. In southeastern Sicily, it is called* la scaccia *(meaning pressed or squeezed). In Catania and its surrounding towns, it is called* la schiacciata *(a variation of the word* scaccia*), while in Palermo it is known as* l'impanata *(a word borrowed from the Spanish* empanada*).*

Among the countless recipes for stuffed focaccia, I've selected two fillings to share. The first involves tomato paste and caramelized onions, a focaccia typically prepared in Ragusa. The second uses potatoes, rosemary, caramelized onions, and vastedda *cheese. The latter is a personal favorite of mine, but then again, I have a weakness for potatoes.*

Other popular fillings are broccoli, sardines, and primo sale cheese, *or anchovies and tuma cheese. In addition to the multiple types of fillings, there are also various ways that the dough can be folded to hold in the contents. Stuffed focaccia sold in* rosticcerie *are rolled out very thinly using sheeting machines and are folded multiple times. For commercial production, the dough is rolled out thin in a machine. At home, they are prepared round, in half-moon shapes, and in rectangular shapes and have a more rustic look to them, as pictured on pages 96 and 97.*

Makes 2 stuffed focaccia

2 cups warm water

2 teaspoons honey

2 teaspoons (0.2 ounce) fresh yeast

1.1 pounds remilled hard wheat semola flour

1 teaspoon salt

3 tablespoons extra-virgin olive oil, plus more for greasing

Tomato and Onion Filling or Potato, Onion, and Cheese Filling (opposite)

1 In a small bowl, combine half of the warm water with the honey. Add the yeast and stir to dissolve.

2 In a stand mixer with a hook attachment, combine the yeast mixture and the flour. With the mixer moving on the slowest possible speed, pour in the remaining water and incorporate it into the flour. As soon as the ingredients are fully incorporated, add the salt and mix well. Slowly pour in the olive oil until it is fully absorbed by the dough. Grease a large bowl with olive oil. Place the dough on a floured work surface and form it into a round ball. Place in the bowl and make a cross on the top of the dough ball with a knife. Cover the bowl with a kitchen towel and let the dough rise in a warm area of the kitchen for about 1 hour, or until doubled in size.

3 Transfer the dough to a floured work surface. Using a knife, cut the dough in half. Roll out each piece with a rolling pin to the shape of a square cross, about 10 inches in length on each side.

4 Preheat the oven to 400°F. Fill the dough in the center of each piece with the filling of your choice, then flip the edges on top of the center of the piece, forming a pocket.

5 Bake for about 30 minutes. The bread is ready when it's golden brown. Let cool on a rack for at least 20 minutes before cutting.

Tomato and Onion Filling

Makes enough filling to stuff 2 focaccia

3 tablespoons extra-virgin olive oil	1 teaspoon Garlic Paste (page 40)
4 yellow onions, sliced into thin rings	1 cup tomato paste
Salt	10 fresh basil leaves, left whole
Sugar	1 teaspoon freshly ground black pepper

1 Heat 2 tablespoons of the olive oil in a saucepan over low heat. Add the onions, 2 cups water, a pinch or two of salt, and a pinch or two of sugar. Cook until the water evaporates. When the onions start to brown, deglaze the pan with a touch of water and continue cooking until the onions are caramelized to taste.

2 In a separate saucepan, gently sauté the garlic paste in the remaining olive oil over low heat until the garlic loses its shiny nature. Make sure not to brown the garlic. Add the tomato paste, the caramelized onions, and 1 cup water and mix well with a wooden spoon. Cook until reduced by two-thirds, about 10 minutes. Add the basil leaves and season with 1 teaspoon salt and the pepper.

3 Store the filling in the refrigerator in an airtight container for up to 1 day.

Potato, Onion, and Cheese Filling

If you can't find vastedda *cheese, you may substitute any soft cheese that melts easily but does not contain too much liquid, such as* provola *or* fontina.

Makes enough filling to stuff 2 focaccia

1 pound Yukon gold potatoes, peeled and thinly sliced	1 cup *vastedda* cheese, cut into small cubes
1½ tablespoons salt	1 sprig fresh rosemary, leaves removed from the stem and roughly chopped
2 cups caramelized onions (see above)	

1 In a pot, cover the sliced potatoes with cold water. Add 1 tablespoon of the salt and bring to a boil. Cook until the potatoes are easily pierced with the tip of a paring knife, about 10 minutes. Fill a bowl with cold water and ice. Transfer the potatoes to the ice bath and let cool. Remove the potatoes from the ice bath and dry on paper towels.

2 In a bowl, combine the boiled potatoes, the remaining ½ tablespoon salt, caramelized onions, cheese, and rosemary. Store the filling in the refrigerator in an airtight container for up to 1 day.

OLD-FASHIONED SICILIAN PIZZA

{ Pizza Antica Siciliana }

PIZZA ANTICA RI SICILIA

In Sicily, pizza comes in many forms and each area has a traditional style, with various names for their specialties. In addition, there is a big difference between the pizza served in a pizzeria, a casual sit-down restaurant, and pizza from a rosticceria, a locale that sells individually portioned fried and baked bread-based bites. Pizza sold in a pizzeria is usually thin, round, and served as a whole, individual-size pie. It is meant to be cut with a knife and fork. This recipe, on the other hand, is for a square cut or small round piece of thick dough that is eaten by hand.

My favorite pizza hails from home ovens, and those served in restaurants cannot compare. Most country kitchens have wood-fired ovens, and unlike the pizzeria-style pizza, home versions are baked in trays lined with olive oil. What we call pizza in Sant'Anna is known by different names, such as guastedda or focaccia, in other parts of Sicily. What I enjoy about pizza night (known as a pizziata) in my relatives' homes is that all of the ladies in the family take part in the preparation, even the younger generation. And usually pizza night implies that neighbors and relatives will join in the meal.

Makes 2 large rectangular pizzas

Dough

2 pounds all-purpose flour

1 pound remilled hard wheat semola flour

³/₄ pound Starter Dough (page 88)

¹/₂ teaspoon honey

2 cups water

1 tablespoon fine salt

Extra-virgin olive oil, for greasing

5 cups Tomato Pulp (homemade, page 70, or store-bought)

Maria's Favorite Topping

16 salted anchovy fillets, cut into small pieces about ¹/₂ inch in length

3 tablespoons dried Sicilian oregano

2 cups grated pecorino cheese

1 FOR THE DOUGH: Mix the two flours together. In a stand mixer, using a paddle attachment combine the starter dough, honey, water, and half of the flour mixture and mix on a low speed. With the mixer still running, slowly add the remaining flour until all the flour is incorporated and the dough is sticky to the touch. Add the salt and mix again. Grease a large bowl with olive oil. Transfer the dough to the bowl and coat with the oil while rolling it into a ball. Cover the bowl with a clean kitchen towel and let the dough rise in a warm area for 1 hour, until doubled in size.

2 Preheat the oven to 400°F. Grease two 18 by 10-inch baking sheets with olive oil.

3 Punch down the dough and transfer it to a floured work surface. Knead the dough for about 10 minutes, until soft and smooth. Divide in half with a knife. You can freeze half of the dough at this stage. Using a rolling pin, or your fists placed underneath one piece of the dough, begin to stretch it to a 20-inch-long size. Transfer to a baking sheet and, using your fingertips, continue to stretch out the dough until it reaches the edges. Repeat with the remaining dough.

4 Using the back of a spoon, spread the tomato pulp over the dough, leaving a 1-inch border on all sides.

5 FOR MARIA'S FAVORITE TOPPING: Evenly arrange the anchovies on top and sprinkle with the oregano, followed by the grated pecorino.

6 Bake the pizzas for 20 minutes. They are done when the bottom of the crust is coppery brown. To check, use a wooden paddle to gently lift the pizza from the baking sheet, being careful not to break the dough. Let the pizzas cool on a rack for about 5 minutes before cutting.

A PIZZA BY ANY OTHER NAME

Here are some of the traditional baked breads that are specific to certain areas of the island. While they are not all called pizza, they are like pizza in style, in that a layer of dough is topped then baked, each with its own unique shape. I suggest tasting each of these baked breads when visiting Sicily, but you can also top the pizza dough on page 105 with any of the traditional condiments described here, as pictured there. (Also, see my list of recommended *pizzerie* around the island on page 324.)

Rianata (Trapani)

In Trapani, a traditional pizza—called *rianata*—is prepared with an abundance of tomato and onion slices, as well as dried oregano, grated aged pecorino cheese, and anchovies. Traditionally, this pizza is served large, in a rectangular shape.

Sfincione Bagherese (Bagheria)

Sfincione bagherese is a traditional thick, round baked bread, which is not called a pizza in Sicilian. Traditionally, *sfincione bagherese* is cooked in wood-burning ovens, fired by dried olive branches. It is available in Bagheria (a city near Palermo) all year round, but tradition holds that *sfincione* is eaten on Christmas Eve. Although hard to mimic the authentic lightly smoky flavor without a wood-burning oven, the topping for this *sfincione* can be used on pizza dough and baked at home.

First place anchovies on the surface of the dough, then top with a layer of fresh sheep's milk cheese and with ricotta, caramelized onions, and coarse breadcrumbs. Tomato sauce is not used in *sfincione bagherese*. When biting into this specialty, the first sensation on the roof of one's mouth is the crispiness of the baked breadcrumbs, which is followed by the softness of the melted cheese and ricotta.

Sfincione Palermitano (Palermo)

Also in Palermo, a thick bread is called *sfincione*, and it's commonly sold on street carts in the historical center of the city. In this version, tomato sauce is used to top the dough. Caciocavallo cheese is first placed underneath the sauce, which is a thick sauce cooked with anchovy, onion, and dried oregano. Breadcrumbs are used as in the version from Bagheria, however in Palermo, fine breadcrumbs are used to coat the surface of the sauce and do not become crunchy during baking.

Focaccia Messinese (Messina)

In Messina, a traditional pizza is called *focaccia messinese*. It is topped with boiled chopped escarole, anchovy pieces, scamorza cheese, and a light layer of fresh cherry tomatoes.

Pizza alla Norma (Catania)

In Catania, a pizza is made in the same name (and with the same ingredients) as the city's famous Norma pasta (page 173). The pizza dough is covered with a very thin layer of tomato sauce, with fried eggplant slices, basil, and grated ricotta salata.

Pizza Muddiata (Ragusa)

In Ragusa, a traditional pizza topping is tomato sauce, oregano, pitted black olives, and *provola* cheese. This pizza traditionally has a softer dough than other versions; in fact the name *muddiata* ("soft" in Sicilian) indicates the pizza's soft consistency. However, the dough is usually crunchy on the bottom.

Guastedda (all over Sicily)

Round in shape, this thick pizza is popular in the interior mountainous areas of Sicily. The most popular way to dress the bread is with a thin layer of tomato sauce, some grated pecorino cheese, and a few salted anchovies. It is also known as *faccia di vecchia*, which translates to "old lady's face."

PAPER-THIN FLATBREAD

{ *Pizza Antica Siciliana* }

CARTA RI MUSICA

Carta ri musica *means "sheet music," an appropriate name for this flatbread because it is as thin as paper. Thin flatbread is more common in Sardinia than in Sicily, but this recipe, which calls for nuts, can be found in some of the island's top restaurants and I've created this version for home cooks. Perhaps this flatbread earned its name not just for its thinness, but due to the musical sounds diners make when they bite into this crisp bread.*

Makes 8 sheets

0.5 ounce (1½ tablespoons) fresh yeast	2 tablespoons shelled pistachios
1 cup warm purified water	2 tablespoons raw almonds
7 tablespoons olive oil, plus more for greasing	2 tablespoons shelled hazelnuts
1 tablespoon wildflower honey	2 tablespoons raw white sesame seeds
1 tablespoon salt	2 tablespoons black sesame seeds
1 pound remilled hard wheat semola flour	

1 Dissolve the yeast in the warm water, oil, and honey. In a separate bowl, mix the salt with the flour. Add the yeast mixture and stir to incorporate it into a dough. Grease a bowl with olive oil and transfer the dough to the bowl. Roll the dough in the oil and then cover the bowl with a kitchen towel. Let the dough rest in a warm spot in the kitchen for about 1 hour, until it doubles in size.

2 Meanwhile, in a food processor, finely chop the pistachios, almonds, and hazelnuts, making sure that the nuts do not turn into a paste. Add the white and black sesame seeds to the nut mixture, tossing to combine.

3 Preheat the oven to 350°F. Grease a baking sheet with olive oil.

4 Punch down the dough. Knead it and then cut the dough into 8 pieces, about 5 ounces each. Working with one piece of dough at a time, use a hand-rolling pasta machine to roll the dough as thinly as possible, until it resembles a lasagna sheet about 24 inches in length. The sheet should be translucent when you hold it up to the light. Alternatively, you can use a rolling pin to flatten the dough; however, it will be difficult to obtain the desired thinness. Place the sheet of dough on the baking sheet. (Keep the remaining dough covered with a clean cloth in a cool environment. You may bake multiple flatbreads at a time if you have multiple baking sheets. Otherwise, work in batches.)

5 Using a kitchen brush, brush a small amount of water on the top of the dough. Sprinkle with the nut mixture. Using your hand, gently press the nut mixture into the dough.

6 Bake for about 10 minutes, until the thin dough is light brown in color. Remove the flatbread immediately from the baking sheet with a spatula and let cool on a wire rack. Repeat the rolling, topping, and baking process with the remaining dough. The flatbread will keep in an airtight container for up to 2 days.

FENNEL-SESAME BREADSTICKS

GRISSINI CU FINOCCHIU E GIUGGIULÉNA

Grissini originated in Torino, in the seventeenth century, and got their name from a Piemontese elongated bread (similar to a French baguette) called gherssa. *According to legend, grissini were invented when the son of the Duke of Savoy fell ill from intestinal disorders. His doctor advised him to eliminate undercooked bread from his diet and eat only crunchy well-baked bread. Chefs devised these thin snacks, in the same form as the* gherssa *but thinner. Initially grissini were a novelty for the upper class, but now they are widely diffused throughout Italy.*

At many restaurants around the country, packaged breadsticks are offered to customers when they first sit down. At finer restaurants, signature breadsticks are prepared in-house by chefs. In Sicily, one chef prepares breadsticks with tumminia flour and extrudes the dough from a pasta machine in the shape of bucatini pasta. Other chefs flavor the dough with Sicilian herbs, such as wild fennel, and sesame.

These long, crisp breadsticks look impressive as a centerpiece on your table. They make nice accompaniments to antipasti such as cured meats and olives. You can replace the fennel and sesame with other herbs and spices, such as fresh rosemary or sage, dried Sicilian oregano, cayenne pepper, black sesame seeds, or poppy seeds.

Makes 30 to 40 breadsticks, depending on length

1 cup warm water

0.5 ounce (1$\frac{1}{2}$ tablespoons) fresh yeast

1 tablespoon honey

1 tablespoon sea salt

$\frac{2}{3}$ cup olive oil, plus more for brushing on the dough

1 pound all-purpose flour, sifted

$\frac{1}{2}$ cup Sicilian wild fennel seeds or other fennel seeds

$\frac{1}{2}$ cup raw sesame seeds

Semolina flour, for sprinkling on the work surface

1 In a stand mixer with the hook attachment, combine $\frac{1}{4}$ cup of the warm water, the yeast, and honey. Let sit for 5 minutes. In another bowl, mix the remaining $\frac{3}{4}$ cup warm water and the salt until the salt dissolves. Add the olive oil, then the all-purpose flour to the yeast mixture. Start the mixer on the slowest speed possible. In a slow stream, add the water and yeast mixture. When the flour absorbs the water, raise the speed of the mixer to medium and combine the ingredients until the dough is elastic looking. Add the fennel and sesame seeds to the mixture.

2 Sprinkle a work surface with the semolina flour. Place the dough on the work surface and roughly form it into a large rectangle. Brush some olive oil on the surface of the dough and cover with a piece of parchment paper. Cover with a kitchen towel and let the dough double in size, about 1 hour.

3 Preheat the oven to 350°F. Line two of your longest baking sheets with parchment paper.

4 Using a rolling pin, roll out the dough to about $\frac{1}{4}$ inch thickness. Using the point of a sharp chef's knife, cut strips of dough, about $\frac{1}{3}$ inch in thickness, from the long side. If your baking sheets are not long enough to accommodate the strips, cut from the short side.

5 The strips of dough might reduce in size after they're cut. If so, grasp both ends of a strip of dough with your hands and pull until the strip is the length of the baking sheets. Continue until all of the dough is cut into strips and stretched.

6 Brush the sticks of dough with olive oil. Bake for about 20 minutes, until the thickest parts of the breadsticks are golden brown.

BAKED CHICKPEA CHIPS

{ Sfoglie di Farina di Ceci }

SFOGGHIE RI FARINA RI CICIRI

Chickpea flour is the base of Sicily's panelle, *a popular street food (page 134). In this recipe, which I learned from David Tamburini, a Tuscan chef formally based in Modica, the flour is used to make thin chips, which are a delicious and healthy snack.*

Makes about 40 chips

1 pound chickpea flour (also called garbanzo flour)

1 cup purified water

1 tablespoon salt

1 Preheat the oven to 350°F. Place a silicone baking mat (such as from Silpat) on a baking sheet.

2 In a bowl, mix together the chickpea flour, water, and salt, making sure that the batter has no lumps.

3 Place 1 teaspoon batter on the silicone mat and, using a metal fish spatula, spread the batter evenly and thinly to make a 5-inch-wide round. Repeat with more batter to fill the baking sheet. Bake for 2 minutes, until the chips are cooked through and start to lift from the silicone mat. Let cool, then gently remove the chips from the silicone mat, one by one.

4 Working in batches, repeat with the remaining batter to make about 40 chips in all. Store in an airtight container until ready to use. The chips will last for up to 4 days.

THE ROADSIDE BANQUET

Widespread throughout the island is *cibo da strada*, or street food. Although present in most Sicilian cities, street food is ubiquitous in Palermo. Dispersed in many corners of the capital, vendors sell a wide range of delicacies that are meant to be eaten while standing. While the majority of street food items tend to be greasy, markets also sell lighter fare, such as coal-roasted artichokes, boiled small potatoes, raw mussels, and sea urchin roe in little cups.

A *rosticceria* is a place where Sicilian-style fast food is sold. Most commonly, fried and baked bites are sold from a counter where they are displayed. The quintessential Sicilian fast food is *arancine* (see page 163), deep-fried rice balls, which in some areas are shaped like cones, making them easier to eat out of hand. Don't leave the island without indulging in these, but be forewarned that they tend to be so substantial that you may not be hungry for any dinner afterward. Nowadays, many guidebooks consider *rosticceria* to be in the same category as street food. However, the types of food sold directly on street carts and in *rosticcerie* varies. The following are among the most iconic Palermitan street food dishes.

Panelle are fried chickpea flour fritters (page 134) served in a sesame-semola roll (page 90). In the past, the best-known *panelle* makers, called *panellari*, used to form the fritters between polished, rectangular wood pieces, decorated with a floral relief, although nowadays, very few street vendors continue this tradition. The pattern they imparted on the *panelle* was not merely decorative, but rather served to indicate freshly fried fritters. When reheated, the floral design faded away. This is an example of how even street food was (and still is) held to the highest standards, just like any other type of food prepared in Sicily.

Cazzilli are fried potato croquettes, which often get stuffed inside a sandwich roll along with *panelle*.

Stigghiole are lamb or goat intestines, wrapped around spring onions and grilled over a charcoal grill. Those who sell them are called *stigghiularu*.

Pani cà meusa are soft round sandwiches filled with chopped veal spleen and lung, which are sold by peddlers known as *meusari*. The offal is boiled in lard and seasoned with lemon. When caciocavallo or ricotta cheese is added, the sandwich is considered *maritatu*, meaning a man who is married. To omit the cheese, ask for it *schettu*, which means a single man.

Spitini are typical snacks served in the *rosticceria* of Palermo. Leftover bread never goes to waste in Sicily. *Spitini* makes use of day-old bread. Slices are layered with a beef and pea ragù, then breaded and fried. The name of this fried snack recalls *spiedini di carne*, which are grilled stuffed rolls of beef. The reason for the similar name comes from the fact that both recipes are prepared by using skewers (*spiedini*) to hold the pieces together during cooking. Neapolitans make a similar dish, by layering leftover bread with mozzarella, known as *mozzarella in carrozza*.

SATCHELS STUFFED *with* LAMB AND CHEESE

{ *I Pastieri di Modica* }

PASTIERI MODICANI

For Easter, Sicilians prepare crown-shaped loaves with whole eggs baked into them called cuddura cu l'ova, *which comes from the Greek word* kulloura, *meaning "crown." The same bread, with the egg in the center, is sometimes shaped like a bird and is known as* aceddu cull'ova. *In some areas, the eggs baked into the bread are colored red, to symbolize the blood of Jesus that was spilled for the salvation of humanity.*

Every town has different specialties prepared for Easter, often meat based, as Lent has come to an end. One of my favorite savory treats for the holiday hails from Modica. Known as pastieri, *these meat-stuffed satchels are traditionally made in homes for Easter. Today, they can be found there in* rosticceria *all year long.*

Makes 10 satchels

Stuffing

1 pound ground lamb, preferably containing some fat so not too lean

1 cup red wine

1 teaspoon Garlic Paste (page 40)

2 cups grated *caciocavallo ragusano* cheese (substitute with grated Parmesan or grana padano)

3 large eggs, beaten

1 teaspoon ground cinnamon

About 2 tablespoons salt

Ground black pepper

1 bunch of fresh parsley, finely chopped

Dough

Focaccia dough (page 102), prepared up to step 2

2 egg yolks, beaten with a pinch of salt

1 FOR THE STUFFING: Heat a large sauté pan over high heat, and when very hot, add the ground meat to the pan. Stir continuously with a wooden spoon until the moisture of the meat evaporates completely. Remove the pan momentarily from the stovetop and deglaze the pan with the red wine, scraping the bottom of the pan with a spatula to remove any brown bits. Return the pan to high heat and let the red wine evaporate.

Remove the pan from the heat and transfer the meat to a mixing bowl to cool.

2 Add the garlic paste, cheese, beaten eggs, and cinnamon to the bowl and mix well with the ground meat. Add about half of the salt and some pepper. Depending on the salinity of the cheese you are using, you might not need any more salt than that. To test, make a small patty of the meat and place it in a nonstick pan over high heat. Taste the meat when cooked through. If you need more salt or pepper, you can add it now. The stuffing may be prepared up to 1 day in advance; keep it covered in the refrigerator.

3 FOR THE DOUGH: Either roll out the dough with a rolling pin to about $1/16$ inch thick or do so with a manual pasta machine, on the number 4 setting. Using a 6-inch cookie cutter, cut out rounds of dough. Placing a dough round in one hand to form a pocket, use your other hand to place 2 tablespoons of the stuffing inside. Close the satchel by making it into a little sack, pleating the edges. The top of the satchel should remain open. Repeat with the remaining dough rounds and filling.

4 Preheat the oven to 350°F. Line a baking sheet with parchment paper. Place all of the satchels on the pan. Make sure to leave at least 2 inches of space between each pocket, as they will expand during baking. Using a pastry brush, spread the egg yolk mixture over the satchels.

5 Bake for about 15 minutes, or until the pastry is golden brown. Cool on a rack. The pastries can be prepared up to 1 day in advance and held in the refrigerator. They should be reheated before serving.

MILK *and* CHEESE CROQUETTES

{ *Crocchette di Latte* }

CROCCHÉ RI LATTI

In Palermo, croquettes are sold as street food, to eat during a passeggiata in piazza, *or stroll in the town square. This is a simple recipe, but the hard part is to fry these snacks without them bursting open in the fryer. The filling must be well coated with flour and breadcrumbs to avoid this. The recipe is based on a basic béchamel, enriched with a lot of cheese. While the most popular types of croquette (from the French* croquet) *are prepared with potatoes—they are known as* cazzilli—*these small bites were introduced to Sicily by the French* monzù *chefs (see page 184).*

Serves 6 to 8

Béchamel

¹/₂ cup (1 stick) unsalted butter

1 cup all-purpose flour

3 cups milk

1 teaspoon salt

¹/₂ teaspoon finely ground black pepper

1¹/₂ cups grated Parmesan cheese

¹/₂ teaspoon grated nutmeg

Croquettes

1 cup all-purpose flour

2 large eggs, beaten

1 cup fine breadcrumbs (page 42)

Vegetable oil, for frying

1 FOR THE BÉCHAMEL: In a thick-bottomed pot, over low heat, melt the butter, then add the flour, whisking it with the butter until fully incorporated. Add the milk slowly in a stream, while continuing to whisk the mixture with the other hand. Bring the mixture to a boil and then lower the heat while continuing to stir the contents of the pot for about 5 minutes to let thicken. Remove from the heat, then add the salt, pepper, cheese, and nutmeg. Let cool.

2 Using a rubber spatula, spread the cooled mixture onto a cold kitchen work surface, such as a clean marble countertop or a chilled baking sheet, to an approximate thickness of 1¹/₂ inches. Cut the mixture into small pieces (about 1 inch wide by 2 inches long), which will yield about 20 croquettes. Moisten your hands with water, then briskly roll each piece between your palms into logs with a rounded edge.

2 FOR THE CROQUETTES: Place the flour, beaten eggs, and breadcrumbs in separate bowls. Dip each croquette in the flour, then in the beaten egg, and finally in the breadcrumbs. Make sure that each piece is well coated with the breadcrumbs. The croquettes can be prepared to this point up to 1 day in advance, but they are best fried just before serving.

3 Pour enough vegetable oil into a large pot to submerge the croquettes in a single layer and place the pot over medium heat. Use a deep-fry thermometer to check the temperature of the oil. Once it reaches 350°F, begin to deep-fry the croquettes, working in batches to avoid crowding the pot. Fry until the outer layer of each croquette turns golden brown, about 5 minutes. Remove the croquettes from the oil using a slotted spatula. Transfer them to a plate lined with paper towels and serve immediately while still hot.

CRISPY POCKETS STUFFED *with* ESCAROLE *and* ANCHOVY

{ *Pitoni alla Messinese* }

PITONI A LA MISSINISI

The following recipe is for a typical snack in Messina. Another type of stuffed bread, these pockets are filled with fresh cheese (typically tuma cheese), tomatoes, escarole, and anchovies. Then they are shaped like half moons and fried. Keep in mind that the lard, which is the traditional ingredient used in such breads, will yield a much flakier dough than butter. However, you may use butter if you prefer. The same dough is used to make calzone, which are widespread in Italy and usually filled with ragù (page 167) or cooked ham and cheese.

Makes 15 to 20 pockets

Dough

0.5 ounce (1¹/₂ tablespoons) fresh yeast

1¹/₂ cups warm water, plus more if needed

2 pounds all-purpose flour

2 tablespoons sugar

¹/₂ cup lard or butter (or half of each)

1 tablespoon salt

Filling

2 pounds escarole, well rinsed and chopped into 1-inch pieces

Salt

15 salted anchovies, crushed into a paste

1 tablespoon extra-virgin olive oil

2 plum tomatoes, thinly sliced

1 cup Tomato Pulp (homemade, page 70, or store-bought)

3 cups mozzarella cut into ¹/₂-inch cubes

1 egg yolk beaten with 1 tablespoon milk, if baking

2 quarts vegetable oil, if frying

1 FOR THE DOUGH: In a stand mixer with a hook attachment, combine the yeast, warm water, flour, sugar, and lard. On the slowest speed possible, mix the ingredients together. When incorporated, turn the mixer to a higher speed, then add the salt and continue mixing. If the mixture is too dense, add a little more water.

2 Transfer the dough to a work surface sprinkled with flour. Form the dough into a ball and place it in a bowl. Using a sharp knife, make an incision in the shape of a cross on the surface of the dough. Cover the bowl with a dishtowel and let sit for 2 hours to rise.

3 In the meantime, PREPARE THE FILLING: Start by lightly blanching the escarole in salted boiling water for 1 minute. Remove the greens from the water and place them in a mixing bowl with the anchovy paste and the olive oil. In another mixing bowl, combine the sliced tomatoes and ¹/₂ teaspoon salt.

4 After the dough rises, divide it into 15 to 20 small pieces, about 4 ounces each in weight. Using a rolling pin, flatten each piece of dough until it reaches a thickness of less than a ¹/₄ inch. The pieces of dough should be as round as possible. If necessary, use a 6-inch cookie cutter to cut out round shapes.

5 In the center of each piece of dough, place a spoonful of the tomato pulp. Spread it around the dough using the back of the spoon. Be careful not to let the tomato pulp reach the edges of the dough or you won't be able to seal the pockets. Top with about 2 tablespoons of the escarole filling, a slice of the salted plum tomato, and 4 or 5 cubes of the mozzarella.

6 Using a pastry brush, spread a thin layer of water around the interior edges of the dough. Flip the top side of the dough circle on top of the bottom, forming the dough into pockets the shape of half moons. Using the back of a fork, press the edges of the dough together to seal.

7 Transfer the pockets onto a baking sheet lined with parchment paper. Let sit in a warm area of the kitchen for 30 minutes so that the dough continues to leaven slightly, which will make the cooked pockets lighter and fluffier in texture.

8 To bake the pockets in the oven, preheat the oven to 375°F. Brush the tops of the dough with the egg yolk–milk mixture and bake for 25 minutes, or until golden brown.

9 Alternatively, to fry the pockets, heat the vegetable oil in a heavy-bottomed pot until it reaches 350°F on a deep-fry thermometer (see Note). Place each pocket in the oil and fry until golden. Depending on the size of your pot, you can fry 2 or 3 pockets at the same time, but keep in mind that this will lower the temperature of your oil. Each batch should take about 5 minutes. When removing the pockets from the oil, place them on a baking sheet lined with paper towels to soak up some of the oil. Let sit for a few minutes and consume when warm.

Note: Keep the thermometer in the oil to regulate the temperature. If it exceeds 350°F, lower the heat, and vice-versa. If the oil is too hot, the dough pockets will start to burn on the outside and the dough and filling will not cook. If the oil is not hot enough, the dough will get soggy from the oil and will not have a crunchy texture on the outer layer.

Chapter 4

ANTIPASTI

AT MY FAMILY TABLE in Sicily, as in most homes, a daily midafternoon *pranzo* commences with a pasta or minestra. Only on feast days do we indulge in appetizers, known as *japri lu pitittu* in Sicilian dialect, meaning that they open up one's appetite. On such occasions, small cold bites, which are comprised of preserved meats, vegetables, or seafood, are enjoyed. Some of the same foods are commonly eaten as a light dinner.

When dining today in restaurants around the island, it's hard to fathom that antipasti are not part of the daily home meal, as is the case in most other regions of Italy. In upscale Sicilian establishments, even before the meal commences, customers are offered a complimentary welcome bite, referred to as *il benvenuto*. Once presented with a menu, diners can then choose from an array of elaborate appetizers, commonly including raw seafood creations.

Within this chapter are recipes from home and restaurant kitchens. Some of the dishes from this book's vegetable chapter (see page 215) also make excellent starters, such as the baked stuffed vegetables (page 223) or the stuffed squash blossoms (page 222). Rice balls (page 165) are another great alternative, especially if you are omitting a pasta course.

SNACKS STRAIGHT FROM THE SEA

For sashimi lovers, Sicilian restaurants—especially those located by the sea—are perfect spots to satisfy a craving for raw seafood of the highest caliber. For purists, raw seafood in Sicily is dusted with local sea salt and drizzled with olive oil and nothing more. Sicilian raw seafood dishes, known as *crudo*, are meant to be savored without masking the pure flavor of the fish. The seafood can be thinly sliced or chopped into a tartare. However, for some chefs the term *crudo* includes seafood that has been marinated with citrus or cured with salt.

While upscale restaurants tend to present raw seafood with cuts that highlight fine knife skills, trattorie serve *crudo* in a more rustic manner. On the Aeolian Islands, small shrimp, known as *gamberi di nassa,* which hail from the surrounding waters, are commonly served with heads on, in their shell, sometimes full of eggs, with a lemon wedge on the side of the plate. These tiny shrimp possess a buttery texture when raw and are so flavorful, making the lemon superfluous. I've witnessed those who express repulsion to raw seafood try just one bite of these shrimp, and then proceed by ripping off the shells and devouring morsel after morsel.

Many Sicilian chefs garnish their *crudo* platters with internationally prized salts, in addition to Sicilian sea salt. Don't be surprised to see black salt from Hawaii, pink salt from the Himalayan Mountains, and French fleur de sel next to Sicilian salt from Trapani or Mozia. It's even common to see a server carry a tray full of colorful salt rocks to the table to grate them over the raw seafood.

Flavored olive oil is also used as a condiment by many chefs. For example, I've tasted a raw red prawn combined with mandarin-infused oil, a small pink shrimp with carob-infused oil, hake with oregano-infused oil, tuna with smoked oil, and squid with ash-infused oil, to name a few.

When selecting fresh fish for a *crudo*, it's of utmost importance to source from a fishmonger you trust. Make sure that the seafood was not previously frozen.

OLIVE SALAD

{ *Insalata di Olive* }

'NSALATA R'ALIVI

This is a home-style rustic dish, one of my favorite antipasti. In Sicily and all around Italy, salads composed of lettuce greens are served as side dishes during the main course, not as appetizers. This salad, however, is abundant with olives, making it a perfect start to a meal.

Serves 4

3 cups cracked, pitted Sicilian green olives

3 to 4 celery stalks, preferably leaf celery, cut on an angle into $1/2$-inch pieces (reserve about a handful of the celery leaves and roughly chop them)

1 red bell pepper, cut into $1/4$-inch-thick slices

$1/4$ red onion, cut into thin strips

1 large carrot, cut in half lengthwise and cut into $1/4$-inch-thick slices

Juice of 1 lemon

1 teaspoon white wine vinegar

Salt

2 tablespoons extra-virgin olive oil

1 Mix the olives, celery and leaves, red pepper, onion, and carrot in a serving bowl.

2 Toss the vegetables with the lemon juice and vinegar. Taste for salt. You might not need to add any if the olives are still very salty from the brine. If you do add salt, stir well to make sure it dissolves into the lemon juice and vinegar, then add the extra-virgin olive oil. Toss again and serve. Alternatively, the salad can be prepared up to 1 day ahead. Cover and refrigerate. Let it come to room temperature before serving.

WARM *and* SPICY BLACK OLIVES

{ *Olive Nere* }

PASSULUNA

In winter months, my cousin Maria serves her salt-cured black olives warm. Both the spiciness and straight-from-the-pan temperature of these olives are warming during the cold. Before heating the olives, make sure to rinse them thoroughly of their salt brine. They should then be well dried before you heat them. To obtain the orange peel, use a Y-shaped vegetable peeler, and gently cut a segment off the orange skin, without removing the bitter white pith.

Serves 4

1 tablespoon olive oil

2 cups unpitted salt-cured black Sicilian olives, rinsed well to remove the salt

1 teaspoon fennel seeds

2 whole spicy red peppers (fresh, preserved in oil, or dried)

2 pieces of orange peel, roughly $1/2$ inch wide and 2 inches long

1 Heat the olive oil in a sauté pan over medium heat. Add the olives, fennel seeds, and spicy red peppers. Twist the orange peels over the pan before adding the two pieces, so that the aromatic oils contained in the skin are released.

2 Hold the pan handle with one hand and continue to move the pan back and forth while heating the olives on all sides. Within about 5 minutes, the cooking is complete. The olives are ready when the skin no longer looks wrinkled, but rather smooth and puffed up. Serve while hot.

EGGPLANT PARMESAN

{ *Parmigiana di Melanzane* }

À PARMIŚCIANA RI MILINCIANI

Most attribute the meaning of the name parmigiana *to the fact that Parmigiano-Reggiano cheese is a crucial ingredient. An alternative explanation is that the name comes from* parmiciana, *a style of wood furniture making that involves inlaid layers, the eggplant layers mimicking this design.*

This dish is said to hail from three regions of Italy: Campania, Sicily, and Emilia Romagna. Outside of Italy, this dish has taken on many variations that are uncommon throughout the peninsula, such as the addition of mozzarella or chicken. In Italy, breadcrumbs are sometimes sprinkled on top of a parmigiana, *but are not used as a breading on each slice of eggplant.*

Around Sicily, in restaurants, I've tried many variations on parmigiana, *some of which even contain layers of seafood. However, the following recipe is a simple and classic way of preparing the dish.*

Traditionally, it's common to soak the eggplants in salted water before frying them, but I opt not to do so, as I harvest them when they are small and have very few seeds. In this manner they tend to be sweet and do not have the bitterness usually associated with eggplants.

1 Preheat the oven to 350°F. Fill a heavy-bottomed saucepan, placed over medium heat, with the olive oil. When the oil is hot, place the eggplant slices in the pan and fry them in batches for 5 to 8 minutes, until they turn a rusty brown color. Remove the fried slices gently with tongs and place them on paper towels to drain the olive oil. While still hot, sprinkle them with salt and pepper. (If you prefer to avoid frying, you can instead drizzle them with olive oil, sprinkle them with salt, and bake them on a sheet pan in a 350°F oven for about 30 minutes, until they soften and turn golden brown).

2 In a 12-inch-long casserole dish, place the eggplant slices, top them with the tomato sauce, and then sprinkle with the cheese. Bake until the cheese is fully melted, about 5 minutes. Remove from the oven, sprinkle the fresh basil leaves on top, and serve immediately.

Serves 4

2 cups extra-virgin olive oil

2 eggplants, sliced into discs
³/₄ inch thick

About ¹/₂ teaspoon salt

Ground black pepper

2 cups tomato sauce
(page 172), warm or
at room temperature

2 cups semi-aged
pecorino cheese

About 10 fresh basil leaves

SAVORY EGGPLANT TRIFLE

{ *Assaggio di Melanzane e Ricotta* }

The following recipe is a modern invention, which I've tried in several upscale restaurants around Sicily. The trifle tastes similar to a parmigiana, *but takes on a new form. It is often presented in a glass or a ceramic ramekin, at room temperature or cold, as a small complimentary welcome dish to guests. In this dish, the eggplant is roasted, pureed, then layered with the other ingredients: cherry tomato pulp and whipped ricotta. The final touch is a crisp made by melting cheese in a nonstick pan and used as a garnish. This is an easy-to-prepare, perfect bite to serve as an hors d'oeuvre. All layers of the dish, including the Parmesan crisps, can be prepared up to a day in advance.*

Serves 8

1 whole eggplant, about 1 pound

2 garlic cloves

Salt

5 tablespoons extra-virgin olive oil

1 pint ripe cherry tomatoes

¹⁄₄ cup Tomato Pulp (homemade, page 70, or store-bought)

Pinch of sugar

2 cups ricotta (homemade, page 80, or store-bought)

1 teaspoon dried Sicilian oregano

3 large fresh basil leaves, plus more for layering

1 cup grated Parmigiano-Reggiano cheese

1 To make the eggplant layer, preheat the oven to 400°F. Cut a small slit in the eggplant skin and insert one of the garlic cloves. Place the whole eggplant on a sheet pan and roast it for 40 minutes. Remove from the oven and let cool. Then cut the stem off the top of the eggplant and peel off the skin, which will remove quite easily. The garlic will also have roasted. Place the eggplant pulp along with the roasted garlic in a bowl. Season with ¹⁄₂ teaspoon salt. Using the back of a fork, smash the eggplant and garlic well, turning them into a chunky mash. Add 2 tablespoons of the extra-virgin olive oil and mix well. Taste for salt and add more if

necessary. Note that each consecutive layer should be seasoned with salt separately.

2 To make the tomato layer, smash the uncooked garlic clove with your hand so that it lightly crushes. In a sauté pan, gently heat up 2 tablespoons of the olive oil over low heat and add the crushed garlic clove. Then squeeze the ripe cherry tomatoes with your hand as they are dropped into the pan. Add the tomato pulp, the pinch of sugar, about ¹⁄₂ teaspoon salt, and about 2 cups cold water. Let the cherry tomatoes cook over medium heat until the water has evaporated, about 5 minutes. Rip each of the basil leaves in half by hand, then add them to the tomato pulp. Taste and add more salt if necessary. Remove the garlic clove and let the chunky tomato mixture cool.

3 To make the whipped ricotta layer, place the ricotta in the bowl of a food processor with the oregano, ¹⁄₂ teaspoon salt, and the remaining 1 tablespoon extra-virgin olive oil. Mix on high speed for 1 minute. Taste for salt. If you add more, mix the ricotta again before removing it from the food processor. Hold in the refrigerator until ready to use.

4 To make the Parmesan crisp, heat a 6-inch nonstick pan over medium heat. Sprinkle half of the grated Parmesan into the pan in an even layer. The cheese will melt and stick together. Using a heat-resistant rubber spatula, flip the layer of cheese, as if you were flipping a pancake. The cheese will get crunchy and golden in color when it is ready to be removed from the pan. Let the crisp cool, ideally on a silicone baking mat. Repeat with the remainder of the cheese. Once cooled, each round piece of melted cheese can be broken into four smaller pieces, which will be used to garnish each serving of the dish.

continued ↓

5 Ideally the eggplant and tomato layers should be at room temperature before you assemble the dish. In a juice glass or in a 1-cup ceramic ramekin, first place ¼ cup of the eggplant pulp. Then add about the same amount of the cooked cherry tomatoes. Finally add a scoop of the whipped ricotta. In between each layer, add a small piece of basil, either a ripped piece of a large basil leaf, or the individual leaves from a basil bush. Top with a piece of Parmesan crisp. Repeat in the same way with seven more juice glasses or ramekins and serve.

SQUASH GREENS FLAN *with a* RAGUSANO CREAM

{ *Sformato di Tenerumi* }

SFORMATU RI TINNIRUMA

A sformato *is an Italian preparation, a savory custard similar to the French soufflé, though slightly less airy due to the addition of ricotta. Numerous types of vegetables are used in preparation of the* sformato, *including spinach, mushroom, and eggplant. I have noticed that this dish can seem intimidating to home cooks, but in actuality, it is quite simple to prepare.* Tenerumi *are the leaves of the* cucuzza *plant (see page 152), a particular type of summer squash that Sicilians love to grow. They may be hard to find off the island, but you can substitute any leafy green, such as spinach, Swiss chard, nettles, or a combination thereof. You will need four 10-ounce ramekins to hold the* sformato.

Serves 4

Sformato	*Ragusano cream*
¹/₂ **pound** *tenerumi* **leaves, or other leafy greens**	**1 cup grated** *ragusano* **cheese (see page 64)**
Extra-virgin olive oil, for greasing the ramekins	**1 cup heavy cream**
¹/₂ **pound ricotta**	
3 large eggs, beaten	
¹/₂ **cup grated pecorino cheese**	
1 teaspoon salt	

1 FOR THE *SFORMATO*: Preheat the oven to 350°F. Blanch the greens in a pot of salted boiling water for about 3 minutes. Meanwhile, using the pointer and middle finger of one hand, rub a small amount of olive oil inside four 10-ounce ovenproof ceramic ramekins. Drain the blanched greens in a colander, letting as much water drain out as possible. Finely chop the greens with a chef's knife or chop them in a food processor. In a mixing bowl, combine the chopped greens, ricotta, beaten eggs, pecorino cheese, and salt. Mix well, then fill the prepared molds with the mixture.

2 Place the ramekins on a baking sheet and bake for 15 minutes. Let cool for 10 minutes. Turn each *sformato* out of its ramekin onto a platter or tray. If they do not release easily, run the tip of a knife around the edges of the *sformato* to help loosen them.

3 FOR THE *RAGUSANO* CREAM: Combine the *ragusano* cheese and heavy cream in a sauté pan. Bring to a boil, then reduce to a simmer, whisking constantly so that the cheese melts. Cook until the cream is reduced by half. The *ragusano* cream can be prepared a day in advance and held in the refrigerator; reheat before serving.

4 To serve the *sformato*, place 2 large spoonfuls of the *ragusano* cream on the bottom of each serving plate. Then use a spatula to place a *sformato* on top of each spoonful of cream.

SEAFOOD SALAD

{ Insalata di Mare }

'NSALATA RI MARI

Seafood salad is a staple appetizer at the rustic seaside trattorie around the island. This recipe combines the classic elements of a Sicilian seafood salad with whipped avocado. Until recently, avocado was not used often in Sicily, but today more and more avocado trees are being grown on the slopes of Mount Etna, where they thrive in the volcanic soil. The creaminess of the avocado complements the citrus and seafood flavors here. If you'd like to make a simpler version of this dish, it will still be delicious without the avocado cream.

Serves 8

Seafood salad

1 cup white wine

2 bay leaves

About 1 teaspoon salt

1/4 pound fresh wild calamari (follow the steps for cleaning calamari on page 129)

1/4 pound mussels, shell on, scrubbed

8 sea scallops

1/2 poached octopus, about 2 pounds (follow the steps for poaching octopus on page 130)

Juice of 1 lemon

2 stalks celery, including the leaves, cut into 1/2-inch pieces

1/2 cup loosely packed fresh parsley leaves (from about 1/2 bunch of parsley)

1 cup Sicilian green olives, pitted and sliced in half

1 tablespoon salted capers, rinsed well

2 pints ripe cherry tomatoes

Smoked sea salt

3 tablespoons extra-virgin olive oil

Avocado cream

2 ripe avocados

2 to 3 tablespoons fresh lemon juice

1/2 teaspoon salt

2 tablespoons extra-virgin olive oil

1 FOR THE SEAFOOD SALAD: Ready an ice bath on the counter near the stovetop. Prepare a poaching liquid in a saucepan by combining 1 gallon water, the wine, bay leaves, and salt. Bring to a boil, then reduce to a simmer. Poach the calamari first for about 2 minutes, then transfer it to the ice bath to stop the cooking. Poach the mussels in their shells for about 3 minutes or until the mussels open and are orange in color. Discard any mussels whose shells do not open completely. Transfer the mussels to the ice bath as well. Poach the scallops until firm (as opposed to rubbery in texture), about 5 minutes, depending on the size of the scallops, then transfer them to the ice bath. Thinly slice the previously poached octopus on a bias using a serrated paring knife or another sharp knife.

2 In a mixing bowl, combine the poached seafood, lemon juice, celery and leaves, parsley, olives, capers, cherry tomatoes, and smoked salt to taste. Mix well, until the salt dissolves into the lemon juice. Then add the extra-virgin olive oil and toss again. Chill in the refrigerator while preparing the remainder of the dish. The salad may be prepared to this point up to 1 day in advance.

3 FOR THE AVOCADO CREAM: In a food processor, combine the avocados, lemon juice, and salt. Turn on the food processor to a high speed and slowly pour in the extra-virgin olive oil in a stream. The oil will emulsify with the avocado and create a soft cream.

4 To plate each salad, spread some of the avocado cream across each dish. Place a scoop of the seafood salad in the center.

SAUTEED SQUID

{ *Calamari in Padella* }

CALAMARA IN PADEDDA

I love both the simplicity and elegance of this sautéed squid appetizer, which is served by Giovanni Guarneri at his restaurant in Ortigia. The key to making this dish delicious is in the sourcing of fresh, wild squid, as opposed to the frozen farmed varieties that are more readily available in North American supermarkets, but tend to be much tougher in consistency when cooked. Ask your local fishmonger to let you know when local fresh squid is available in your area, and it will make this simple dish shine. Chef Guarneri serves the dish in small glass jars with lids on them. On the walk from the kitchen to the table, the jar starts to fill with steam, which exudes a pleasant seafood aroma when the lid is removed at the table.

While most fish markets in the United States sell cleaned squid, follow the steps below if you're purchasing it whole. Fresh squid appears plump and slippery. It has a clean aroma, reminiscent of the ocean, but not overly fishy. The body of a whole squid is covered with a purplish film, which is edible but often removed in restaurants for aesthetic purposes.

Serves 4

16 whole squid (about 1¹/₂ pounds total)	**About 16 fresh basil leaves, torn in half**
6 ripe plum tomatoes	**Salt**
1 tablespoon olive oil	**Extra-virgin olive oil, for finishing**
2 garlic cloves	
1 cup white wine	

1 CLEAN THE SQUID: It is advisable to wear an apron, as the innards contain a small amount of black ink that can easily stain clothes. Hold the tail firmly with one hand while pulling the head with the other. With a twisting motion, the head, which is attached to the innards, will slip out of the tail cavity. Next, remove the head and innards from the tentacles by using a sharp knife to cut on top of the eyes of the squid. A small piece of cartilage, known as a beak, is located at the base of the tentacles, where it was connected to the head. Squeeze this part to easily remove the beak from the tentacles. To clean the tail, first remove the inedible clear piece of cartilage that looks like a sliver of plastic by pulling it out of the tail. Finally, remove the outer dark skin of the squid tail. Rinse the inside of the tail and slice the squid into ¹/₂-inch segments. Repeat with the remaining squid.

2 To peel the tomatoes, bring a large pot of water to a boil. With a paring knife, core each tomato by cutting out the part that is connected to the stem, and cut an X into the bottom of each tomato. Place them in the pot of boiling water for 1 minute. Remove with a slotted spoon and let cool for a few moments. The skin of the tomatoes should get soft, and you can peel it off by gently pulling it up with your knife from the point where you cut the X. After the skin is removed, cut each tomato in half crosswise and remove the seeds with a small spoon or with the back of your thumb. Dice the peeled tomatoes into ¹/₂-inch cubes.

3 In a large sauté pan, heat the olive oil over medium heat. Add the garlic and let it cook for 2 minutes, then add the peeled tomatoes and simmer for another 2 minutes. Finally, add the cut pieces of calamari to the pan along with the white wine. Cook for about 5 minutes, until the calamari is cooked through and the wine has evaporated. The calamari will appear somewhat rubbery when cooked through.

4 Add the torn basil, some salt to taste, and the extra-virgin olive oil. Stir the contents of the pan and serve while hot, removing the garlic cloves before serving.

GRILLED OCTOPUS *with* CHICKPEA PUREE

{ *Polipo con Crema di Ceci* }

PURPU CU I CICIRI

I first came across the flavor pairing of this addictive charred octopus, brilliantly counterpointed by a simple creamy rosemary-laced chickpea puree, at a port-side restaurant in Sciacca.

In Sicily, fresh octopus is easy to come by. Off the island, frozen octopus is much more common, but when poached gently it yields a similarly delicious, meaty flavor. There are many opinions about how to cook octopus the so-called right way (adding a cork to the water is a common tip), but I've come to the conclusion that all that is required is for the octopus to be gently poached until tender. You know it is ready when its surface is soft to the touch and feels similar to the skin between one's thumb and pointer finger. The bigger the octopus, the more poaching time it requires. If you find small, fresh baby octopi, you can skip the poaching step and grill them directly.

Serves 8

Octopus

1 large octopus (about 4 pounds), thawed if frozen

1 (750 ml) bottle red wine, such as Nero d'Avola

2 stalks celery, cut into chunks

1 carrot, unpeeled, cut into chunks

1 fennel bulb, quartered

1 large yellow onion, quartered

1 bunch flat-leaf parsley

3 bay leaves

¼ cup black peppercorns

½ cup extra-virgin olive oil, plus extra for finishing the plate

1 sprig fresh rosemary, stemmed and finely chopped, plus 8 small sprigs for garnish

Salt and freshly ground black pepper

Chickpea puree

1 cup dried chickpeas

1 teaspoon baking soda

Juice of 1 lemon

1 garlic clove, crushed into a paste

Sea salt

2 tablespoons extra-virgin olive oil

1 TO POACH THE OCTOPUS: Fill a large stockpot with water. Add the octopus, wine, celery, carrot, fennel, onion, parsley, bay leaves, and peppercorns and bring to a boil. Lower the heat to a simmer and cook for 20 minutes, or until the octopus is soft to the touch, like the skin between your pointer finger and thumb. Remove from the heat, cover the pot, and let the octopus rest in the poaching liquid for 20 minutes. Remove the octopus from the poaching liquid with large tongs and let it cool on a baking sheet. Then marinate the octopus for at least 1 hour in the olive oil and rosemary. (The octopus may be prepared to this point up to 2 days in advance and refrigerated.)

2 FOR THE CHICKPEA PUREE: Place the chickpeas in a container with 2 cups water and soak overnight. Drain the chickpeas and transfer to a pot. Cover with about 1 inch of fresh water and add the baking soda. (Do not add salt.) Bring to a boil, then lower the heat to a simmer and cook until tender, about 1 hour depending on the age of the dried beans. Drain the chickpeas, reserving about 2 cups of the cooking liquid for pureeing. Let cool to room temperature.

3 Transfer the chickpeas to a food processor. Add the lemon juice, garlic paste, about ½ teaspoon sea salt, and the olive oil and pulse until the chickpeas form a very smooth puree. It should be thinner than store-bought hummus but thicker than a pureed soup. If too thick, add a few tablespoons of the bean cooking liquid. Taste, adding more sea salt if needed.

4 TO GRILL THE OCTOPUS: Prepare a medium-hot fire in a grill, spreading the coals evenly for direct-heat cooking. Alternatively, use a grill pan to cook the octopus, preheated over high heat. Coat the octopus in the olive oil and rosemary marinade and season with salt and pepper. Place the octopus on the grill and cook until the exterior is slightly charred and crunchy and the center is hot, about 4 minutes per side. While grilling, brush the octopus occasionally with the marinade.

5 To serve, spoon about 5 tablespoons of the chickpea puree in the center of each plate. Using the back of the spoon, spread the puree into a circle. Slice the octopus on the bias into pieces about ¾ inch thick. Divide the slices among the plates, placing the curved part of the tentacle on top. Garnish each plate with a sprig of rosemary and a drizzle of olive oil.

MARINATED SARDINES *with* CHILLED CANTALOUPE SOUP

{ Sarde Marinate }

I SARDI MARINATI

Chef Angelo Pumilla of Sciacca creates appetizers composed of raw or marinated seafood with cold fruit soups during the summer months. In addition to this dish, which incorporates marinated sardines with a cantaloupe puree, he also prepares a raw shrimp dish with basil and a tomato-peach soup. The marinated sardines can also be enjoyed with some toasted bread.

Either ask your fishmonger to clean and debone the sardines, or fillet them yourself. Look for fish with a firm, silver-blue, iridescent skin and clear eyes.

Serves 4

Sardines

6 fresh whole sardines, filleted, tails removed

1/2 tablespoon white wine vinegar

1/4 teaspoon salt

1 tablespoon extra-virgin olive oil

Cold melon soup

1/2 cantaloupe, peeled and cut into pieces

Juice of 1/2 lemon

1/4 cup plain whole-milk yogurt

1 teaspoon red wine vinegar

1 teaspoon wildflower honey

Cold melon soup, **continued**

2 tablespoons extra-virgin olive oil

Salt

5 fresh mint leaves, finely chopped

To assemble

Salt

1 celery stalk, finely sliced

1 spring onion, finely sliced

1 carrot, peeled and finely sliced into long thin strips

1 teaspoon extra-virgin olive oil

1/2 cup ricotta (homemade, page 80, or store-bought)

1 FOR THE SARDINES: In a glass container (don't use a reactive metal container), toss the sardine fillets with the vinegar and salt. When the salt dissolves, add the extra-virgin olive oil.

2 Cover the container with plastic wrap and marinate in the refrigerator for at least 1 hour but no more than 6 hours.

3 FOR THE COLD MELON SOUP: In a food processor, blend the cantaloupe along with the lemon juice, yogurt, vinegar, and honey. Then, from the top of the food processor, add the extra-virgin olive oil in a slow, steady stream, blending until the contents become very smooth.

4 Transfer the melon soup to a mixing bowl. Stir in about 1/2 teaspoon of salt before adding more according to your taste.

5 Add the finely chopped fresh mint leaves and stir well. Chill the cantaloupe soup in the refrigerator to for at least 1 hour before serving.

6 TO ASSEMBLE: Bring a pot of salted water to a boil over high heat. Blanch the celery, spring onion, and carrot separately. Prepare a bowl filled with cold water and ice. When each vegetable is blanched for about 1 minute, remove it from the boiling water and place it in the ice bath to stop the cooking. Transfer the vegetables from the ice bath to a plate lined with paper towels to remove the excess moisture. Finally, toss the blanched vegetables with the extra-virgin olive oil.

7 To plate the dish, start by lining the bottom of each soup bowl with the cold cantaloupe soup. In the center of each bowl, place a dollop of the ricotta. Top each serving with 3 sardine fillets and some of the blanched vegetables as a garnish. Serve immediately.

SALAD OF TUNA, POTATOES, *and* STRING BEANS

{ Insalata Pantesca }

'NSALATA PANTESCA

Located both spatially and culturally between the western coast of Sicily and Tunisia, the volcanic island of Pantelleria possesses a rugged terrain, adorned with jagged lava stones, white domed dwellings, trellised vineyards, ancient caves, and titanic seaside cliffs and grottos, framed by uncontaminated turquoise-tinged waters. When visiting Pantelleria, expect to discover a pristine land, a place where time seems to stand still. The late novelist Gabriel Garcia Marquez declared that Pantelleria was more beautiful than the moon. The island's natural beauty is indeed breathtaking but is not limited to its landscape. It extends to the quality and concentrated flavor of its local fruits, vegetables, and famous capers, which profit from the fertility of the volcanic soil.

This salad is a classic dish in Pantelleria, but can be found in several variations. The staple ingredients are the ripe tomatoes, the capers and olives, and some form of preserved fish, most commonly tuna or mackerel belly. If you want to make your own preserved tuna, poach a piece of tuna (preferably about a pound of tuna belly) in salted water, then place in a jar and submerge with olive oil (it will keep up to five days in the refrigerator). Jarred tuna in olive oil, preferably Italian, can be substituted.

Serves 4

¼ **pound waxy potatoes, cut into 1-inch chunks**

Salt

¼ **pound string beans, ends removed**

1 cup green Sicilian olives, pitted and sliced in half

¼ **red onion, thinly sliced**

1 pint ripe cherry tomatoes, cut in half

2 tablespoons salted capers, well rinsed

2 tablespoons white wine vinegar, plus more if needed

2 tablespoons dried Sicilian oregano

Cracked black pepper

2 tablespoons extra-virgin olive oil, plus more if needed

¾ **pound preserved tuna**

1 Place the potatoes in a large pot and cover them with cold salted water. Bring to a boil over high heat and let them cook for a few minutes after the water comes to a boil. The potatoes should be cooked through at this point, but to ensure that they are ready, slip a paring knife in the center of one chunk. If it slips through quickly, the potato is ready. Drain the potatoes thoroughly so that no water remains on them, and place them in a mixing bowl.

2 Meanwhile, in another pot, bring more salted water to a boil over high heat, then cook the string beans in the boiling water for a few minutes. Set up a bowl filled with cold water and ice. If you prefer the string beans to be firm, remove them quickly, or if you prefer that they cook through and are soft, leave them in the water a little longer. I prefer the string beans to have a crunch to them, but ultimately either way is fine and is just a matter of personal taste. After removing the string beans from the boiling water, place them in the bowl filled with ice water in order to stop them from cooking further. Drain them well so that no water remains on them before adding them to the mixing bowl with the potatoes.

3 To the mixing bowl with the potatoes and string beans, add the olives, red onion, cherry tomatoes, capers, vinegar, oregano, cracked pepper, and olive oil. Toss well and taste, adding salt accordingly. Add more vinegar and olive oil, if necessary and toss again. Top or toss with the preserved fish. Serve immediately.

CLASSIC CHICKPEA FRITTERS

{ Panelle }

PANEDDE

Typically prepared as a street food on the western side of Sicily, panelle *are thin fried fritters prepared from a batter made of chickpea flour, water, salt, and olive oil. As a street food, they are served in semola panino rolls with sesame seeds (page 90). I like to serve the fritters warm as an appetizer, preparing them thicker than the street-food version.*

Serves 6

¹/₂ **pound chickpea flour, sifted**

1 teaspoon salt

1 tablespoon olive oil, plus more for greasing

1 cup finely chopped fresh parsley leaves (optional)

Vegetable oil, for frying

2 cups Crunchy Caponata (recipe opposite)

1 In a thick-bottomed saucepan, combine the chickpea flour with 5 cups cold water, the salt, and olive oil. Whisk all the ingredients together briskly and continue whisking for the entire cooking process, otherwise the mixture will stick to the bottom of the pan. Turn the heat to medium. When the batter starts to boil, lower the heat slightly and cook for another 10 minutes. If it becomes difficult to whisk, stir the mixture with a wooden spoon instead. If clumps arise, use an immersion hand blender to break them up. If adding chopped parsley, stir it into the chickpea mixture, which should be thick and sticky at this stage.

2 Rub a 12 by 18-inch sheet pan with 1-inch sides with olive oil. Working quickly, as the mixture will firm up quickly, transfer the hot chickpea mixture to the sheet pan, using an offset spatula to spread it evenly and to flatten it. Let cool in the refrigerator for at least 30 minutes.

3 Using a paring knife or a cookie cutter, cut the chilled chickpea mixture into equal-size pieces, no more than 3 inches in length.

4 To fry the *panelle*, pour enough vegetable oil into a large pot so the *panelle* can be submerged in the oil when frying. Place the pot over medium-high heat. When the oil is hot and the surface is shimmering, begin to fry the *panelle*, working in batches to avoid crowding the pan. After a few minutes, when the chickpea fritters are golden brown, use a slotted spoon to remove them from the oil. Place each piece on a plate lined with paper towels so that any excess oil can drain. Serve immediately, with the caponata alongside.

CRUNCHY CAPONATA

{ Caponata Croccante }

This caponata omits the tomato sauce and replaces the olives and capers with raisins and pine nuts. I call it "crunchy" because it is not stewed and the fresh vegetables still have a bite to them. That's also why this version is not meant for preservation. The warm, somewhat nutty flavor of the chickpea fritter com-plements the sweet-and-sour vegetables of the caponata, and I often serve these two dishes on one appetizer plate, although this is nontraditional.

Serves 4 as an appetizer

Extra-virgin olive oil

2 medium eggplants, cut into ¹/₂-inch cubes

1 zucchini, cut into ¹/₂-inch cubes

2 red bell peppers, cut into ¹/₂-inch pieces

1 large onion, cut into ¹/₂ inch pieces

3 celery stalks, cut on an angle into ¹/₂-inch pieces

¹/₄ cup *agrodolce* (page 46)

¹/₂ cup golden raisins or currants

1 teaspoon Garlic Paste (page 40)

1 cup of semi-oven-dried tomatoes (page 73; optional)

¹/₄ cup Italian pine nuts, toasted

6 fresh basil leaves, hand-ripped or delicately sliced into thin strips

Salt

1 Heat about 1 cup olive oil in a sauté pan over medium to high heat and fry the eggplants until golden brown on all sides, about 6 minutes. Remove from the oil using a slotted spoon and drain the excess oil from the eggplant on paper towels or by placing the cooked vegetables in a strainer placed over a deep pan. Then sauté the zucchini, bell peppers, onion, and celery, each separately, adding more oil between batches as needed. It is best to cook all the vegetables separately because they have different cooking times. Do not overcook the vegetables for this preparation. A gentle sauté over high heat is sufficient. They should not be soggy, but rather cooked yet still crunchy and firm.

2 Meanwhile, in a saucepan, heat the *agrodolce* with the raisins. In a separate large sauté pan, heat about 1 tablespoon olive oil, add the garlic paste, and gently fry for about 30 seconds. Avoid browning the garlic. Add the cooked vegetables, the semi-oven-dried tomatoes, and the pine nuts. Slowly add the *agrodolce* mixture. Turn up the heat and let the mixture cook together for about 5 minutes over medium heat. Add salt to taste; I find 1 teaspoon salt is usually sufficient.

3 Let cool to room temperature and serve. The caponata can be prepared up to a few hours in advance; however, the longer it sits, the less firm the vegetables will remain.

SAVORY POTATO CAKE

{ Gatò di Patate }

GATÒ RI PATATI

A potato gatò, *from the French term* gateau, *meaning "cake," is a savory pie with a stuffing of cured meats, evidence of the French* monzù *chefs (see page 184) in Sicilian aristocratic homes of time past. This dish can be served as an appetizer, on its own for a light meal, or as second course. I usually prepare* gatò *after a big holiday party as a way to use the end pieces of cured meats.*

In Sicily's rosticceria *tradition, this potato cake is commonly stuffed with fried eggplant,* primo sale *and caciocavallo cheese, or with a beef and pea ragù (page 167). If you choose to stuff it with either eggplant or ragù, omit the cured meats from the potato mixture.*

Serves 6

3 pounds Yukon gold
potatoes, peeled

1 cup grated
Parmesan cheese

1/2 teaspoon
grated nutmeg

1/4 pound end pieces
of salame or other cured
meats, finely ground in a
food processor

Salt

4 large eggs, beaten

4 tablespoons
unsalted butter

1 1/2 cups fine breadcrumbs
(page 42)

1/2 pound *primo sale* cheese
(substitute with mozzarella
or smoked mozzarella), cut
into 1/4-inch cubes

1/4 pound *prosciutto cotto*
(Italian ham), cut into
1/4-inch cubes

Olive oil

1 Preheat the oven to 350°F. In a pot of cold water to cover, bring the potatoes to a boil. When cooked through and the tip of a paring knife slips easily through the potatoes, drain them and let them cool. Place the potatoes in a hand-held ricer or in a food mill fitted with a medium disc over a mixing bowl so that the potatoes are mashed and fall into the bowl. Or you can smash the potatoes with the back of a fork. Avoid blending them with an electric mixer, as that will puree them too much. A ricer keeps the potatoes light and airy.

2 Mix the potatoes with the grated cheese, ground nutmeg, and the ground salame. Taste for salt and season to taste. Add the beaten eggs and mix well.

3 Use the butter to generously grease one large baking pan or six 10-ounce ceramic ramekins. Sprinkle the pans with the breadcrumbs and turn so that all sides are evenly coated, reserving some of the breadcrumbs for later use.

4 Fill the baking pan or ramekins with the potato mixture halfway, then add a layer of the *primo sale* cheese, a thin layer of the *prosciutto cotto*, followed by another layer of the potato mixture. Sprinkle the remaining breadcrumbs on top.

5 Bake for about 30 minutes, until the breadcrumbs on the top of the potato cake are light brown. Remove from the oven to cool slightly before unmolding. The *gatò* can be prepared up to 1 day in advance and baked to serve. To unmold the *gatò*, turn each mold upside down on a plate and gently tap the bottom.

ORANGE *and* LEMON SALAD

{ *Insalata di Limone ed Arancia* }

'NSALATA RI LIMUNI E ARANCIA

My mother learned this old Sicilian rustic dish from her grandfather and often prepared it for me as an afternoon snack when I was a kid. With its sweet, piquant, and salty notes, it also makes a great antipasto. I've always found this salad very invigorating. After chewing on a sour chunk of lemon, I like to follow with a sweet bite of orange and I always make sure that I save an orange piece for last. I also enjoy eating this with bread to soak up the salty juices and olive oil.

In Sicily, I love to prepare this salad with the addition of citron, which has thick, sweet rinds. The citrus fruit should be cut into chunks, but first remove the outer peel using a sharp paring knife or a peeler. Make sure that the spongy white pith that sits under the rind is left on the fruit. The peels—if you are using organic fruit—can be saved to flavor other dishes or to make Candied Orange Peel (page 306). Keep fresh in an airtight container for a few days in the refrigerator. Otherwise, dry the peels by leaving them on a plate fully exposed to air for about one week. Then you can keep them for months in spice jars and use them in recipes that call for orange or lemon peel.

Serves 4

3 lemons

3 sweet oranges

1 tablespoon Sicilian dried oregano

Sea salt

Cracked black pepper

2 tablespoons fine extra-virgin olive oil

1 Remove the peel from the lemons and oranges. Cut each fruit into four sections, removing the seeds. Continue by cutting into bite-size pieces.

2 In a bowl, combine the lemon and orange chunks and the oregano. Add sea salt and cracked pepper to taste. Mix well. Add the extra-virgin olive oil and toss again before serving.

Variation

A popular Sicilian winter salad consists of orange chunks, sardines preserved in olive oil, extra-virgin olive oil, and cracked black pepper. Some cooks also add raw onion. The saltiness of the sardines is a perfect accompaniment to the sweet, tangy oranges.

Chapter 5

SOUPS & RICE

CLOCKWISE FROM TOP LEFT:
*White beans, black beans,
red beans, chickpeas, lentils
from Ustica, brown lentils,
red lentils, black lentils,
grass peas, fava beans, black
chickpeas, cranberry beans*

A NUMBER of Italian terms indicate different types of soup. Minestra is prepared with rice, pasta, or whole grain, in addition to vegetables and broth. Minestra, in all its variations, has always been a humble dish and its name comes from the verb *minestrare*, that is, "to administer," because it was served or "administered" by the householder. Minestrone, born after contact with the New World introduced potatoes, corn, and beans to Italy, is a thick, more abundant version of a minestra.

Zuppa is usually served with pieces of bread, but does not contain rice or pasta. It is usually denser than a minestra, because less broth is used in its preparation, but the types of vegetables included may be the same. The name, *zuppa*, similar in all European languages, is derived from the Gothic word *suppa*, indicating that the slice of bread soaks up the soup.

Vellutata is a pureed soup that is prepared from the mixture of two or three blended components and broth. A *crema* is a puree of one component (meat, fish, or vegetable), which can be thickened with potato. In Sicilian home cooking, cream is rarely used in such preparations, but in upscale restaurants sometimes chefs will add it sparingly.

BEANS AS THE BASE

Beans are popular in Sicily, not only because they are nutritious and hearty, but also because the plants add to the fertility of the soil by bringing nitrogen gas from the atmosphere into the earth. At Feudo Montoni, as part of a system of organic farming, favas and chickpeas are planted in between the rows of the vineyard during during the winter months. In the early spring, the flowering legumes are plowed into the earth, where they provide nutrients to the vines awakening from their long rest. During winter, I prepare bean soups at home almost every day. I love that each type of bean possesses its own unique flavor.

Beans	Italian Name	Sicilian Name
Badda bean*	Fagioli badda	Fasoli badda
Grass peas	Cicerchie	Rumanedda o ciciruòccolo
Chickpeas*	Ceci	Ciciri
Black chickpeas	Ceci neri	Ciciri nivuri
Cranberry beans*	Fagioli borlotti	Borlotti
Beans from Scicli	Fagioli cosarusciaru	Cosarusciaru ri Scicli
Lupin beans	Lupini	Lupini
Fava beans*	Fave	Favi
Brown lentils	Lenticchie	Linticchi
Lentils from Ustica	Lenticchie di Ustica	Linticchi ri Ustica
Black lentils	Lenticchie nere	Linticchi nere
Red lentils	Lenticchie rosse	Linticchi rosse
Black beans	Fagioli neri	Fasoli nivuri
White beans	Fagioli di Ustica	Fasoli ri Ustica
Tabaccara beans	Fagioli Tabaccara	Fasoli Tabaccara
Peas*	Pideddi	Piselli

* These bean varieties are also consumed fresh, especially the peas, fava, and cranberry beans.

LENTILS *Lenticchie* LINTICCHI

Multiple varieties of lentils are grown in Sicily, but my favorite is one that originated around a town called Villalba, known as *lenticchie di Villalba.* These large, hearty green lentils do not get mushy when cooked. In fact, even when cooked for long periods, they retain their meaty texture and shape.

The smallest lentils in all of Italy are cultivated on Ustica, a small island off the north coast of Sicily. Sown in January and picked in the first half of June, *lenticchie di Ustica* are a key ingredient in the local peasant cuisine. Dark brown with delicate shades of green, these legumes are always grown on the fertile lava soil and always the technique is completely manual, in accordance with the environment and nature. No fertilizers or herbicides of any kind are used. Weeds are removed with a hoe.

Black lentils have been grown since the 1950s in the province of Enna, but are not favored by farmers, who tend to prefer more resilient varieties. Around the turn of the century, they were nearing extinction. Since then, the cultivation of black lentils has experienced a slight resurgence, but because all operations— from planting to harvesting and cleaning—must be done by hand, it is a highly labor-intensive process.

Lentils need no presoaking and cook much more quickly than other dried legumes. Just be sure to choose the right type for each dish. Red lentils, which are hulled, tend to break down during the cooking process, thus, are most commonly used in soups. Green and brown lentils hold their shape best and are used in salads as well as soups. If using hearty lentils, such as those from Villalba, cook them with vegetables that have a long cooking time and then mix the soup with ditalini pasta.

BEANS OF SCICLI *Fagioli Cosarusciaru* COSARUSCIARU RI SCICLI

The Sicilian word *cosarusciaru* translates as "sweet thing." These beans are recognizable by their creamy white color with small brown streaks. In the nineteenth century, these beans played a major role in the local economy of the area between Modica and Scicli. Although cultivation plummeted when peasants emigrated in the early twentieth century, the beans are slowly regaining their popularity, thanks to efforts by the Slow Food organization to reestablish a market for them. A popular vegetable soup is made with these beans, with the addition of pork rind in the broth for flavor.

BADDA BEANS *Fagioli Badda Bianchi e Neri* FASOLI BADDA BIANCA E NIURA

Badda in Sicilian dialect means "ball." Farmers from the town of Polizzi Generosa, in the Madonie Mountains, have been growing badda beans in small family gardens and farms for centuries. Ivory colored and spotted, fruity and herbaceous in flavor with notes of almond and chestnut, badda beans are consumed fresh or dried and are known for being easily digested. Lighter varieties, with orange-colored spots, are known as *badda bianca,* while darker beans with deep purple spots are known as *badda niura.* Typical dishes prepared with the beans include fresh tagliatelle pasta with green badda beans and cherry tomatoes and a soup with dried badda beans, wild fennel, and pork rinds.

CHICKPEAS *Ceci* CICIRI

The term *cicer* is believed to derive from the Greek work *kikus,* which means "power." In ancient times, chickpeas were considered a sacred bean and an aphrodisiac. According to folklore, during the Sicilian vespers in the thirteenth century, French-speaking Angevin enemies, who dressed in similar garments as the Sicilians in order to blend in, were pinpointed when they could not pronounce the Sicilian word for chickpea, *ciciri.*

Chickpeas are consumed fresh, but they are more commonly dried and used in soups or cooked with rice. Their flour is used to make the well-known street food, *panelle* (page 134), as well as in a traditional minestra from Palermo known as *cicirata,* which combines chickpea flour with broth, ground pork, spicy pepper, and parsley.

Black chickpeas are also grown in Sicily in small quantities, although they are more popular in Puglia.

FAVA BEANS *Fave* FAVI

In ancient Greece, fava beans were considered an aphrodisiac by some and food of the dead by others. Pythagoras forbade his disciples to come into contact with the beans. In Sicily even today, fava beans are typically prepared on November 2, the Day of the Dead, which is devoted to honoring loved ones who've passed away.

Like chickpeas, fava beans are consumed fresh or dried. But fresh fava beans, which grow in the spring, are more commonly prepared and have a longer season than other beans. (For a dish using fresh fava beans, see page 218.) They are stewed, pureed, and prepared with pasta and soups. Dried fava beans can be found with both their skin on and off, but the latter is more popular, used in soups and pasta preparations. Dried fava beans with their skin intact are hard and are dark brown in color, but when the outer skin is removed the inside beans are creamy white in color and soft in texture. It's common to stew fava beans with their skin intact, then eat them by hand, removing the skin with one's fingertips.

Badda beans

BROTH

{ Il Brodo }

Ù BRORU

A Sicilian folktale tells the story of a peasant from a mountain town who was carried by his relatives to Palermo after falling ill so that he could seek help from a doctor. Before the visit, they stopped at a shop selling broth. The patient felt immediately, even miraculously, better after drinking the broth, and walked back on his own feet to his village, without ever seeing the medic. In line with the tale, an old Sicilian proverb is, "A lu malatu brodu di picciuni, ca all'omu sanu cci abbasta lu pani." ("Feed pigeon broth to the sick, but to the healthy man, bread is enough.") Even today, broths are still commonly fed to the sick in Sicily.

In addition to their healing uses, broths are the base of many soups. Rice is commonly boiled first then served in chicken broth, while meatballs and small dumplings that include rice or bread are cooked in the broth.

I prefer to use homemade broth, rather than dried or packaged bouillon in my soups, braises, and other recipes calling for broth, and have shared four basic recipes below. You can prepare the broths in advance and keep them in the refrigerator for up to a week, or for months in the freezer. A few days before preparing them, set aside any vegetable pieces or stems in your kitchen, as they can be thrown into the broth. In a container, collect vegetables such as carrot tops, leek greens, scallion tops, cabbage, turnip, and fennel pieces. The stems of herbs like oregano, parsley, sage, or thyme also make complementary flavor additions.

When the broths are ready, strain out the solid ingredients. Most vegetable pieces should be discarded, but those that stay intact, as well as the meat or chicken pieces, can be eaten and enjoyed.

All four recipes make about 2 quarts broth each

Meat Broth

2 1/2 pounds lean beef or veal, cut into 3-inch chunks	2 celery stalks, cut into chunks
1 beef bone with marrow	1 bunch fresh parsley
2 to 3 garlic cloves, crushed	2 bay leaves
1 to 2 ripe tomatoes, crushed	1 whole clove
3 to 4 carrots, cut into chunks	1 teaspoon whole black peppercorns
2 large onions, cut into quarters	1 tablespoon salt
	1 sprig fresh basil

1 Place all the ingredients except the salt and basil in a stockpot with 1 gallon plus 1 quart cold water and bring to a boil over high heat, skimming off the foam that rises to the top of the pot. Lower the heat to medium and simmer for 3 to 4 hours. About halfway through the cooking period, add the salt. The broth is done when the meat is very soft and can be cut in half with a fork.

2 Let the broth cool in the pot, adding the basil sprig for flavor. Filter the cooled broth through a fine-mesh strainer. Remove the pieces of meat and carrots gently with kitchen tongs and reserve to enjoy separately; all the other solid ingredients can be discarded.

Chicken Broth

1 whole 3-pound chicken, quartered

2 ripe tomatoes, cut in half

3 to 4 carrots, cut into chunks

2 large onions, cut into quarters

2 celery stalks, cut into chunks

1 tablespoon whole black peppercorns

1 bunch fresh parsley

2 bay leaves

1 whole clove

1 tablespoon sea salt

1 Place all the ingredients in a stockpot with 1 gallon cold water and bring to a boil over high heat, skimming off the foam that rises to the top. Lower the heat to medium and simmer for 2 to 2¹/₂ hours.

2 Let the broth cool in the pot, then filter it through a fine-mesh strainer. Remove the chicken and carrot pieces and reserve to enjoy separately. Alternatively, the meat can be pulled off the chicken bones and used in salads, pasta, or rice timbales.

Vegetable Broth

To prepare a vegetable broth, replace the chicken in the recipe above with at least 3 more pounds of vegetables. The vegetables should be mainly those already called for in the chicken broth recipe, but feel free to add other vegetable pieces that you have on hand. In my refrigerator, I always keep a bag full of vegetable scraps that can be anything from a piece of a pepper to fennel greens to zucchini pulp. The cooking time is about the same as for the chicken broth; the vegetables need time to infuse their flavor into the water.

Fish Broth

2 pounds bones and heads of fish, fillets removed (non-oily fish with white flesh such as John Dory, grouper, or monkfish is best)

2 carrots, cut into chunks

2 large onions, cut into quarters

4 celery stalks, cut into chunks

2 bay leaves

1 bunch fresh parsley

1 tablespoon whole black peppercorns

1 teaspoon salt

Place all the ingredients in a stockpot with 1 gallon cold water and bring to a boil over high heat, skimming off the foam that rises to the top of the pot. Lower the heat to medium and cook 20 to 30 minutes. To test if the broth is done, taste a spoonful. If the broth has a pleasant fish flavor, you can stop cooking. Strain the broth and discard the solids.

SEAFOOD SOUP

{ Minestra di Pesce }

MINESTRA RI PISCI

In Sicily, there are a few types of seafood typically added to this dish, especially scorpion fish, or scorfano in Italian; however, it is difficult to find in U.S. markets. When selecting shellfish for this soup, choose your favorite types that are available from your fishmonger. Clams and mussels work very well and can be used on their own. Make sure that all mussels and clams have closed shells, which indicates that they are still alive and fresh. If the shells are open, discard them, as they could contain harmful bacteria. If using lobster, cut it in half lengthwise. If using lobster tail, cut the cartilage so that the meat is easy to remove from the shell when eating. Baby octopus cooks quickly and is tender.

Serves 6 to 8

4 baby octopus, thawed if frozen and rinsed under cold water (optional)

1 bay leaf (for cooking the octopus)

¹/₂ onion, finely chopped

3 tablespoons olive oil

2 garlic cloves, crushed with the palm of your hand

2 pounds assorted shellfish of your choice

1 cup white wine

1 cup ripe cherry tomatoes, stems removed, cut in half

3 cups Tomato Pulp (homemade, page 70, or store-bought)

3 cups Fish Broth (page 147)

Salt

Cracked black pepper

12 ounces dried spaghetti, broken into 1-inch pieces, or small soup pasta, such as ditalini

Finely chopped fresh parsley

1 Cook the baby octopus, if using: Bring water to a boil in a large pot and add the bay leaf. Add the octopus, reduce the heat, and simmer for about 1 hour, until the tentacles can be easily pierced with a fork.

2 Meanwhile, in a 5- to 6-quart heavy pot over low heat, gently sauté the onion in the olive oil until translucent. Add the garlic and cook for another minute. Add the shellfish and wine. Stir with a wooden spoon, then cover the pot to let the shellfish steam slightly.

3 Squeeze the cherry tomatoes with your hand and add them to the pot along with the tomato pulp, broth, and cooked baby octopus. Add salt and black pepper to taste. Cook over low heat, stirring often, for about 10 minutes, until the shellfish is cooked. Clams, razor clams, and mussels are cooked when their shells open. Lobster, scallops, and spiny lobster are done when the meat feels firm not mushy when touched with your pointer finger.

4 Meanwhile, cook the pasta according to the package instructions in a separate pot of boiling salted water until very al dente.

5 Add the pasta and chopped parsley to the soup and let cook for another minute, until the pasta begins to soak up some of the broth. Stir well. Remove the garlic cloves from the soup and serve.

SAINT JOSEPH'S SOUP

MINESTRA RI SAN GIUSEPPI

Classically prepared on March 19 for Saint Joseph's Day, this soup is linked to San Giuseppe, the saint who embodies humility and poverty. It was traditionally offered to those in need.

Since the holiday falls during Lent, the soup is cooked without meat. The amount of broth in the soup can be regulated, depending on whether you prefer a thick or a thin soup. For the pasta, I use a small, round cut that's shaped like peppercorns and appropriately called acini di pepe. *Traditionally, ditalini are preferred.*

Serves 8 to 10

1 cup dried chestnuts

1 cup dried chickpeas

1 cup dried cranberry beans

1 cup shelled dried fava beans

1 cup dried brown lentils

4 cups broccoli florets

2 to 3 cups Vegetable Broth (page 147), heated

2 cups very finely chopped leafy greens, preferably Swiss chard, borage, or beet greens

1 tablespoon dried fennel seeds (traditionally the soup is prepared with fresh wild fennel, in season in Sicily when this holiday takes place)

2 to 5 spicy red chile peppers, fresh or preserved in oil, chopped (optional)

Salt

Cracked black pepper

$^1/_2$ pound small pasta, such as *acini di pepe* or ditalini, for the broth

Extra-virgin olive oil, for drizzling

1 Soak the chestnuts and all the beans (except the lentils) overnight in a separate bowls of water.

2 The next day, drain the chestnuts and the beans. (Since each type of bean requires a different cooking time, keep them separate.) Bring a large pot of water to a boil. Reduce the heat to low and add the chestnuts and chickpeas; simmer for 45 minutes. Add the cranberry beans and cook for 45 minutes more. Add the fava beans and cook for 15 minutes. Add the lentils and cook for another 30 minutes. Do not add any salt while the chestnuts and beans are cooking.

3 Meanwhile, blanch the broccoli in salted boiling water for 3 minutes. Drain and and add it to the pot of beans after they are done cooking.

4 Add about 2 cups of the vegetable broth to the soup pot, along with the greens, fennel seeds, and chile peppers, if using. Keep in mind that the chicken broth already contains salt, so taste the soup before salting and add more according to taste. Also add the black pepper to taste. Cook for another 10 minutes.

5 Add the pasta and cook for about 8 minutes, until the pasta is al dente. If the soup looks too thick, add more broth.

6 Ladle into individual bowls and drizzle with a fine extra-virgin olive oil.

**CLOCKWISE FROM BOTTOM
LEFT:** *Seafood Soup (page 148);
Saint Joseph's Soup (page 149);
Sicilian Squash Soup (page 153);
Creamy Chickpea Soup (page 159);
Grass Pea Soup with Pork Sausage
(page 155)*

AN ABUNDANT AND VERSATILE SQUASH

Cucuzza is a type of calabash popular in Sicily. The fruit, which grows out of delicate white flowers on a vine, has pale green, smooth skin. Its flesh is white, soft, and, during the summer months, lined with edible tender seeds. Later in the season, when mature, a *cucuzza* can grow to more than three feet long and its seeds can become hard. While most resemble cucumbers in shape, some *cucuzza* grow to look like thick, curving serpents. The shape ultimately depends on how the squash are grown. When the plants are left on the ground, the squash tend to curl and grow thick. To grow long and skinny, the squash plants are trained to vine on nets or wood reeds, which allow the fruit to hang straight down to the ground.

High in vitamin C, this nutritious gourd has a mild flavor and retains a firm texture when cooked, even when peeled. Like zucchini, *cucuzza* can be sautéed, fried, baked, stuffed, and added to soups. In certain parts of Sicily, *cucuzza* is also candied and used in some of the island's most opulent desserts. The nuns of Monastero Santo Spirito—a cloistered convent in Agrigento—use finely chopped candied *cucuzza*, known as *zuccata* (page 313), to stuff shell-shaped almond marzipan cookies. Other Sicilian pastry chefs use thick chunks of *zuccata* to decorate cassata, the famous ornate cake made with layers of sponge cake and sweet ricotta cream (see page 311).

In early summer, when the plants first start to grow, the leaves of the *cucuzza* vine, called *tenerumi,* are tender (as their Sicilian name suggests) and are also used in Sicilian cooking. When cooked, *tenerumi* have a delicate taste with a light citrusy flavor.

For years, I searched endlessly for *cucuzza* and *tenerumi* in New York. A few years leading up to my move to Sicily, they became more readily available in the United States. I was finally able to feature them in dishes at my restaurants, thanks to Guy Jones of Blooming Hill Farm, who grows these Sicilian squash in abundance during summer months. Occasionally, I've found them in grocery stores and at New York City's Union Square Greenmarket. The squash and their seeds are also available for purchase online (see Sources, page 326).

In Sicily, I now grow an abundance of Sicilian squash. At the end of the summer, I hang a few gourds from fruit trees and allow the seeds to dry out. After about one month, I remove the seeds, lay them out on a wire mesh rack, and dry them in the sun for a few days to remove any additional moisture. In the spring, I then plant the seeds, which sprout readily.

SICILIAN SQUASH SOUP

{ Pasta con i Tenerumi }

PASTA CU I TINNIRUMI

In the summertime, when cucuzza *is in season, this recipe is one of my favorites. While the Sicilian squash can be substituted with gray zucchini, available in supermarkets and farmers' markets, the leaves, or* tenerumi, *do not have a direct substitute. Therefore, I recommend preparing this dish only when you can procure the Sicilian squash and its tender vines.*

Serves 4 to 6

Sea salt

2 cups squash leaves (*tenerumi*) from a Sicilian squash vine, finely chopped

2 tablespoons olive oil

2 garlic cloves, smashed

3 cups Tomato Pulp (homemade, page 70, or store-bought)

4 Yukon gold potatoes, peeled and cut into ¹/₂-inch chunks

1 pound Sicilian *cucuzza* squash, peeled, seeds removed, and cut into ¹/₂-inch-thick chunks

¹/₂ pound soup pasta (I prefer ditalini)

Extra-virgin olive oil, for drizzling

1 Bring a 5- to 6-quart pot of salted water to a boil. Add the squash leaves and let them cook for about 10 minutes. Remove them from the boiling water and hold until ready to add to the sauce. Do not discard the cooking water.

2 Meanwhile, in a large sauté pan, heat the olive oil over medium heat. Add the garlic and gently sauté it. Before the garlic turns brown, add the tomato pulp, a touch of salt (a light touch as more will be added later), 3 quarts cold water, and the potatoes. Raise the heat and bring to a boil. As soon as the liquid starts to boil, lower the heat slightly and add the squash. Cook for about 15 minutes, until the squash is tender and soft to the touch.

3 Bring the cooking water from the greens to a boil, add the pasta to the pot of boiling water, and cook until the pasta is al dente, about 8 minutes. Drain and add the pasta and the cooked squash leaves to the sauté pan and stir well. Add about two large ladlesful of the salted pasta water. Taste for salt and add more to taste.

4 Remove from the stovetop and serve immediately, with a drizzle of fine extra-virgin olive oil.

USTICAN WINTER LENTIL SOUP

{ *Zuppa Invernale di Lenticchie di Ustica* }

ZUPPA 'NVIRNALI RI LINTICCHI

On the island of Ustica, lentils are harvested in June, but are cooked all year round with different vegetables, depending on the season. However, herbs and vegetables are used in moderation so as to not mask the delicate flavor of the lentils. Traditionally, the soup always contains onion, garlic, tomato, and either summer or winter squash. In the warmer months, cucuzza *and* tenerumi *are the squash of choice with basil added.*

This cold-weather version uses winter squash or pumpkin along with beet greens or Swiss chard. Cauliflower or broccoli are also common winter additions. Potatoes are also commonly found in this soup, but are omitted in some households on Ustica. Islanders add either wild fennel or rosemary in the winter to aromatize the soup.

If you like, serve the lentil soup with toasted bread rubbed with a clove of garlic.

Serves 6

3 tablespoons olive oil

$1/2$ **pound peeled, seeded cheese pumpkin or butternut squash, cut into $1/2$-inch cubes**

$1/2$ **head cauliflower, cut into small florets**

2 cups Soffritto (page 40)

1 garlic clove, smashed

$1/2$ **pound brown lentils**

2 Yukon gold potatoes, peeled and cut into $1/2$-inch cubes

2 sprigs fresh rosemary

4 cups Meat Broth (page 146), heated

Salt

2 cups Swiss chard or beet greens, finely chopped

Extra-virgin olive oil, for drizzling

1 Heat half of the olive oil in a sauté pan over medium heat. Add the pumpkin and cook, turning the pieces occasionally, until soft and lightly browned, about 5 minutes. Transfer to a plate and set aside. Heat the remaining olive oil in the pan and add the cauliflower. Cook, turning occasionally, until lightly brown but still crunchy. Transfer to another plate and set aside.

2 Meanwhile, prepare (or reheat) the soffritto in a 5- to 6-quart pot over low to medium heat. Add the smashed garlic and sauté for a few minutes, until the ingredients are soft but not brown. Add 4 cups cold water, the lentils, potatoes, and rosemary. Simmer over medium heat until the lentils are soft but not fully cooked, about 30 minutes, depending on the size of lentils you are using.

3 Add the seared cauliflower florets, the broth, and salt to taste. Simmer for another 10 minutes, then add the pumpkin and Swiss chard. Cook the soup for another 10 minutes, until it starts to thicken. Serve immediately with a drizzle of fine extra-virgin olive oil.

GRASS PEA SOUP *with* PORK SAUSAGE

{ *Zuppa di Cicerchia e Salsiccia* }

ZUPPA RI CICIRUÒCCOLO E SASIZZA

Grass peas are a very old crop, historically cultivated in the interior parts of Sicily. Today, production of these peas on the island is modest; in fact, very few Sicilians have cooked with these beans. Nonetheless, they can be found in specialty stores in the United States (see Sources, page 326).

Also known by their Italian name, cicerchia, *grass peas resemble a cross between peas and chickpeas, but are slightly more bitter. You can swap in dried chickpeas in this recipe if you cannot get ahold of grass peas. A flour is also made from these beans, which in certain areas of Sicily is prepared as a polenta, known as* la patacò.

Serves 4 as a main course

2 cups dried grass peas or chickpeas

1 teaspoon baking soda

1 pound pork sausages (see page 265)

1 cup Soffritto (page 40)

1 cup fresh wild fennel (see page 29 for substitution ideas), finely chopped, or 1 tablespoon dried wild fennel or fennel seeds

About 1 cup white wine

2 cups Tomato Pulp (homemade, page 70, or store-bought)

2 cups Meat or Chicken Broth (page 146 or 147)

3 bay leaves

2 to 5 spicy red chile peppers, fresh, dried, or preserved in olive oil, chopped (optional)

Salt

Extra-virgin olive oil, for drizzling

1 Soak the grass peas overnight in about 5 cups water mixed with the baking soda.

2 The next day, drain the beans and place them in a small pot with 2 quarts unsalted water. Bring to a boil and then reduce the heat to a simmer. Cook the beans for about 1 hour, until they are easily crushed with a fork. Drain, saving the cooking liquid.

3 Meanwhile, sear the sausage in a nonstick pan for 5 to 7 minutes, until browned on all sides. Let cool, then slice into $1/2$-inch-thick slices.

4 In a 5- to 6-quart pot, heat the soffritto with the fennel. Add the sausage pieces and deglaze with the white wine, scraping the bottom of the pot with a spoon.

5 After the wine evaporates, add 2 cups of the cooking liquid from the beans, the tomato pulp, broth, bay leaves, and chile peppers, if using. Let cook for about 10 minutes, then add the grass peas. Cook for another 10 minutes, until the broth becomes thick and dense. Taste for salt and add accordingly.

6 Serve immediately, drizzling each portion with some extra-virgin olive oil.

PESTO BROTH *with* BREAD DUMPLINGS

{ Brodo di Nepitella con Palline di Pane }

NEPPITEDDATA

This old recipe comes from the Caruso family on the island of Salina. It's a soup prepared in the spring when the herb nepitella *(also called* calamint*) is in season. The main element of the soup is the bread dumplings, which are cooked in a broth mixed with the* nepitella *pesto. I enjoyed this soup because of its simplicity, but also because of the soft texture and delicate flavor of the dumplings that allow the herbed broth to shine. In the absence of* nepitella*, I've found that a mixture of basil and mint makes a fine substitute.*

Serves 4 to 6

Dumplings

2 cups fine breadcrumbs (page 42)

1 tablespoon extra-virgin olive oil

1 tablespoon finely chopped fresh parsley

1 large egg, beaten

1 cup grated Parmesan cheese

1 teaspoon salt

1 teaspoon black pepper

Pesto and Broth

2 cups fresh *nepitella* leaves (or a mixture of basil and mint)

1 garlic clove

2 tablespoons extra-virgin olive oil

2 quarts Chicken or Vegetable Broth (page 147)

1 FOR THE DUMPLINGS: In a bowl, mix together the breadcrumbs, olive oil, parsley, egg, cheese, salt, and pepper. With your hands, roll the mixture into about 30 (³/₄-inch) ball-shaped dumplings. Refrigerate while preparing the broth.

2 FOR THE PESTO AND BROTH: In a mortar using a pestle or in a food processor, grind or process the *nepitella*, garlic, and olive oil into a paste.

3 Combine the *nepitella* pesto in a pot with the broth and bring to a boil over high heat. Add the dumplings and reduce the heat. Simmer for 10 to 15 minutes, until the dumplings are sponge-like in texture. Serve immediately in the broth.

CREAMY FAVA BEAN SOUP

{ Macco di Fave }

MACCU RI FAVI

Macco is a typical Sicilian soup of pureed fava beans with either wild fennel or bitter greens such as escarole or beet greens. The name comes from the Latin verb maccare, *which means to reduce to a paste.*

The soup hails from the province of Ragusa, but it is now popular in all parts of the island. In some areas, macco *is typically served on Saint Joseph's Day. In the Madonie Mountains, many families prepare the soup with tomatoes, while in Palermo it can be found with squash added to it. In several upscale restaurants around the island, the dish is served with seafood, most commonly shrimp and octopus, which both pair well with the earthiness of the dried fava beans. I have also sampled a version of* macco *blended with some fresh sheep's milk ricotta, which added a pleasant creaminess.*

Serves 4 to 6

1 pound dried fava beans, shelled

1 large onion, cut into small chunks

2 celery stalks, cut into small chunks

1/2 pound escarole or fresh wild fennel, roughly chopped

Salt

1/4 cup extra-virgin olive oil

Garnishes

2 ounces pancetta, cut into very small pieces

1/2 pound leftover bread, crust removed, sliced, and left to dry out overnight

1 garlic clove

Pinch of fine sea salt

1 tablespoon olive oil

Extra-virgin olive oil, for drizzling

1 Soak the shelled fava beans in water overnight.

2 Drain the beans and place them in a 5- to 6-quart stockpot. Add the onion and celery. Cover with water to come 2 inches above the beans and vegetables. Bring to a boil over high heat, then lower to a simmer. Cook for about 45 minutes, until the fava beans are easily mashed with the back of a fork. Add the escarole. Cook for another 15 minutes, until the escarole is cooked through. Remove from the heat and add about 1 tablespoon salt. Let cool to room temperature.

3 In a blender, working in batches, puree the soup with the extra-virgin olive oil on high speed until smooth. Pour the soup into a clean pot and taste, seasoning with more salt if needed.

4 PREPARE THE GARNISHES: For the pancetta and croutons, preheat the oven to 350°F. Place the pancetta on a baking sheet and bake for about 10 minutes, until the pancetta is crispy. For the croutons, rub the clove of garlic on the surface of the bread and cut it into 1/2-inch cubes. Toss the bread cubes with the salt and olive oil and place on a small baking sheet in a single layer. Bake alongside the pancetta for about 5 minutes, until golden brown. Remove the pancetta and bread cubes from the oven and let cool to room temperature.

5 While the croutons and pancetta are cooking, bring the pureed soup to a boil over a low heat. Make sure to continuously stir the soup so that it doesn't stick to the bottom of the soup pot. If necessary, add a touch of water to the pot to thin it out.

6 To plate, top each bowl of *macco* with some croutons and crispy pancetta pieces. Drizzle with fine extra-virgin olive oil and serve immediately.

CREAMY CHICKPEA SOUP

{ Zuppa di Ceci }

ZUPPA RI CICIRI

During the long harvest period at Feudo Montoni, which lasts from late summer well into the fall, the temperature and weather tend to change drastically. One of my favorite recipes to prepare when the season changes is this dish, which warms the body and is easy to prepare during the busy season, when work in the fields and in the cellar continues into the nighttime. This soup can sit unattended on the stovetop while the beans are cooking, as the chickpeas soften during the cooking process and don't need to be stirred.

The most important factor in this recipe is to source high-quality chickpeas, which tend to be full in flavor, as opposed to supermarket brands. See Sources, page 326, for where to purchase Italian chickpeas from either Sicily or Umbria. I harvest a local variety of chickpea at Montoni every spring, which works perfectly in this recipe. For a vegetarian version, simply omit the pancetta.

Serves 4 to 6

1 pound dried chickpeas

1 teaspoon baking soda

About 4 ounces Yukon gold potatoes, peeled and cut into 3/4-inch cubes

1 garlic clove, smashed

1 sprig fresh rosemary

2 tablespoons olive oil

2 ounces pancetta, finely chopped

1 onion, finely chopped

Sea salt

Extra-virgin olive oil, for drizzling

Cracked black pepper

1 Put the chickpeas, baking soda, and 6 cups water in a large pot. Soak the chickpeas overnight.

2 The next day, add the potatoes, garlic, and rosemary to the pot and bring to a simmer over medium heat. Cook until the chickpeas are soft to the touch but not fully cooked, about 1 hour, depending on the variety of chickpeas you're using. Remove three-quarters of the contents from the pot and puree it in a blender or food processor. Return the pureed ingredients to the pot with the soup.

3 Meanwhile, in a sauté pan heat the olive oil over medium heat. Add the pancetta and onion and cook until the onion starts to turn golden brown and the pancetta softens, releasing its fat into the pan, about 10 minutes.

4 Add the pancetta and onion mixture to the soup pot and stir well. Let the ingredients simmer over medium heat until the chickpeas are completely soft to the touch and break easily between your thumb and pointer finger, about 30 minutes. Taste for salt and add more accordingly. Serve with a drizzle of olive oil and some cracked black pepper.

A SOUTHERN WAY WITH RICE

Rice is a main ingredient in many traditional Sicilian dishes, such as in the fried and stuffed rice balls called *arancine* (page 165), a festive baked rice casserole known as *timballo*, and the sweet rice fritters from Catania known as *crispeddi* (see page 300), which are prepared during Carnival. In home-style recipes, boiled rice is used in simple broths, which are sprinkled with grated cheese, or in minestre, in lieu of pasta or grains. A cold rice salad that incorporates boiled rice with pickled vegetables and tuna, cheese, and hot dog pieces is prepared all over Italy in the summer months. In Sicily, we often pack this salad in our picnic basket when heading to the beach.

In restaurants around Sicily, rice is prepared as a risotto, employing the cooking technique imported from Northern Italy. The flavors and basic ingredients used, however, are typically Sicilian, making Sicilian risottos hybrids that merge Sicilian and mainland cuisines. For example, in Northern Italy, butter is used to amalgamate the rice, a process known in Italian as *mantecare*. In Sicily, some chefs pride themselves on adding creaminess to their risotto dishes with extra-virgin olive oil instead of butter.

First introduced to Sicily during Muslim rule, rice was cultivated on the island for centuries, but when Italy was unified, new laws were passed to limit the spread of malaria. The watery lands needed for rice growing were no longer allowed to be located near populated areas. By the Fascist period, the rice industry in Sicily had completely disappeared.

Over the past few years, the Manna family of Leonforte—located in central inland Sicily—successfully reinitiated rice cultivation. Angelo Manna and his father, Giuseppe, researched historical documents belonging to noble families to understand the techniques used in rice cultivation on the Sicilian terrain. The rice is not grown in wet swamps, but in moist soil with a water-drip system, which is the same technique used for growing vegetables. Although production is limited, chefs around the island are eager to purchase the rice so that they can source all their ingredients from local purveyors. Nonetheless, the majority of rice used in Sicily is imported from Northern Italy.

The main types of rice used in Sicilian cooking are the short- and medium-grain varieties that are used in the making of risotto, due to their high starch content and their ability to soak up liquid. Arborio (the variety grown by the Manna family) is the most commonly found rice, and the least expensive. It is short-grained, rounded, and can absorb liquid as much as five times its weight. Carnaroli is the highest quality and is medium in grain. It is extremely absorbent and contains a complex starch structure, thus it is considered the best rice for risotto. Vialone nano has a longer grain than arborio, but is shorter and fatter than carnaroli. Also extremely absorbent, vialone nano retains its shape during the cooking process and is therefore great for timbales and rice balls.

RICE DUMPLINGS *in* BROTH

{ *Palline di Riso in Brodo* }

BADDUZZI RI RISU 'NTO BRORU

The round dumpling shape of a meatball is a recurring theme in Sicilian cuisine. In this recipe, similar to the Pesto Broth with Bread Dumplings (page 156), little balls are formed from rice, egg, and breadcrumbs, then served in a chicken broth. This recipe is prepared during the Christmas season by Sígnora Anna Maria of Sciacca. Her son Giacomo says, "After eating this, it's fundamental to just sit in silence for a few moments to contemplate the goodness of the dish."

In Sicily, these rice balls are fried in olive oil instead of vegetable oil. If you choose olive oil, which creates a more authentic Sicilian flavor, make sure not to let the oil rise above 400°F, which is the smoke point for a good-quality olive oil.

Serves 4 to 6

Rice Dumplings

2 tablespoons olive oil

1 onion, very finely chopped

$^1/_2$ pound arborio rice

1 cup white wine

4 cups lightly salted Vegetable Broth (page 147), heated

1 cup grated Parmesan cheese

1 egg yolk

Salt

2 egg whites, beaten

$1^1/_2$ cups fine breadcrumbs (page 42)

Vegetable oil, for frying

2 quarts Chicken Broth (page 147)

$^1/_2$ cup grated Parmesan cheese

1 FOR THE RICE DUMPLINGS: To make the risotto, in a large pot, heat the olive oil over low to medium heat and add the onion. Gently sauté until the onion is translucent, but not brown, about 4 minutes. Add the rice and cook, stirring rapidly with a wooden spoon and being careful not to brown the rice, for 2 minutes. Add the wine, being careful not to let any wine splatter on the stove. When the wine evaporates, add a ladleful of the hot vegetable broth and reduce to a simmer. Cook, stirring with a wooden spoon until you notice the rice has absorbed the broth, then add additional broth. Do not allow any grains of rice to remain on the side of the pot. Continue adding broth and stirring constantly for about 25 minutes. Taste the rice and see if it is cooked. It should be soft in texture but slightly crunchy in the center. By continuously stirring the rice with the broth, the starches exude from the kernels and make the risotto creamy in texture. Let the risotto cool.

2 Add the Parmesan, egg yolk, and salt to taste to the cooled risotto and mix to incorporate all the ingredients. Using your hands, roll the rice into very small balls, no more than $^3/_4$ inch in diameter. Dip the rice balls into the beaten egg whites, then roll in the breadcrumbs.

3 To fry the dumplings, fill a large thick-bottomed pot three-fourths full with vegetable oil and place it over high heat. A candy thermometer can be attached to the side of the pot to help ensure that the oil does not exceed 360°F and does not fall below 350°F. Fry the dumplings in batches, making sure that the rice balls do not overlap. When golden brown on the outside, 4 to 6 minutes, remove them from the oil and drain on paper towels.

4 In a stockpot, bring the chicken broth to a boil over high heat. Divide the fried rice dumplings equally among serving bowls. Pour the hot broth around the rice balls and sprinkle with the Parmesan.

SEAFOOD RISOTTO *with* MINT PESTO

{ *Risotto ai Frutti di Mare* }

RISOTTU CU I FRUTTI RI MARI

This dish is a popular offering at a trattoria on the island of Lipari. Seafood risotto can be found in countless restaurants around Sicily, but the less traditional addition of a mint pesto adds a pleasant freshness to the dish.

Serves 6 as a main course or 8 as a first course

Mint Pesto

1 cup loosely packed fresh mint leaves

¹/₂ cup loosely packed fresh parsley leaves

1 garlic clove

1 teaspoon grated lemon zest

¹/₂ cup extra-virgin olive oil

Seafood Risotto

1 pound mussels and clams, cleaned

2 quarts Fish Broth (page 147)

1 tablespoon olive oil

2 cups carnaroli or vialone nano rice

3 cups dry white wine

¹/₂ pound fresh small shrimp, shells removed and deveined

¹/₂ pound fresh whole calamari, cleaned and cut as per the directions on page 129

Salt

1 FOR THE MINT PESTO: In a food processor, combine the mint, parsley, garlic, lemon zest, and olive oil. Blend all the ingredients together until they form a smooth paste. The pesto will hold for up to 1 day in the refrigerator.

2 FOR THE SEAFOOD RISOTTO: Add the mussels and clams to a large pot of water. Cover the pot and cook over medium heat until the shells open up, 5 to 8 minutes; discard any that do not open. Let the shellfish and cooking water cool down before discarding the shells. Strain the cooking liquid and reserve it. The cooked mussels and clams will keep for up to 1 day in the refrigerator.

3 Combine the fish broth and strained cooking liquid in a large saucepan and bring to a boil over high heat.

4 In another large pot, heat the olive oil over low heat. Add the rice and stir rapidly with a wooden spoon for 2 to 3 minutes, being careful not to brown the rice. Add the wine, being careful not to let any wine splatter on the stove. When the wine evaporates, add a ladleful of hot broth and reduce the heat to a simmer. Cook, stirring with a wooden spoon, until you notice the rice has absorbed the broth, then add additional broth. Do not allow any grains of rice to remain on the side of the pot. Continue adding broth and stirring constantly for about 25 minutes. Taste the rice and see if it is cooked. It should be soft in texture but slightly crunchy in the center. By continuously stirring the rice with the broth, the starches exude from the kernels and make the risotto creamy.

5 Stir in the shrimp and calamari. Continue to cook just until the shrimp turn pink. Remove from the heat and stir in the mussels and clams.

6 Just before serving, add half of the mint pesto to the pot of risotto and stir well. Do not add the mint pesto earlier, as it will turn brown in color. Taste and decide if you'd like to add more of the pesto. It's a matter of your own taste. (If some pesto remains, you can serve it at the table for those who want to add more, or you can hold it in the refrigerator for up to 2 days.) Add salt to taste. Serve the risotto immediately.

SPINACH RICE BALLS STUFFED *with* PROVOLA

{ *Arancine con gli Spinaci* }

ARANCINE CU I SPINACI

The pleasant flavor of spinach balances well with the lightly sweet provola *cheese in this variation of the rice balls on page 165. I've also prepared these rice balls with nettles or Swiss chard instead of spinach. Making a puree out of green leafy vegetables is a good way to use them if they are starting to wilt. Look for Sicilian* provola *cheese for this recipe; it's soft, delicate, and lightly sweet. If you can't find* provola, *substitute any other mild white cheese.*

Makes 10 to 12 rice balls

Salt

1 pound spinach

3 tablespoons extra-virgin olive oil

$^1/_2$ onion, finely chopped

2 cups carnaroli or vialone nano rice

1 cup white wine

6 cups Vegetable Broth (page 147), heated

2 tablespoons extra-virgin olive oil

4 ounces *provola* cheese, cut into $^3/_4$-inch cubes

2 tablespoons all-purpose flour

$^1/_4$ cup milk

1 large egg, beaten well

1$^1/_2$ cups fine breadcrumbs (page 42)

Vegetable oil, for frying

1 Bring a pot of salted water to a boil. Add the spinach and cook for 2 minutes. Remove the greens and place them in an ice bath to stop the cooking process. Remove as much water as possible by placing the spinach in a cheesecloth and squeezing out the water. Transfer the spinach to a food processor and blend on high speed into a smooth paste. Hold the puree at room temperature until the risotto is ready.

2 To prepare the risotto, in a large pot, heat the olive oil over low to medium heat and add the onion. Gently sauté until the onion is translucent, but not brown, about 5 minutes. Add the rice and cook for 2 minutes, stirring rapidly with a wooden spoon and being careful not to brown the rice. Add the wine, being careful not to let any wine splatter on the stove. When the wine evaporates, add a ladleful of hot broth and reduce to a simmer. Cook, stirring with a wooden spoon until you notice the rice has absorbed the broth, then add additional broth. Do not allow any grains of rice to remain on the side of the pot. Continue adding broth and stirring constantly for about 25 minutes. Taste the rice and see if it is cooked. It should be soft in texture but slightly crunchy in the center. By continuously stirring the rice with the broth, the starches exude from the kernels and make the risotto creamy. After the rice is cooked, add salt to taste and then add the spinach puree and stir well with a wooden spoon for a few minutes to fully incorporate the ingredients. To add an additional creaminess to the risotto, add the extra-virgin olive oil. Stir well until fully absorbed.

3 To proceed with forming, stuffing, coating and frying the *arancine*, follow the directions for Rice Balls Stuffed with Beef-Pea Ragù on page 165, beginning with step 3, but using a small piece of the *provola* cheese instead of the ragù to stuff each ball.

IN THE ORBIT OF ARANCINE

Rice balls (known as *arancine* or *arancini*) are a typical street food in Sicily, sold year round in *rosticcerie* and bars all around the island. Most commonly, *arancine* are round and ball shaped. However, they are also commonly found shaped as a cone, easy to eat while walking around, like an ice cream cone. Traditional rice balls are prepared with saffron-infused rice stuffed with a beef-pea ragù (page 167).

In Messina, tomato sauce is added to the rice, but this touch is not common in other parts of the island. *Arancine di burro* are made from rice mixed with butter and then stuffed with prosciutto cotto (Italian ham) and cheese. In Palermo, on December 13, for the Feast of Saint Lucia, when milled grain is not consumed, rice balls are traditionally eaten, along with a wheat berry pudding known as *cuccia* (see page 314).

Some food historians believe that the rice ball took shape during Muslim rule, when rice flavored with saffron was eaten by hand, along with pieces of lamb. Legend claims that rice balls were invented by a Muslim-Sicilian emir who reconfigured the rice timballo into a smaller form. Other historians argue that the breadcrumb crust became a popular way to prepare food for long voyages during the reign of Frederick II in the thirteenth century. Rice balls are first described in Sicilian books in the eighteenth century, which leaves its exact origins to speculation.

In restaurants, rice balls are often served as appetizers, but they can also replace a pasta course since they are basically individual rice timbales. Alternatively, they can be prepared in mini sizes and passed out as perfect little hors d'oeuvres. It's only to be expected that creative chefs have added their own twist to the flavors used in rice balls, swaying from the traditional and using the rice ball form to invent new appetizers.

In Ortigia, Chef Giovanni Guarnieri prepares saffron rice balls stuffed with pulled veal. Several restaurants flavor the rice with black squid ink and stuff the rice balls with a seafood ragù. Sweet versions for dessert with chocolate and pistachio are also common. In Terrasini, at the restaurant Il Bavaglino, chef Giuseppe Costa prepares a couscous ball, stuffed with a seafood ragù. From the outside, it appears like a rice ball, but when open the couscous shell is revealed.

RICE BALLS STUFFED *with* BEEF-PEA RAGÙ

{ *Arancine alla Carne* }

ARANCINE CU A CARNI

Some Sicilian cooks believe that the best rice balls are prepared with all three varieties of rice. In my attempts, this technique creates unevenly cooked arancine, *unless the three types are cooked separately. So I like to stick to just one variety. While most recipes call for boiling the rice, I learned to prepare rice balls by stirring the rice during the cooking process, as if preparing a risotto. Although more labor intensive, I find that the creaminess of the rice when cooked in this manner makes for a very moist and luscious rice ball.*

Makes 10 to 12 rice balls

Risotto Base

3 tablespoons olive oil

¹⁄₂ onion, finely chopped

2 cups carnaroli or vialone nano rice

1 cup white wine

6 cups Vegetable Broth (page 147), heated

¹⁄₂ teaspoon saffron threads

About 2 tablespoons extra-virgin olive oil (optional)

Salt

2 cups Beef-Pea Ragù (page 167)

2 tablespoons all-purpose flour

¹⁄₄ cup milk

1 large egg

1¹⁄₂ cups fine breadcrumbs (page 42)

Vegetable oil, for frying

1 To prepare the saffron risotto, in a large pot, heat the olive oil over low to medium heat and add the onion. Gently sauté until the onion is translucent, but not brown, about 5 minutes. Add the rice and cook for 2 minutes, stirring rapidly with a wooden spoon and being careful not to brown the rice. Add the wine, being careful not to let any wine splatter on the stove. When the wine evaporates, add a ladleful of hot broth and reduce the heat to a simmer. Cook, stirring with a wooden spoon until you notice the rice has absorbed the broth, then add additional broth. Do not allow

any grains of rice to remain on the side of the pot. Add the saffron. Continue adding broth and stirring constantly for about 25 minutes. Taste the rice and see if it is cooked. It should be soft in texture but slightly crunchy in the center. By continuously stirring the rice with the broth, the starches exude from the kernels and make the risotto creamy.

2 To add an additional creaminess to the risotto, add the extra-virgin olive oil. Stir well until fully absorbed. Test the risotto for salt (remember that the broth may contain salt) and add some more, if necessary, to taste.

3 Grease a baking sheet with olive oil. When the risotto is done, transfer it to the baking sheet by holding the pot in one hand and using a rubber spatula to drop and spread the cooked rice on the pan. Let cool. As soon as the rice reaches room temperature, place the baking sheet in the refrigerator so that the rice stiffens.

4 To shape the rice balls, wet your hands with water so that the rice does not stick to your fingers and scoop up a ball of rice. I like to use a 4-ounce spring-loaded scoop in order to measure the correct amount of rice for each ball. This way, the rice will not stick to the scoop and each rice ball will end up approximately the same size. With a teaspoon measure, scoop up some ragù. Place the rice in one hand and flatten it with the other. Put a spoonful of ragù in the middle of the rice and close the ball, making sure that the liquidy ragù stays inside. If necessary, moisten your fingertips between each rice ball. I like to keep a small bowl of warm water on the counter while rolling the rice balls. Repeat to make 10 to 12 stuffed rice balls.

continued ↓

5 To coat the balls with breadcrumbs, mix the flour, milk, and egg in a bowl to create a paste. Place the breadcrumbs in another bowl. Roll the balls in the flour-egg mixture so that they are fully coated. Immediately transfer to the bowl with the breadcrumbs and coat evenly. You can cover and refrigerate the rice balls at this stage for up to 1 day if you choose and fry them when you are ready to serve them.

6 To fry the rice balls, preheat the oven to 400°F. Add enough vegetable oil to a large thick-bottomed pot to fill it three-fourths full (or see Note below); the rice balls will need to be submerged in the oil to cook. A candy thermometer can be attached to the side of the pot to help ensure that the oil does not exceed 360°F and does not fall below 350°F. Fry the balls in batches until golden brown in color, about 5 minutes. Using tongs, remove each ball from the oil and place it on a baking sheet. Transfer to the oven and bake for an additional 3 minutes to ensure that the stuffing has heated through. Remove from the oven and serve.

Note: If you plan on preparing rice balls or other fried foods often, you might want to invest in an electric countertop fryer. The advantage of an electric fryer over a pot on the stovetop is that you can easily regulate the temperature.

BEEF-PEA RAGÙ

{ Ragù }

RAÙ

This ragù is the filling for traditional arancine, *or saffron rice balls (page 165), and is added to several other fried snacks such as* spitini *(see page 110), appetizers, and pastas. Ideal pasta shapes for this sauce are penne, rigatoni,* mezze maniche, *or any other short pasta cut. To dress one pound of pasta, you will need just half this recipe; you could easily freeze the remaining half for future use. Some cooks in Sicily use pork instead of beef, or a mixture of both.*

Makes 2 quarts

1/2 cup tomato paste

3 cups water, Chicken Broth, or Vegetable Broth (page 147)

About 2 cups Soffritto (page 40)

1/2 pound 85% lean ground beef

1 cup red wine

1 bay leaf

2 whole cloves

Salt

1 cup shelled fresh peas or frozen peas

1 In a bowl, dissolve the tomato paste in the water. Set aside.

2 Heat the soffritto in a large pot over medium heat. Add the beef to the pot. As the meat cooks, water is often exuded. Raise the heat to high and allow any moisture to evaporate and the meat to cook through. Add the red wine and use a wooden spoon to scrape the bottom of the pot to release any stuck meat.

3 When the wine has evaporated and been absorbed, add the tomato mixture to the pot, then add the bay leaf and cloves. Cook the ragù for over medium heat for about 20 minutes, stirring every few minutes to make sure the meat does not stick to the bottom of the pot. Season with salt.

4 Meanwhile, bring a small pot of water to a boil. Salt the water, add the peas, and cook for about 2 minutes. Drain the peas and stir them into the ragù. Remove the pot from the heat.

5 Let the ragù rest for at least 10 minutes and remove the cloves and bay leaf before using. Store in the refrigerator for up to 3 days or freeze for up to 3 months.

Chapter 6

PASTA

During my childhood summers in Sant'Anna, I was fascinated by how cousin Maria began the midday meal with a different pasta preparation every day. Using eggplants, squash, tomatoes, herbs, and more from her garden, Maria created a broad spectrum of pasta dishes. I was her rapturous student at the table, absorbing the tastes and aromas while learning about the versatility of the ingredients. Her spaghetti laced with pungent fresh tomatoes, olive oil, garlic, and basil, executed with perfection every time, unleashed an unforgettable perfume in the house. Her pasta with fried eggplants and tomato sauce was utterly satisfying when topped with a fresh grating of aged black-peppercorn-laced pecorino cheese. Each dish she prepared not only tasted different but exuded its own unique aromatic footprint.

Back in New York, I came into contact with many people who imagined Sicilian food to be nothing more than "red sauce"–based pasta dishes. From a young age I began a crusade to debunk such myths, armed with the firsthand knowledge from Maria's kitchen that such stereotypes are unfounded. Later on as an adult, during my extensive travels around the island, I began to confirm that Sicilian cuisine overflows with an incalculable number of pasta preparations. It would take volumes of books to list the plethora of pasta dishes prepared throughout the island. For every savory ingredient, there exists a classic Sicilian pasta dish: pasta with potatoes, pasta with artichokes, pasta with fava beans, pasta with cauliflower, and so on.

Sicilians have had centuries to experiment with pasta making. During the ancient Greek period, strips of unleavened bread, known as *laganon*, were baked and cut into tagliatelle-like strips. Romans adopted the dish, calling it *laganum*. Evidence of pasta making in Sicily hails from the island's Muslim rule, and most Sicilian food historians now believe Marco Polo's role in the trajectory of pasta making is mere legend.

The first-known ship inventory listing pasta (written by a Genovese merchant) dates almost twenty years prior to Polo's return to Italy. Historians presume that Muslim Sicilians learned the art of pasta making during their trade with the Chinese and Persians, and hence introduced it to Europe. In A.D. 1154, the court geographer under Roger II, Muhammad al-Idrisi, documented that vermicelli pasta was made in Sicily, noting that a pasta factory existed in Trabia, near Palermo, which produced thin, long noodles. The Arabic name for the noodles was *itryia*, and today *tria* is the word for "pasta" in Sicilian dialect.

I'd like to offer a few key tips for cooking pasta of any type: First, make sure that the cooking water is well salted. I suggest tasting the water before adding the pasta. If you can't taste the salt, then you need more. After partially cooking fresh or dried pasta, to the point of just before "al dente" (see page 172), let the pasta finish cooking in the sauce over a low heat. This technique allows the sauce to absorb into the pasta. Finally, you can prepare sauces in advance, but you should never precook pasta.

Dried Pasta

There are two main categories of pasta used throughout Italy: fresh and dried. The latter—prepared in Sicily with hard wheat semola flour and water—is at its best when produced in machines equipped with bronze extruders that shape the pasta. You will most likely see this noted on product labels as "trafilata al bronzo." The surface of the metal gives the pasta a somewhat rough exterior, which allows the pasta to adequately absorb the sauce it is served with. Fresh pasta can also be produced in machines with bronze extruders, but in Sicily it is more commonly prepared by hand (see page 192).

Dried pasta can be naturally dried on racks under the heat of the sun. However in order to be packaged for commercial use, the pasta must be dried in machines that adequately remove the moisture. I prefer to dry the pasta I produce—which I prepare with heritage Sicilian grains (see page 94)—in the oven at a low temperature of approximately 100°F for an average of 30 hours. This way I find the pasta not only cooks quickly, similar to a fresh pasta, but also holds its shape during the cooking process. When purchasing packaged dried pasta—whether Sicilian or from another region of Italy—look for artisanal products made from small producers who use organic grain.

The best way to enjoy dried pasta is when cooked to al dente, however the cooking time of each brand of pasta varies, depending on the method used to dry the pasta. Packages often note the cooking time, but in reality, the only way to test for al dente is to place a piece of pasta between your teeth. If it's hard to bite into, the pasta is undercooked. If it's mushy when you bite into it, it is overcooked. Al dente refers to the moment when the pasta is between under- and overcooked. With a little practice, its easy to discern when the pasta is cooked to perfection.

THE ESSENTIAL SAUCE

Although tomato sauce is not the only sauce used in Sicily, the importance of this condiment cannot be underestimated. On page 70, I explained how to prepare tomato pulp. However, the pulp is plain and still needs to be seasoned before it's ready to use as a sauce. Not surprisingly, there is no single agreed-upon way to prepare tomato sauce.

Start by simmering either shaved garlic or slivered onion in olive oil over a low heat until lightly cooked. Add tomato pulp (either the homemade version or a high-quality bottled tomato pulp or *passata*) along with an equal amount of water and raise the heat in order to bring the liquid to a boil. Reduce the heat to a simmer, add a pinch of salt and some fresh basil leaves, and cook for nearly an hour, stirring every 10 minutes with a wooden spoon, until it has reduced in volume by half. Add more fresh basil when the sauce is ready. This sauce can be tossed with spaghetti and sprinkled with grated aged cheese, or you might use it as a base upon which to serve fried zucchini or eggplant.

I'm often asked what brands of tomato pulp I prefer, and my answer is always to bottle your own with organic tomatoes that are fully ripe. However, when purchasing tomato pulp in a supermarket, look for Vantia, Cento, or La Valle. When in Sicily, I encourage you to purchase and try cooking with pulp made from the *siccagno* variety of tomato, which has a concentrated tomato flavor and produces a rich, intense sauce.

PASTA *with* EGGPLANT, TOMATO SAUCE, *and* BAKED RICOTTA

{ *Pasta alla Norma* }

PASTA CU I MILINCIANI

This is my favorite dish in the summer, when eggplants are in season. Pasta is tossed with basil-laced tomato sauce then topped with a heaping portion of fried eggplant morsels. In my cousin Maria's home, and throughout rural Sicily, this dish is referred to as pasta cu milinciani, *which translates simply to pasta with eggplants. In Catania, and in restaurants around the island, this dish is known as* pasta alla Norma, *named after Bellini's highly regarded nineteenth-century opera* Norma. *The story goes that after performers were served this dish in a Catania restaurant, to express their delight in its perfection, they exclaimed, "This is Norma!"*

Over the past few years, I've tried countless adaptations of the dish in restaurants around this island, once in the form of a ravioli, a few times with smoked eggplants, and once with tiny meatballs, the size of pennies, added to the tomato sauce. I've heard on more than one occasion that the latter was the original version of the dish. The type of pasta for the sauce varies from long and thin to short and wide. Each and every version I tried was unique, perfection in itself, but my favorite remains the simple version of my cousin Maria.

When Maria serves this dish, she places freshly grated aged pecorino cheese and a chunk of the milder ricotta salata on the table alongside a grater, so that guests can choose their garnish. During my travels, I discovered another option for topping the dish: baked ricotta. I like how the smoky yet sweet baked ricotta complements the sauce, without masking the sweetness of the tomato and eggplants.

Serves 4

Salt

About 2 cups olive oil, for frying

1 large eggplant, unpeeled and cut into 1-inch cubes

1 pound dried short pasta, such as paccheri

3 cups tomato sauce (page 172)

8 fresh basil leaves, roughly torn in pieces

Ricotta salata or Baked Ricotta (page 81), for serving

1 Bring a large pot of salted water to a boil over high heat.

2 Meanwhile, heat about 3 inches of the oil in a heavy-bottomed pan over high heat. Add the eggplant in batches and fry, turning occasionally, until golden brown, 5 to 8 minutes. With a slotted spoon, transfer the eggplant to paper towels to drain the excess oil. Sprinkle the fried eggplant with salt to taste.

3 Add the pasta to the pot of boiling water and cook until not quite al dente.

4 Meanwhile, heat the sauce in a pot over low heat. Before the pasta is al dente, drain it (reserving some of the cooking water) and add it to the sauce, continuously moving the pan back and forth over the stovetop so the pasta does not stick to the bottom of the pan. If the pasta is not yet cooked but the sauce is very thick, add some pasta cooking water. Season with salt to taste. Add the basil leaves and some of the fried eggplant to the sauce.

5 Place the pasta, coated with the tomato sauce, on a platter or on individual serving plates. Top with the remainder of the fried eggplant, then shaved ricotta salata or baked ricotta.

PASTA *with* CAULIFLOWER, PINE NUTS, *and* RAISINS

{ *Pasta con i Cavolfiori* }

PASTA CU I VROCCULI ARRIMINATI

In Sicilian dialect, the word broccolo *is used to denote cauliflower, which is available in multiple color variations. This dish is a classic wintertime pasta, prepared with minor variations around the island. The use of the Sicilian dialect word* arriminati *("stirred") implies that the cauliflower is mixed with the pasta in a large pan. The recipe calls for one head of cauliflower, but when preparing this dish for a larger group, try mixing florets from white, green, and purple cauliflowers, which give the pasta a festive appearance. For vegetarians, the anchovies can be omitted without jeopardizing the goodness of the dish.*

Serves 4

Salt

1 medium-sized cauliflower head, cut into small florets, stem cut into fine pieces

2 tablespoons olive oil

1 large white onion, finely chopped

3 preserved anchovies in olive oil, crushed with the back of a fork into a paste

2 tablespoons pine nuts

2 tablespoons golden raisins, soaked overnight in water or wine and drained

$1/2$ teaspoon saffron threads

1 pound of any short cut pasta, such as rigatoni or ziti

1 cup grated *ragusano* or aged pecorino cheese

4 tablespoons coarse breadcrumbs (see page 42)

1 Bring a large pot of salted water to a boil over high heat. Add the cauliflower and blanch until slightly tender, about 2 minutes. To test if ready, remove one floret from the water and insert a paring knife inside the stem. If the knife is smoothly inserted with ease, the cauliflower is ready. Transfer the cauliflower with a slotted spoon to a strainer to drain excess water. Reserve the pot of boiling water to cook the pasta.

2 In a sauté pan, heat the olive oil over low to medium heat. Add the onion and cook until translucent, about 5 minutes. Add the anchovies, pine nuts, raisins, and saffron threads. Let all the ingredients simmer together for a few minutes, then add the blanched cauliflower florets. Add about 1 cup of the boiling pasta water to the pan and let simmer until the water is reduced by half and the sauce appears amalgamated but not dry.

3 Meanwhile, cook the pasta until al dente; drain. Add the pasta to the sauce along with the cheese and toss together until the pasta is coated with the sauce. Taste for salt and add more accordingly.

4 Plate the pasta and top with the coarse breadcrumbs.

PASTA *with* PRESERVED TUNA

{ *Pasta con Tonno sott'Olio* }

PASTA CU TONNU SUTT'OGGHIU

When in my Palermo home, away from the country garden, this is one of my go-to meals on busy days when I don't have time to purchase fresh vegetables. Redolent with capers, green Sicilian olives, and herbaceous dried oregano, this dish is Sicily on a plate, and is quick and simple to prepare. It is traditionally prepared using jarred or canned preserved tuna belly, known in Italian as ventresca di tonno. *However, you can preserve your own tuna belly for this dish if you like (see page 133).*

Serves 4

Salt

2 tablespoons salted capers

2 to 3 tablespoons extra-virgin olive oil

1 red onion, thinly sliced

2 cups cherry tomatoes, cut in half

1 cup Tomato Pulp (homemade, page 70, or store-bought)

2 tablespoons Sicilian dried oregano

1/2 pound preserved tuna belly

8 Sicilian green olives, pitted and sliced

1 pound dried long pasta, such as busiate

1 Bring a large pot of salted water to a boil over high heat.

2 Put the capers in a fine-mesh strainer and rinse them under cold running water for a couple of minutes to remove the excess salt. Squeeze out the excess water.

3 In a wide shallow pot, heat 1 tablespoon of the olive oil over medium heat. Add the red onions and sweat until translucent, about 4 minutes. Add the cherry tomatoes, squeezing them with your hands first so that the pulp falls into the pot. Add the tomato pulp, oregano, tuna belly, olives, and capers, along with 1 cup of the boiling water. Simmer for about 10 minutes, until the tomato sauce has thickened enough to coat the back of a spoon.

4 Cook the pasta in the boiling salted water until al dente. Drain the pasta, reserving about 1 cup of the cooking water. Add the pasta to the sauce with some of the reserved cooking liquid if the sauce appears dry. While constantly stirring, simmer the pasta and sauce together until the sauce gently coats the pasta. Taste, seasoning with more salt if needed.

THE ICONIC DISH OF SICILY: PASTA WITH SARDINES

Pasta with sardines, better known as *pasta cu li sardi*, is a highly flavorful dish composed of inexpensive elements. It is well known in Sicily and beyond as an iconic dish of the island's traditional cuisine. In many areas of the Mediterranean, wild fennel grows profusely. Sardines swim in abundance and are often used as bait to catch bigger fish. In Sicily, these and other meager ingredients become the base of many classic dishes.

One legend of the origin of this classic Sicilian preparation revolves around a ninth-century Muslim general, Eufemio, and his chef. When landing in Sicily during the conquest of the island, Eufemio was forced to feed his troops with a combination of foods brought from North Africa and fruits of the Sicilian island. His chef thus combined Sicilian sardines and wild fennel with his supply of raisins, pine nuts, and saffron.

As with all Sicilian dishes, countless versions of this pasta recipe exist, ranging from province to province, village to village, and family to family. There is no right or wrong version, although most cooks tend to swear that their adaptation is the only authentic version. The difference in execution of this pasta dish is roughly divided into two main categories: with and without tomato. In Palermo, it is highly frowned upon to add tomatoes in any form. In other areas, tomato paste, fresh tomatoes, or tomato sauce are common, as in the following recipe, which uses a touch of tomato paste and hails from a village next to Palermo.

Finally, in upscale restaurants, chefs create their own adaptations of this classic dish, so don't be surprised if you find versions with seared or breaded fresh sardines perched on top of the pasta. I've also enjoyed variations with carrots in the sauce, and with a breadcrumb topping made from *panettone*, a typical Italian fruit cake popular during the Christmas season.

As iconic as this dish is, like caponata (page 74), the many forms it takes demonstrate that authenticity is relative.

PASTA *with* SARDINES

{ *Pasta con le Sarde* }

PASTA CU I SARDI

I learned a version of pasta with sardines from my Zia (meaning aunt) Franca Belliotti, who hails from Monreale, a village above Palermo. She uses fresh anchovies in this dish, which are slightly smaller than sardines and taste less fishy, but are often referred to interchangeably in Sicily. Because fresh anchovies are hard to come by in the United States, I replaced them by combining a few salted anchovies with 1/2 pound of fresh sardines instead of using 1 pound of fresh anchovies.

For the aromas used in the sauce, Franca uses cinnamon, black pepper, and nutmeg in lieu of saffron. She does, however, stay true to the wild fennel, which in reality has no substitute. In New York, I tried all types of replacements when lacking the wild fennel, but the dish just isn't the same. As I mentioned earlier, you can source cultivated "wild" fennel in farmers' markets around the country, especially on the West Coast. Otherwise, the best way to find wild fennel is to either grow it yourself or source it from local farmers, then blanch it and freeze it for use during winter months. This might sound extreme, but it's the only way to stay true to the flavors that are required to make this dish successful.

Before serving, topping the pasta with some sugar-laced toasted breadcrumbs turns this into a gastronomic delight. Of all the versions of this dish I've tried, this one is my personal favorite.

Serves 4

Sweet breadcrumbs

2 tablespoons olive oil

2 cups plain fine breadcrumbs

1 tablespoon sugar

Pasta

Salt

3/4 pound wild fennel, finely chopped (see page 29 for substitution ideas)

2 tablespoons olive oil

2 salted anchovies

1 large onion, chopped into very fine pieces

Pasta, continued

1 tablespoon tomato concentrate

2 tablespoons pine nuts

2 tablespoons raisins

1/2 teaspoon cinnamon

1/2 teaspoon freshly ground black pepper

About 1/2 teaspoon grated nutmeg

1/2 pound fresh sardines, filleted with tails removed

1 pound dried pasta in a long shape, such as wide bucatini

1 FOR THE SWEET BREADCRUMBS: In a sauté pan, heat the olive oil over low to medium heat and add the breadcrumbs and sugar. Cook, stirring occasionally with a wooden spoon, until they turn light brown in color, about 5 minutes. Remove from the pan and let cool.

2 FOR THE PASTA: In a large pot, bring salted water to a boil over high heat. Add the fennel. After about 5 minutes, remove the fennel with a fine-meshed hand-held strainer and reserve all of the cooking liquid, keeping it at a boil. In a sauté pan, heat the olive oil over low heat. Add the salted anchovies and onion and cook until the onion is soft, about 8 minutes. Add the tomato concentrate, a ladleful of the boiling water (from blanching the wild fennel), the pine nuts, raisins, cinnamon, black pepper, and nutmeg. Let cook for 5 to 8 minutes. Add the fresh sardines and the fennel, along with another ladleful of the boiling liquid. Cook for about 10 minutes. If the sauce looks dry, add more of the boiling liquid.

3 Add the pasta to the boiling water and cook until al dente. Drain and add to the sauce. Toss and let them amalgamate for 2 minutes so that the pasta soaks up sauce. You might need to add more of the boiling water if the pasta appears dry and sticks to the pan.

4 To plate the dish, top with the sweet breadcrumbs and serve immediately.

SPAGHETTI *with* SARDINES IN THE SEA

{ *Spaghetti di Perciasacchi con Sarde al Mare* }

SPAGHETTI RI PERCIASACCHI CU I SARDI AL MARI

The ingredients in this dish are similar to those used in some versions of pasta with sardines, but here the sardines are omitted. Therefore, with a touch of irony, Sicilians have dubbed this dish "pasta with sardines in the sea." This was originally a rustic dish, but to give it a modern touch, the wild fennel is pureed and placed beneath the spaghetti, a simple but elegant touch that I've seen repeatedly in restaurants around the island. (The wild fennel can be substituted with parsley for a different flavor profile.) Kamut, which is called by the name perciasacchi *in Sicily, is an ancient variety of hard wheat that has a special nutty flavor. If you can't find Kamut spaghetti, it's fine to substitute the more common spaghetti made from durum wheat.*

Serves 4

Salt

2 cups loosely packed roughly chopped wild fennel (or substitute finely chopped parsley leaves)

1 pound dried Kamut (*perciasacchi*) spaghetti

1/4 cup extra-virgin olive oil

1 teaspoon Garlic Paste (page 40)

1/4 cup anchovy paste (see page 31)

1/4 cup crushed almonds

Spicy dried chile pepper

1/2 cup fine breadcrumbs, toasted (see page 42)

1 In a large pot, bring salted water to a boil over high heat. Add the wild fennel and blanch for less than 1 minute. Remove the fennel with a slotted spoon and place it in an ice bath to stop the cooking. Reserve the boiling water to cook the pasta. Transfer the wild fennel to a blender and add 1 cup water. Blend on high speed until the fennel is fully pureed. Transfer to a heavy-bottomed saucepan and simmer over low heat until reduced by half. Keep warm until ready to use.

2 Cook the spaghetti in the salted boiling water until al dente.

3 Meanwhile, in a sauté pan over low heat, gently heat the olive oil, making sure not to overheat the oil. Add the garlic paste and cook until golden brown. Add the anchovy paste, crushed almonds, and chile. Cook for about 1 minute, then add 1 cup of the boiling pasta water. Due to the saltiness of the anchovies, and since the pasta water is salted, you will probably not need to add extra salt.

4 Drain the spaghetti, transfer to the sauté pan, and toss well so that the sauce fully coats the pasta.

5 To serve, spread the warm wild fennel puree around the bottom of each plate. Place the spaghetti on top, leaving an edge around the plate so that the puree is visible. Sprinkle the breadcrumbs on top of each serving.

PASTA *with* SALT-PRESERVED SARDINES

{ *Pasta con Sarde sotto Sale* }

PASTA A LA MILANISA

In my grandmother's village and in other inner-island villages, pasta with sardines prepared with tomato sauce is also known as pasta a la Milanisa, *or in the style of the Milanese. One tale explains that the dish got its name when immigrants from Sicily to Northern Italy could not find fresh sardines for this dish and thus replaced them with salted sardines. Upon their return to Sicily, they gave the dish its Milanese moniker. Another possible explanation is that the Normans— who were categorized as Milanese since they arrived from the north—introduced salted sardines to the interior areas of the island. In the past, fresh seafood was not commonly found outside of port cities, so salted fish was the norm inland.*

When using the salted sardines preserved in oil, you can add more or less, depending on your taste. I prefer to use preserved Sicilian sardine fillets that are held in oil and sold in glass jars (see Sources, page 326). However, whole, gutted Sicilian sardines are also packed in coarse sea salt and canned. The latter need to be rinsed very well in water, and their heads and spines need to be removed before using as an ingredient in this recipe.

Serves 4

Salt

2 tablespoons olive oil

1 large onion, finely chopped

2 cups Tomato Pulp (homemade, page 70, or store-bought)

4 to 5 fresh basil leaves, torn

Pinch of freshly ground black pepper

4 to 6 salted sardine fillets in oil, slightly broken into pieces with a fork

1 pound dried pasta in a long shape, such as spaghetti or thin bucatini

1 In a large pot, bring salted water to a boil over high heat.

2. In a sauté pan, heat the olive oil over medium heat. Add the onion and cook until translucent, about 5 minutes. Add the tomato pulp, basil, black pepper, and sardines. Add a ladleful of the boiling water. Let cook for about 5 minutes, stirring occasionally.

3 Cook the spaghetti in the boiling water until al dente. Drain, add to the sauce, and continue cooking for a minute or two until the pasta soaks up some of the sauce. If the sauce appears too dry, add a little more of the boiling pasta water.
Serve immediately.

SPAGHETTI *with* SEA URCHIN

{ *Spaghetti con Ricci di Mare* }

SPAGHETTI CU I RIZZI RI MARI

As a kid, I learned to dive for sea urchin around coral reefs near the local beach in Sciacca. Once back at the beach, I used to crack open the shells and devour the roe within minutes. Sometimes I would even do so while swimming, as I found the flavor of this delicacy to be addictive. Today the taste of the roe is yet another sensation that instantly brings me back to my childhood summers in Sicily.

Sea urchin roe, also called coral, are innards found in both males and females. The bright orange edible parts are not eggs, but rather reproductive gonads, which are laid out in five symmetrical rows that form the shape of a star. Around the world, numerous types of sea urchin species exist. In Sicily, you'll find a variety known as purple sea urchins; these are small, with bodies the size of a golf ball. In the Atlantic and Pacific Oceans, larger sea urchins exist, but the roe of these red or green sea urchin possesses a very similar taste to that of their Mediterranean counterparts. In most American seafood stores, sea urchin roe is sold in flat containers of cleaned pieces. In Sicily, merchants often sell the roe in little cups.

When in Sicily, don't miss the sensory experience of eating this ultra-simple pasta dish, which almost every portside restaurant offers in some version or another. In Sciacca, at one of my favorite spots, La Lampara, the spaghetti is served with an optional sprinkle of toasted breadcrumbs (page 42), as pictured. Note that in May and June of most years, Sicilian fishers must cease harvesting sea urchin to allow the species time to reproduce. During this period, this dish is of course harder to find.

Serves 4

Salt

1 pound dried spaghetti

¹/₄ cup extra-virgin olive oil

2 whole garlic cloves, peeled and crushed slightly with the palm of your hand

¹/₄ pound sea urchin roe

2 tablespoons finely chopped fresh parsley leaves

1 Bring a large pot of salted water to a boil over high heat. Add the spaghetti and cook until al dente.

2 Meanwhile, start the sauce by gently heating the olive oil in a saucepan over low heat. Add the garlic and fry for a few minutes, making sure not to brown the garlic.

3 Drain the pasta and add it to the saucepan, followed shortly after by the sea urchin roe. Briskly stir the spaghetti in the pan with a wooden spoon so that the pasta is well coated with the sea urchin and the olive oil, which will transform into a creamy textured sauce.

4 Remove the garlic from the pan. Add the parsley to the pan and stir briskly into the spaghetti. Serve immediately.

Baked Pasta

Another traditional way to cook pasta in Sicily is baked in the oven, *pasta al forno*. In Sicily, the word *lasagne* refers specifically to the long flat pasta sheets, not the baked dish as a whole. It's common to serve baked pasta—which can be prepared in many forms from the meager to the lavish—on holidays or on Sundays with many guests. My favorite part is ripping off the crunchy ends that overcook in the oven and eating them with my fingers before serving the dish.

As a kid, I had an adverse reaction to my cousin Maria's *pasta al forno*—prepared with lasagna sheets, béchamel, and a meat sauce—because it contained peas, which I detested at the time. I used to pick them out one by one with my fingers when I thought she wasn't looking, stuffing them in my napkin. Maria admitted to me when I grew up that she knew all along I hated the peas and that she served them to me until I finally got tired of picking them out. It was her way of teaching me to enjoy peas, and she succeeded.

At home in Palermo, I prepare baked pasta with seasonal local vegetables. Although not traditional in Sicily, I roast or grill slices of vegetables and layer them with fresh pasta sheets or toss them with short pasta cuts or *annelletti* (small pasta rings). I add sauce, Sicilian cheese, and sometimes ricotta béchamel. In the early fall, I prepare luscious mushroom, eggplant, and roasted tomato baked pastas, while in winter months, I make versions of lasagna with Sicilian cauliflower and squash. In the spring, I use fresh peas, favas, artichokes, onions, and wild asparagus. The possibilities are endless, so allow your creativity to come through.

DELICIOUS MOCKERY: THE ROOTS OF PEASANT COOKING

Beyond its multi-ethnic makeup, Sicilian cuisine is characterized by a mélange of both simple and complex preparations. Traditional Sicilian cooking stems from two main sources: from aristocratic kitchens, where splendor and spectacle were of utmost importance, and from the homes of the peasants, who were bound more by necessity but mustered a creative imagination that embodies Sicilian identity.

The aristocratic strain can be traced back to 1805, when Maria Carolina, the wife of Ferdinand I, the king of Sicily and Naples, and the sister of Marie Antoinette, imported French chefs to the royal court in Palermo. These chefs became known as *monzù*, a corruption of the word *monsieur* and a title used to emphasize the chefs' superior status among the servants of the house. The elevated cuisine that resulted in Sicily due to the presence of the *monzù* chefs was refined but bold, combining French technique with Sicilian ingredients. Gradually the cooks who had apprenticed under the French *monzù* took over the aristocratic kitchens and continued to bear the prestigious title.

Peasant cuisine, on the other hand, was meager and unrefined, but it too contained typical Sicilian ingredients. Like in most regions of Italy, there is a profound difference in the elaborate and embellished quality of aristocratic dishes with those of the masses, which were simple ingredient-driven dishes. In Sicilian cuisine, however, several peasant dishes mirror foods of the upper class. In such preparations, expensive main ingredients are substituted with those of lesser value, and the name of the meager dish reflects its aristocratic origins. For example, birds are exchanged with sardines in *sarde a beccafico* (see page 249), and rabbit is replaced with salted codfish in *Cunigghiu Polizzano* (page 76). There is an underlying paradox when naming and modeling a peasant dish after an expensive aristocratic preparation, reflecting a sense of irony and cunningness that Sicilians value highly.

SAVORY CRÊPES BAKED *with* RICOTTA FILLING

{ *Cannelloni Ripieni* }

CANNIDDUNA O MANICOTTI

There are two common names for this dish in Italian. One is cannelloni, *meaning "big reed," and the other is* manicotti, *or "cooked hands," probably because the cook's fingers can get scorched when preparing the crêpes. This dish has always been a staple dish on our family table, in Sicily and in New York. My grandmother never let a religious holiday or large family gathering go by without preparing her manicotti. Today I like to carry on her tradition. As a start to a long multicourse meal, these savory baked crêpes are not overly filling. Grandma's secret to making the dish exquisite was preparing her own sheep's milk ricotta, which adds a richness and creaminess that store-bought ricotta simply cannot imitate. If you don't make your own (page 80), try to source the best-quality ricotta possible.*

This recipe will yield approximately twelve 8-inch crêpes. Although only eight crepes are needed for four servings, when serving crêpes, it's best to overestimate the amount of batter required, since commonly the first few crêpes don't come out as expected because the pan is either too hot or too cool. This particular sauce for the manicotti contains just a bit of meat, although many families prepare the dish with a plain tomato sauce. The meat is meant as a flavor accent, not to be the predominant taste.

Serves 4 (about 12 filled crêpes total)

Crêpes

$1^1/_2$ cups all-purpose flour

$^1/_2$ teaspoon salt

2 large eggs, beaten

2 cups milk

Vegetable oil, for the pan

Filling

3 cups strained ricotta

1 cup cubed mozzarella cheese

1 cup grated pecorino or Parmesan cheese

2 large eggs, beaten

2 tablespoons finely chopped fresh basil

1 teaspoon salt

Sauce

1 teaspoon olive oil

$^1/_2$ cup finely chopped onion

1 cup ground beef

$2^1/_2$ cups Tomato Pulp (homemade, page 70, or store-bought)

Salt

To assemble

About 1 tablespoon vegetable oil, for greasing

$^1/_2$ cup grated pecorino cheese

1 FOR THE CRÊPES: Sift the flour and mix it with the salt in a large mixing bowl. Make a well in the flour and pour in the beaten eggs. Beat the eggs to slowly incorporate the flour mixture that surrounds them. Be gentle, otherwise lumps of flour could form. Once the egg and flour are mixed, slowly add the milk, a little at a time, whisking all the time. After all the milk is added, keep whisking until small bubbles form on the surface. The batter can be prepared a day in advance, if necessary, and stored in an airtight container in the refrigerator.

2 Heat an 8-inch nonstick pan over medium heat. Pour a little vegetable oil on a folded paper towel, and wipe it evenly inside the pan. Pour in about 3 tablespoons batter. Using your wrist to tilt the pan, slightly remove the pan from the heat and spread the batter evenly to cover the whole surface with a

continued ↓

thin layer. Return the pan to the stovetop over low to medium heat and cook the batter for about 1 minute. Flip and cook the other side for about 30 seconds, until the crêpe is golden in color. It's best to flip the crêpe with your fingers, because it's very delicate. Transfer the crêpe to a plate. Repeat these steps until you are out of batter, stacking the cooked crêpes on the plate. The stacked crêpes can be covered with a damp paper towel, then with plastic wrap, and refrigerated for up to 1 day.

3 FOR THE FILLING: In a mixing bowl, combine the ricotta, mozzarella, pecorino, beaten eggs, basil, and salt and stir to combine. The filling can be prepared up to 2 days in advance and stored in the refrigerator until you are ready to stuff the crepes.

4 FOR THE SAUCE: In a saucepan, heat the olive oil over low heat. Add the onion and gently sauté over low to medium heat until translucent. Raise the heat, add the beef, and let brown until the meat is cooked, about 5 minutes. Add the tomato pulp and $2\frac{1}{2}$ cups water. Let cook over low heat for 45 minutes, until the sauce has reduced by half. Salt to taste and set aside.

5 TO ASSEMBLE THE CRÊPES: Spread 2 tablespoons ricotta filling on a crêpe, distributing the filling evenly and leaving a 1-inch border around the edge. Roll the crêpe into a cylinder, or fold it into a pocket by folding the left, right, and bottom sides toward the center of the crêpe before rolling it. Repeat with the remaining crêpes and filling.

6 Preheat the oven to 350°F. Brush the bottom of a 10 by 16-inch baking pan with a very thin coating of vegetable oil. Place the filled crêpes, seam sides down, in the baking pan. Do not worry if they are tightly packed. The tighter the crêpes are packed, the less chance they will unfold during the cooking process.

7 Top the crêpes with the tomato-meat sauce, but leave the edges of the crêpes bare so that they will get crispy when baked. Sprinkle with the cheese. Cover with aluminum foil and bake for 20 minutes. Remove the foil and bake for an additional 20 minutes, until the top of the crêpes where the cheese has melted is browned. Serve immediately.

Variation

My cousin Maria uses the same tomato-meat sauce as above for her *pasta al forno*. She layers sheets of pasta dough and the sauce in a baking pan with fresh or frozen peas, béchamel (page 113), and grated caciocavallo cheese, then bakes the pasta for about 50 minutes at 350°F. Her version most closely resembles what Americans call "lasagna," as it's prepared with sheets of pasta. This dish is best when using uncooked fresh pasta sheets (page 192). If you can't find the fresh pasta from a local vendor and don't want to prepare it yourself, dried pasta will do just fine. However, if using the type of packaged dried pasta that does not need to be boiled before use, I suggest placing it in salted boiling water anyway for about 2 minutes; otherwise the pasta soaks up too much of the sauce and can cause your lasagna to turn out dry and bland.

THE LEOPARD TIMBALE

{ *Timballo del Gattopardo* }

TIMBADDU RU GATTUPARDU

This timale recipe, with its pastry crust and French sauces, is a perfect example of the French influence on noble Sicilian cuisine. The dish was described in Giuseppe Tomaso di Lampedusa's novel The Leopard, *which was first published in 1958 and tells the tale of a fictional Sicilian prince and his family in the 1860s. Every year during the summer months, the family traveled to a palace where a feast commenced upon their arrival. Friends of the noble family were invited to an opulent meal, where elaborate creations were served, one of which was this timbale, described as follows:*

The burnt gold casing, the fragrance of sugar and of cinnamon that emanated from it, was just the prelude of the sensation of delight that burst from the depths of the timbale when the knife broke the crust: first streams of smoke erupted, filled with bold aromas. Then the chicken livers, the hard-boiled eggs, the fine layers of prosciutto, the chicken and the truffles were revealed in a united, scorching hot mass of *maccheroni* pasta, colored with a precious suede-like hue by the meat extract.

When preparing the recipe below, feel free to omit any of the ingredients, such as the black truffle or chicken livers, and substitute with greater quantities of any the other ingredients listed. Although it's not described in the novel, I've adapted the recipe to include sausage meat, devoid of fennel seeds or spicy pepper, in the stuffing, which adds some moisture in the form of fat.

Serves 8 to 10

Pastry dough

4 cups all-purpose flour

1 tablespoon salt

1 tablespoon sugar

1 teaspoon ground cinnamon

$^3/_4$ cup lard or 1$^1/_2$ sticks unsalted butter

2 egg yolks (reserve the egg whites for assembling the timbale)

Sauce

3 cups Meat Broth (page 146)

$^3/_4$ cups good-quality dry Marsala

3 tablespoons unsalted butter, cut into small tabs

Pasta

Salt

1 pound short tubular dried pasta of your choice (rigatoni, ziti, penne, *mezze maniche*)

1$^1/_2$ tablespoons olive oil

Stuffing

1$^1/_2$ tablespoons olive oil

$^1/_2$ onion, finely chopped

1 cup plain sausage meat, casings removed

1 cup chicken livers, cut into small slivers

$^3/_4$ cup good-quality dry Marsala

1 cup pulled boiled chicken (cook as in the Chicken Broth recipe on page 147; pull the chicken into small shreds and discard the bones)

$^1/_2$ cup prosciutto cotto (Italian ham), cut into small ($^1/_4$ by 1-inch) strips

1 cup grated Parmesan cheese

1 tablespoon preserved black truffle shavings

3 tablespoons tomato paste

To assemble

2 tablespoons unsalted butter, at room temperature

4 soft-boiled eggs, shells removed

2 egg whites, beaten

1 Several hours before you plan to bake the timbale, MAKE THE PASTRY DOUGH: In a bowl, stir together the flour, salt, sugar, and cinnamon. Place the lard and egg yolks in a stand mixer with a hook attachment and mix on high speed to incorporate, about 1 minute. Reduce the speed to low and add the flour mixture, little by little, mixing slowly so that the flour does not fly out of the bowl. When the ingredients are incorporated into

continued ↓

a unified mass, transfer it to a work surface and form the dough into two equal-sized balls. Wrap each ball of dough in waxed paper and chill in the refrigerator for up to 2 hours, until you are ready to assemble the timbale.

2 FOR THE SAUCE: In a small heavy-bottomed saucepan, combine the broth and Marsala. Bring to a boil over high heat, then reduce to a simmer over low to medium heat. When the liquid is reduced by three-fourths, add the butter and whisk well. Remove from the stovetop and let the sauce cool.

3 FOR THE PASTA: In a large pot, bring salted water to a boil over high heat. Add the pasta and cook until not yet al dente, about 4 minutes less than the time suggested on the package. Drain the pasta and cool it down quickly in a strainer under cold running water to stop the cooking. Immediately transfer the pasta to a mixing bowl (do not let it sit in the cold water), and toss the pasta with the olive oil so that it doesn't stick together. Let the pasta sit uncovered.

4 FOR THE STUFFING: In a sauté pan, heat the olive oil over medium heat. Add the onion and about 2 tablespoons water and cook until translucent. Add the sausage meat, raise the heat to medium-high, and cook until browned, about 8 minutes. Add the chicken livers and continue cooking for about 2 minutes. Add the tomato paste and carefully pour in the Marsala. Using a wooden spoon, dislodge any pieces of sausage or liver that are stuck to the bottom of the pan. Keep the pan on the stove for a few minutes more, until the Marsala is reduced enough to coat the liver. Remove the pan from the stovetop and let it cool.

5 When the sausage mixture is cool, in a large mixing bowl, combine the sauce, pasta, and sausage mixture with the chicken, prosciutto cotto, Parmesan, and truffle shavings. Set the filling aside in a cool place while assembling the timbale.

6 TO ROLL OUT THE PASTRY CRUST: Remove the pastry dough from the refrigerator about 15 minutes before you are ready to roll it out. Dough that is too cold will crack as you attempt to roll it out. The dough is ready to be rolled out when you touch it and your finger leaves an imprint. Flatten one piece of dough into a disc, and place it between two pieces of waxed paper. Start by placing the rolling pin in the center of the dough. Roll upward, applying more pressure in the center of the dough disc, and less as the rolling pin approaches the edges. Do not roll the pin back to the center, but rather pick it up and start each roll out from the center point. Next roll downward, then to the right, and then to the left. Continue rolling out the dough until it forms a circle about 15 inches in diameter that is about $1/8$ inch thick. Roll out the second piece of dough to the same shape, size, and thickness.

7 Preheat the oven to 350°F. Use the 2 tablespoons butter to grease a 10-inch springform baking pan.

8 TO ASSEMBLE THE TIMBALE: Place one piece of rolled-out dough on the bottom of the pan, allowing the sides to protrude slightly from the pan. Place half of the stuffing mixture on top of the dough and spread it out evenly. Top with the soft-boiled eggs, placed at equal distances from each other. Cover with the remaining stuffing. Finally, place the other piece of dough on top, and pinch the edges of the bottom and top layers of dough together to seal. Make sure that the two pieces of dough are adequately attached to one another to keep the filling inside during the baking process. Using a kitchen brush, brush the beaten egg whites on top of the dough in a thin layer. Gently pierce the top piece of dough with a fork five or six times, so that small holes are created to allow steam to escape from the timbale during baking.

9 Bake the timbale for about 45 minutes, until the crust is deep golden in color. Cool on a rack for about 10 minutes, then remove the timbale from the springform pan and serve immediately.

RING PASTA TIMBALE

{ Timballo di Anelletti }

TIMBADDU RI ANEDUZZI

While the timbale in the previous recipe has a golden brown pastry crust, here a layer of thinly sliced fried eggplant forms the "crust." The recipe can be prepared in a simple baking dish or in a decorative cake ring mold. Anelletti are a typical Sicilian pasta, rings of about ¾ inch in diameter. Classically this pasta shape is used exclusively for baked pasta dishes. Many specialty Italian stores sell anelletti imported from Sicily (see Sources, page 326), but if you can't find this shape, replace with any small cut of pasta. For a vegetarian version, substitute a simple tomato sauce (page 172) for the beef ragù.

Serves 8

Blend of olive oil and vegetable oil, for frying

2 large eggplants (about 1 pound each), one thinly sliced, the second cubed

Salt

1 pound dried anelletti pasta

2 cups Beef-Pea Ragù (page 167)

¼ cup grated Parmesan cheese

1 cup ricotta

1 cup cubed *Vastedda del Belice* cheese, *provola,* or mozzarella

1 tablespoon unsalted butter

10 fresh basil leaves

1 Heat about 1 inch of the oil in a heavy-bottomed sauté pan over medium-high heat. Add the sliced eggplant and fry, stirring occasionally, until dark golden brown on all sides, about 5 minutes. The eggplant needs to be well browned for the deepest flavor. Transfer the eggplant slices to a paper towel–lined baking sheet. Add more oil to the pan, and fry the eggplant cubes in the same way.

2 Bring a large pot of salted water to a boil over high heat. Add the anelletti and cook until not yet al dente, about 4 minutes less than the suggested time on the package. Drain the pasta and cool it down quickly in a strainer under cold running water to stop the cooking. Immediately transfer the pasta to a mixing bowl (do not let it sit in the cold water) and stir in the eggplant cubes, ragù, Parmesan, ricotta, and cubed cheese.

3 Preheat the oven to 400°F. Butter a 10-inch ring mold with the butter.

4 Cover the base and sides of the mold with slices of fried eggplant, overlapping them slightly. Place the basil leaves on top of the eggplant slices. Fill the mold with the pasta mixture, then cover the top with more eggplant slices.

5 Bake the timbale for about 20 minutes, until the eggplant starts to darken slightly in color. Let the timbale set inside the mold for 5 minutes before turning it over and serving the eggplant timbale whole on a serving platter.

Fresh Pasta

During my travels around the island, I've come across countless grandmas who, like mine, learned how to prepare fresh pasta from a very young age. But, due to the time constraints faced by many working mothers and the widespread use of packaged pasta, handmade versions are rarely prepared today. My best friend, Maria Grazia, is adamant that the handmade pasta her grandmother taught her how to make must continue as a family tradition. On Sundays, she unites her grandmother, mother, and small daughter at her country home outside Sant'Anna, and together they prepare different variations of handmade pasta (along with countless other family recipes that rotate based on the season). Her three-year-old daughter simply plays with the pasta dough for now, but that's the way that most handmade pasta makers start out in Sicily.

HARD WHEAT PASTA DOUGH WITH EGG

{ *Impasto per Pasta di Grano Duro con l'Uovo* }

Most pastas in Sicily are prepared with flour and water; however, egg is added to a few types of traditional pasta doughs, in certain areas of the island. The egg makes the pasta chewier and richer. I prefer the lighter consistency of an eggless pasta, as it's less filling. Ultimately, it's a matter of taste—experiment with eggless and egg-based pasta dough to see which version you prefer.

Makes about 1¹/₃ pounds dough (6 servings of pasta)

1 pound remilled hard
wheat semola flour, plus
more for kneading

¹/₂ teaspoon salt

4 large eggs, beaten

1 Place the flour in a mound on a clean work surface and create a deep indentation in the center. Add the beaten eggs and salt to the indentation and mix the flour and eggs with a fork. Pay careful attention that the egg does not spill out of the mound of flour. Continue to draw flour from the sides of the well until all of the flour is incorporated with the eggs. Once the dough becomes thicker and starts sticking to your fingers, knead the dough with both hands and form it into a single mass. Continue kneading on a lightly floured surface, until the dough becomes smooth and elastic-like in texture, about 10 minutes. Use a pastry scraper to remove any dough that sticks to the work surface.

2 If the dough feels to dry and is not fully sticking together, add a touch of water. If the dough feels too wet and pasty, add some more flour. In either case, add a little at a time. Form the dough into a ball, cover with a clean kitchen towel, and let it rest for about 1 hour at room temperature.

3 Roll the dough and shape it into the cut of your choice, such as tagliolini, lasagne, or tagliatelle (see "Rolling and Cutting Fresh Pasta Dough," page 197).

HARD WHEAT PASTA DOUGH WITHOUT EGG

{ *Impasto per Pasta di Grano Duro senza Uovo* }

Throughout Sicily, hard wheat flour is the most common choice for making fresh pasta, although soft wheat flour is used in dough flavored with vegetable pulp. I prepare these pastas with heritage stoneground Sicilian hard wheat (tumminia, perciasacchi, bidì, russello, or biancolilla flour), instead of the remilled semola flour. For an explanation of these ancient grain varieties, as well as the differences between hard and soft wheat flours, see pages 86 and 94, in the bread chapter.

Makes about 1 pound dough (4 servings of pasta)

1 pound remilled hard wheat flour of your choice, plus more for kneading	About 1 cup room-temperature water
	1 teaspoon salt

1 Place the flour in a mound on a clean work surface and create a deep well in the center. Add the room-temperature water and salt to the well and mix the water into the flour with the tips of your fingers. Pay careful attention that the water does not spill out of the mound of flour. Continue to draw flour from the sides of the well until all of the flour is incorporated. Once the dough becomes thicker and starts sticking to your fingers, knead with both hands and form into a single mass. Continue kneading on a lightly floured surface, until the dough becomes smooth and elastic-like in texture, about 10 minutes. Use a pastry scraper to remove any dough that sticks to the work surface.

2 If the dough feels too dry and is not fully sticking together, add a touch more water. If the dough feels too wet and pasty, add some more flour. In either case, add a little at a time. Form the dough in to a ball, cover it with a clean kitchen towel, and let it rest for about 1 hour at room temperature.

3 Roll the dough and shape it into the cut of your choice, such as tagliolini, tagliatelle, or lasagne (see "Rolling and Cutting Fresh Pasta Dough," page 197).

Variations

CHESTNUT FLOUR PASTA DOUGH: Replace half of the flour with chestnut flour. This dough is best prepared in the shape of tagliatelle. The pasta has a slightly earthy and nutty flavor.

SQUID-INK PASTA DOUGH: Mix $^1/_4$ cup black squid ink into the water before incorporating it into the flour. Fresh squid ink is better, but bottled squid works fine. The pasta bears a subtle taste of the sea. Not only is it a perfect accompaniment to seafood pasta dishes, the black color is attractive and dramatic, making it perfect for entertaining.

COCOA OR CAROB PASTA DOUGH: Mix $^1/_2$ cup unsweetened cocoa or carob powder into the flour before mixing the dough and use about 3 tablespoons additional water. Bitter cocoa-flavored pasta in the shape of tagliatelle is commonly paired with pork ragù (page 202) or rabbit ragù. Carob is traditionally used to flavor tagliatelle and gnocchi.

PARSLEY PASTA

{ Impasto per Pasta al Prezzemolo }

In Sicily, it is not common to flavor fresh pasta at home. However, nowadays, more and more restaurants are including dishes prepared with pastas flavored with Sicilian tastes and aromas. With an abundance of wild greens that grow at Feudo Montoni, I'm always looking for ways to utilize vegetables in creative ways. This recipe flavors pasta with parsley, but you could easily substitute any other leafy green such as spinach, chard, mustard greens, borage, nettles, and/or basil.

If you would like to flavor the pasta with a non-leafy vegetable such as carrots or beets, first peel the vegetables, cut them into chunks, and cook them in boiling salted water until tender and easily pierced with a paring knife. Puree the vegetable pieces in a food processor, then pass the puree through a fine-mesh strainer to rid it of any lumps.

Makes about 1¹/₂ pounds dough (6 servings of pasta)

About ¹/₂ pound parsley stems and leaves (to make about 1 cup parsley puree)

Salt

¹/₂ pound 00 flour

¹/₂ pound remilled semola flour

About ³/₄ cup room temperature water

1 To make the flavoring puree, lightly blanch the parsley stems and leaves in boiling salted water for about 1 minute. The salt helps to retain the color of the leaves. Do not overcook or the leaves will lose their color. Strain the parsley out of the boiling water and make sure to drain off all the water. One way to remove the water is by placing the blanched parsley in cheesecloth and squeezing out the water by hand.

2 Puree the leaves and stems in a food processor and pass them through a fine-mesh strainer to rid the puree of any lumps or fibrous pieces.

3 To incorporate the vegetable pulp with the two flours, it's best to use a stand mixer with a hook attachment. First place the puree in the mixer, along with the room-temperature water and 1 teaspoon salt. Add the two types of flour little by little, mixing them in until the dough forms a ball. The dough should be smooth and elastic in texture. If the dough feels too dry and is not fully sticking together, add a touch more water. If the dough feels too wet and pasty, add some more flour, of either variety. In either case, add a little at a time. Form the dough into a ball, cover it with a clean kitchen towel, and let it rest for about 1 hour at room temperature.

4 Roll the dough and shape it into the cut of your choice, such as spaghetti, tagliolini, or tagliatelle (see "Rolling and Cutting Fresh Pasta Dough," page 197).

FROM TOP: *Fresh flavored pastas, typically prepared in restaurants and not part of the Sicilian home cooking tradition: parsley, carrot, roasted beet, squid ink, and cocoa.*

ROLLING AND CUTTING FRESH PASTA DOUGH

A hand-cranked pasta machine is used to roll pasta dough and cut it into flat noodles of varying widths. Electric versions of this machine are manufactured, but the ones that are strong and worth buying tend to be expensive, ten to fifteen times the price of a hand-cranked machine. The difference between electric and hand-cranked machines lies in the speed of the pasta making. Hand-cranked machines are the best bet for home use, unless you prepare pasta in large quantities every day, in which case an electric machine would better suit you. To roll and cut fresh pasta, start with 1 to 2 pounds fresh pasta dough of your choice (see pages 192–194) and follow these directions:

1 Cut the dough into four chunks. Roll each piece through a hand-cranked or electric pasta machine, starting with the thickest setting.

2 Each time you pass the dough through the machine, tighten the setting so that the thickness gets smaller and smaller, until it reaches the thinnest setting on the machine.

3 Lay each piece of flattened dough on a floured work surface and let it dry for about 10 minutes.

4 Use the machine to cut the dough to your desired shape, following the manufacturer's instructions. Or cut the pasta by hand by rolling the flattened dough into a tight log and using a knife to cut the pasta noodles to the desired width (see the chart below).

5 Spread the pasta out on a lightly floured surface or hang the pasta on a rack to dry for about 30 minutes before cooking. This helps prevent the pasta from sticking together. You can pre-portion the pasta, wrap it in plastic wrap, and refrigerate it for up to 2 days before cooking.

TRADITIONAL SICILIAN FLAT PASTA SIZES

In Sicily, lasagne are long, wide pasta ribbons, essentially the same as what is known elsewhere in Italy as pappardelle. *Maltagliati* literally means "poorly cut"—you can cut these into any shape you like (roughly triangular shapes are common), but try to keep them of a relatively uniform size so that they will cook evenly. *Sfoglia* are pasta sheets that you can use to make a type of *pasta al forno* (see page 186).

Taglierini (capelli d'angelo)	$1/16$ inch wide
Bavette	$1/8$ inch wide
Tagliolini	$1/5$ inch wide
Tagliatelle	$1/4$ inch wide
Lasagne	$1^{1}/_{2}$ inches wide
Sfoglia	6 to 8 inches wide
Maltagliati	varies

TAGLIOLINI *with* RED MULLET *and* BOTTARGA

{ *Tagliolini con le Triglie e Bottarga* }

TAGGHIULINI CU I TRIGGHI E BOTTARGA

Along the winding mountainous streets that crisscross the island of Lipari, I happened upon an ideal family-operated trattoria offering creations prepared with local seafood, such as this flavorful fresh green pasta with mullet and bottarga. The subtlety of the white-fleshed red mullet balances perfectly with the saltiness of the bottarga, the nuttiness of the pine nuts, and the acidity and sweetness of the orange. In lieu of making the fresh parsley tagliolini, use dried spaghetti tossed with freshly chopped parsley.

Serves 4

6 red mullet fillets
(3 whole fish), cleaned
of all scales and bones

2 tablespoons olive oil

2 garlic cloves, crushed
slightly with the palm of
your hand

1/4 cup pine nuts

2 tablespoons pitted cured
black olives, cut in half

1 cup dry white wine

Grated zest of
1 organic orange

Salt

1 teaspoon vegetable oil

1 pound fresh Parsley Pasta
(page 194), cut into 1/5-inch-
wide tagliolini

2 ounces tuna bottarga

1 To make the sauce, cut two of the fish fillets into pieces about 1 inch in size. In a large sauté pan over low heat, heat the olive oil and add the garlic. Let cook for a minute or so, making sure not to brown the garlic. Add the pine nuts, olives, and the chopped mullet and cook for about 1 minute. Remove the pan from the heat and add the wine, then return the pan to the stovetop. Add the orange zest, reduce the heat to low, and simmer until the wine has reduced, about 3 minutes. Remove the sauce from the heat.

2 In a large pot, bring salted water to a boil over high heat.

3 The key to a good sear is a hot pan and fillets that have been removed from the refrigerator about 10 minutes prior to cooking. Pat the fillets dry with a paper towel to make sure no moisture remains on them and salt them lightly just before cooking.

4 To sear the fish, heat a thick-bottomed skillet over high heat for 1 minute, until very hot. Add a small amount of vegetable oil and heat for a few seconds. Add the four remaining fillets, skin side down, and reduce the heat to medium so that the fish sears but doesn't burn. Cook for 2 to 3 minutes, shaking the pan slightly so that the fish doesn't stick and pressing down on each fillet with a fish spatula so that the skin sears evenly. Use a fish spatula to flip the fillets to the other side and finish cooking, about 1 minute. When done, the fillets will be firm in texture and will flake easily if touched on the meat side. If the skin sticks to the bottom of the pan, remove it with the fish spatula. Hold in a warm place while finishing the dish.

5 Add the fresh pasta to the boiling water and cook for about 1 minute, until the pasta is not quite al dente. Drain, transfer to the sauce, and add salt to taste. Let the pasta finish cooking with the sauce, stirring or tossing the pasta constantly over low heat so that it absorbs the sauce and doesn't stick to the pan. Remove the two cloves of garlic and discard.

6 Divide the pasta among four individual plates and top each serving with a seared red mullet fillet. Shave or grate the bottarga on top of each dish.

CHESTNUT TAGLIATELLE *with* PORCINI

{ *Tagliatelle di Farina di Castagne con Porcini* }

TAGGHIATEDDI RI CASTAGNI CU I FUNCI PORCINI

Throughout the mountainous areas of Sicily, autumn is marked by strong rains combined with warm temperatures, which promote the growth of mushrooms. During this time, it's common to find small roadside stands selling fresh porcini mushrooms in all sizes.

When cooking with porcini, the stem and cap are used, both of which have a smooth texture and meat-like firmness to them. Make sure to rub the dirt off the mushrooms with a damp cloth instead of washing them with water, which can make them mushy. Porcini do not disintegrate but rather retain their shape when cooked.

I do not suggest substituting dried porcini, which have a significantly bolder flavor and will overpower the taste of the chestnut flour. Rather, substitute other fresh mushrooms such as chanterelle or trumpet mushrooms. Although their flavors differ from that of porcini, they will nonetheless complement the sweetness and nuttiness of the chestnut flour pasta. The sausage can be omitted in this dish for a still hearty, and traditional, vegetarian option.

Serves 4

Salt

$1/2$ pound fresh porcini mushrooms

$1/4$ cup olive oil

2 garlic cloves, peeled and left whole

$1/2$ pound sausage (store-bought or homemade, page 265), cut into bite-sized pieces

$1/2$ cup dry white wine

1 pound fresh Chestnut Flour Pasta (variation on page 193), cut into $1/4$-inch-wide tagliatelle

1 tablespoon grated caciocavallo cheese

2 tablespoons finely chopped fresh parsley or thyme

Spicy dried chile pepper (optional)

1 Bring a pot of salted water to a boil.

2 If the porcini are small enough to fit in your hand, cut them lengthwise into $1/4$-inch-thick slices. For larger mushrooms, rather than slicing them, cut them into $1/2$-inch-square chunks. In a large sauté pan, heat the olive oil over low heat. Add the garlic cloves, then the sausage pieces and sear for a few minutes to render some of the fat. Add the porcini and cook over low heat for about 10 minutes, until the porcini are soft in texture. Raise the heat and brown the sausage and cook the porcini for about 2 minutes. Remove the pan from the heat, add the white wine, and quickly return the pan to the stove. Keep warm.

3 Cook the fresh pasta in the boiling water for about 1 minute, until just short of al dente. Drain (preserving some of the cooking water) and transfer to the sauce, adding the cheese and about $1/2$ cup of the pasta cooking water. Toss the pasta in the pan to amalgamate the sauce, pasta, and cheese. Taste for salt and add more to taste.

4 Add the parsley, toss the pasta a few more times, and remove the pan from the stove. If you like spicy food, tear the chile pepper into small pieces and toss with the pasta to taste. Remove the garlic cloves before serving.

PASTA RIBBONS *with* PORK RAGÙ

{ *Pasta con Ragù di Maiale e Ricotta* }

LASAGNI CU RAÙ RI MAIALI E RICOTTA

*This typical Christmas dish traditionally hails from Modica, a splendid Baroque city in the southeast corner of the island, known for its centuries-old chocolate production (see page 318). Although typically prepared with an egg-based fresh pasta, it is also delicious with bitter cocoa-flavored pasta ribbons, which add another layer of flavor. The tomato-based ragù contains both pulled pork and sausage meat, but many home cooks add meat rolls (page 264) or meatballs as well to cook while the meat braises, so that one single dish contains both a pasta and a main course. Some cooks prepare the ragù using pork skin (*cotenna di maiale*) instead of sausage, or with veal pieces instead of the pork butt.*

Serves 4

2 tablespoons lard or unsalted butter

1/2 pound pork butt, cut into 3-inch chunks

1/4 pound plain sausage meat, casings removed

2 cups Soffritto (page 40)

2 garlic cloves, crushed

1/2 cup tomato paste

1 1/2 cups full-bodied red wine

1 cup Meat Broth (page 146)

1 cinnamon stick

3 whole cloves

1 tablespoon fennel seeds

2 bay leaves

1 tablespoon whole black peppercorns

Salt

1 pound fresh Hard Wheat Pasta Dough with Egg (page 192) or Cocoa Pasta (variation on page 193), cut into 1 1/2-inch-wide lasagne ribbons

1 cup fresh ricotta, at room temperature

1 In a large heavy-bottomed pot, heat the lard over medium to high heat. Add the pork and sear on each side until a brown crispy outer layer is formed. Make sure to leave adequate space between the pieces so that they do not steam instead of searing. It's important to get an adequate brown on each side so that the meat flavors lock into each chunk. Remove the pork chunks from the pot and add the sausage meat. Cook, stirring briskly, until the sausage browns. Add the soffritto and return the seared pork cubes to the pot, along with the garlic and tomato paste. Using a wooden spoon, stir all the elements together until the tomato paste starts to darken slightly in color, 2 to 3 minutes. Add the wine, and scape any stuck pieces of meat or tomato paste from the bottom of the pan as the wine evaporates.

2 Add the broth along with 4 cups water. Wrap the cinnamon stick, cloves, fennel seeds, bay leaves, and peppercorns in some cheesecloth, tie with a piece of butcher's twine, and add to the pot. Bring to a boil, then reduce the heat to low, cover, and let cook for about 3 hours, until the pork is very tender. Throughout the cooking process, constantly check on the sauce, and use the wooden spoon to make sure that nothing sticks to the bottom of the pot. About halfway through the cooking time, add salt to taste. When done, the meat will be very tender, and will shred into pieces easily with a fork.

3 Remove the pork, shred all the chunks, then return the meat to the ragù, adding a touch of hot water if the sauce appears too thick. Remove and discard the cheesecloth containing the spices. Keep the ragù warm over low heat while preparing the pasta.

4 Bring a pot of salted water to a boil over high heat. Add the fresh pasta to the boiling water and cook for about 1 minute, until just short of al dente. Drain the pasta and transfer to the hot ragù. Taste the sauce to see if it needs any additional salt, then toss the pasta gently with the ragù until well combined.

5 Transfer to serving plates and place a dollop of ricotta on top of each plate. Serve immediately.

Stuffed Pasta

Ravioli are the most common type of stuffed pasta. They can be prepared round, when formed with ravioli cutters, or they can be cut into square shapes with a pasta knife, which resembles a small pizza cutter. Ravioli are relatively easy to make in batches and can be prepared in advance and held for a day in the refrigerator. However, they should be well sprinkled with durum wheat flour before refrigeration.

Other types of stuffed pasta—caramelle, which resemble wrapped caramels, and tortelli, which resemble hats—need to be formed individually by hand, and in Sicily are more commonly found in restaurants than in home kitchens.

RICOTTA RAVIOLI

{ Ravioli Ripieni di Ricotta }

RAVIOLI RI RICOTTA

Ravioli are typical all throughout Italy, but they are a specialty in Sicily, where they are commonly prepared with sheep's milk ricotta. In the province of Ragusa, sweetened ricotta is stuffed inside ravioli and served with a meaty pork ragù. Traditionally, the ricotta filling is laced with sugar to help balance the salty pork sauce.

When served with tomato sauce, ravioli are commonly stuffed with minted ricotta, devoid of spices and sugar. Both filling recipes follow, but I encourage you to experiment by preparing ricotta-based stuffings with your favorite Sicilian flavors, just as chefs do around the island. Try adding basil to the ricotta and serving it with tomato sauce and fried eggplants.

If it's readily available from your cheesemonger, use sheep's milk ricotta to make the filling, which will impart a flavor and consistency reminiscent of Sicily.

Makes about 40 ravioli (serves 4 to 6)

1 recipe Hard Wheat Pasta Dough with Egg (page 192)

Filling of choice (opposite)

2 egg yolks, beaten

Remilled semola flour, for dusting the work surface and ravioli

1 Roll out the dough into eight 8 by 25-inch sheets with a hand-cranked pasta machine, following the instructions on page 197. Place the sheets on a lightly floured work surface.

2 Spoon 10 mounds of the filling by the tablespoon onto one sheet of pasta, keeping the mounds 3 inches away from each other. The filling should be in rounded mounds that take up no more than 2 inches of space. Brush a thin layer of the beaten egg yolks in a circle around each mound. Place a second sheet of pasta directly on top. Use your fingertips to gently press together the top sheet and the bottom sheet in the egg-washed spots that surround the mounds of filling. The egg will help the top and bottom sheets stick to each other. Using a hand-held ravioli cutter (see Sources, page 326), cut out ravioli shapes one by one, pressing down on the dough surrounding the mounds of filling so that the filling is contained. Repeat with the remaining 6 sheets of pasta and the filling to make about 40 ravioli.

3 Dust the ravioli with flour, spread them out on a baking sheet, and let them sit for 30 minutes. If the kitchen is hot, place the baking sheet in the refrigerator. The ravioli can be held in the refrigerator for up to 2 days or frozen for up to 1 week.

4 Bring a pot of salted water to a boil. Delicately place the ravioli in the boiling water in batches. Cook until the ravioli float to the top of the pot, usually about 2 minutes. Using a slotted spoon, transfer the cooked ravioli to their sauce and cook for another minute in the sauce before serving.

Spiced Sweet Ricotta Filling

Toss ravioli stuffed with this filling with pork ragù (page 202) and top with additional grated ragusano *cheese.*

1 large egg

1 tablespoon sugar

1 teaspoon salt

$^1\!/_2$ pound strained ricotta

1 tablespoon finely chopped fresh marjoram

$^1\!/_8$ teaspoon ground cinnamon

1 cup grated *ragusano* cheese

In a mixing bowl, beat the egg with the sugar and salt. Add the ricotta, marjoram, cinnamon, and grated cheese and mix well with a rubber spatula. Store covered in the refrigerator for up to 1 day.

Minted Ricotta Filling

Toss ravioli stuffed with this filling with a simple tomato sauce (page 172) or a walnut pesto.

1 large egg

1 teaspoon salt

$^3\!/_4$ pound strained ricotta

2 tablespoons finely chopped fresh mint

In a mixing bowl, beat the egg with the salt. Add the ricotta and mint and mix well with a rubber spatula. Store covered in the refrigerator for up to 1 day.

Hand-formed Pasta

There are numerous traditional Sicilian hand-formed pastas, the making of which has been passed down from generation to generation. The techniques of forming *maccheroni* (medium-length tubular pasta) and busiate have been shared, mother to daughter, over the decades. Today, however, such pastas are usually prepared only on feast days and have become a dying art. Some shapes do live on, as they have a dried pasta version. For instance, *ziti*, meaning "betrothed" in Sicilian dialect, once referred to a tubular-shaped pasta served at celebrations for engagements and weddings. Today, ziti are, of course, a common cut of dried pasta.

In the province of Ragusa, *maccarruna a ciazzisa* are prepared one at a time by folding the flap of a square piece of dough around the pointer finger and sealing the dough with the other hand. In some families of noble lineage, each piece of pasta was pressed on a stencil containing the family's coat of arms. This type of pasta was typically cooked in a pork broth. Also prepared in the province of Ragusa is a small pasta that resembles wheat grains, called *pizziliatieddi*. It is prepared by sliding pieces of dough between the thumb and pointer fingers. A similar pasta, a *pasta rattata*, is made by rubbing pasta dough on a hand-held grater.

Cavati, also known as *cavatieddi*, are prepared by forming an indentation inside a small chunk of dough. Instead of preparing cavati by hand, you can purchase an inexpensive hand-cranked machine that turns logs of dough into individual pieces. Dried cavati are also available and are delicious with a sauce prepared with lightly cooked swordfish cubes, sautéed eggplant, fresh mint, garlic, cherry tomatoes, and extra-virgin olive oil.

BUSIATE

Busiate, one of the island's classic pasta shapes, owe their name to the busa, *or knitting needle. This short, thin spiral is traditionally made by twisting pieces of dough around a very thin piece of hard grass that grows in the wild in the Sicilian countryside, but using a knitting needle (busa) is common as well. In my grandmother's village, the name of this pasta is shorter,* busi. *But because it is so labor-intensive to make, nowadays it is commonly found as a dry pasta. (If busiate are unavailable, gemelli or casarecce are good substitutes.) In Trapani, busiate are traditionally tossed with Trapanese Pesto (page 39). It also pairs well with these sauces: tomato sauce (page 172), or pasta with tuna (page 175).*

**1 recipe Hard Wheat
Pasta Dough without Egg
(page 193)**

1 Cut the dough into chunks about the size of a fist.

2 Roll out each chunk of dough into long logs the thickness of a cigarette. Cut the long dough logs into 3-inch pieces. Press a well-floured knitting needle or a wooden skewer into each piece of dough lengthwise to create an indentation. Roll the needle or skewer briskly, allowing the pasta to form around the tool.

3 Using your hand, remove the pasta from the tool. Repeat with all the other pieces of dough.

4 Spread the pasta out on a lightly floured surface and let it dry for about 30 minutes before cooking. This helps prevent the pasta from sticking together. You can also cover the pasta in plastic wrap and refrigerate it for up to 2 days before cooking.

GRATED PASTA *with* PUMPKIN *and* FRESH RICOTTA

{ *Pasta Grattata con Zucca Rossa e Ricotta* }

PASTA RATTATA CÀ CUCUZZA RUSSA E RICOTTA

Grated pasta is reminiscent of a risotto and should be cooked in a similar fashion. The tiny pieces of pasta do not need to be cooked in boiling water. Rather, they can be cooked directly with the pumpkin and broth, allowing the starches inside the pasta to thicken the sauce. This pasta is not actually grated (although it looks like it has been), but instead formed by rubbing pasta dough between the palms of your hands.

Serves 4

1 pound Hard Wheat Pasta Dough without Egg (page 193)

1/2 pound unpeeled pumpkin or butternut squash, seeds removed and cut into chunks

1 teaspoon grated nutmeg

1/2 teaspoon salt, plus more as needed

1/2 cup olive oil, for frying the sage leaves

12 fresh sage leaves

2 tablespoons extra-virgin olive oil, plus a touch more for drizzling

1 large onion, thinly sliced

3 cups Chicken Broth or Vegetable Broth (page 147), heated

1/2 cup grated aged pecorino cheese

1 cup strained ricotta cheese, at room temperature

1 Cut the dough into small pieces, about the diameter of a quarter. Over a large bowl or sheet pan, rub each piece of dough between the palms of your hands, breaking the dough into small particles. Allow the pieces to fall onto the sheet pan. Continue until the entire batch of dough is broken down into small pieces, each about the size of a blueberry. To further break down the pasta pieces, place handfuls between the palms of your hands and continue to rub the pasta together, until each piece is around the size of a peppercorn. Dust the pasta with some flour and let it sit at room temperature to dry out while you prepare the pumpkin. Or you can cover the pasta in plastic wrap and refrigerate for up to 2 days before cooking.

2 Preheat the oven to 375°F. Sprinkle the pumpkin pieces with the nutmeg and salt. Arrange in a single layer on a baking sheet and roast for about 30 minutes, until the squash pulp is soft. Scrape the pumpkin flesh off the peel with a spoon. Transfer the flesh to a bowl, mash it, and hold until ready to use.

3 While the squash is roasting, heat the 1/2 cup olive oil in a saucepan over high heat. Fry 8 of the sage leaves in the hot oil until they shrivel up, less than 1 minute. Drain on paper towels and hold for the garnish.

4 In a heavy-bottomed saucepan, heat the 2 tablespoons extra-virgin olive oil over low heat. Add the onion and cook until translucent. Add the mashed pumpkin, 2 cups of the broth, the 2 remaining sage leaves, and the pasta. Raise the heat to medium and using a wooden spoon, stir for 1 minute. Add the pecorino and continue to cook and stir for 5 minutes, adding more broth to the pot if it becomes dry. Taste a piece of the pasta. The pasta should be cooked through, and the sauce should be moist but well reduced to coat the pasta. When it is finished cooking, taste for salt and add accordingly, then stir in the room-temperature ricotta. Serve immediately, garnished with the fried sage leaves and a drizzle of extra-virgin olive oil.

LITTLE GNOCCHI *with* BEEF RAGÙ *and* CHEESE FONDUTA

{ *Chicche al Ragù e Formaggio* }

CHICCHE AU RAÙ E CACIU

Chicche are about half the size of gnocchi. They are usually prepared only with potato and flour, like gnocchi, but in this recipe, roasted eggplant is added to the dough, contributing a pleasantly bitter flavor profile that contrasts with the rich ragù and the creaminess of the fonduta (Italy's version of fondue, which is used as a sauce, rather than for dipping). The ragù can also be enjoyed separately, tossed with homemade tagliatelle (page 193). Start the recipe at least a day before you intend to serve it, as the beef needs to marinate overnight.

Serves 8

Chicche

Salt

4 Yukon gold potatoes, peeled and cut into 2-inch chunks

1 large egg, beaten

$^1\!/_2$ cup grated Parmesan cheese

1 cup all-purpose flour, plus more for dusting

Beef ragù

$^1\!/_4$ cup unsweetened cocoa powder

$^1\!/_2$ cup olive oil, plus more for cooking

2 pounds beef short ribs, on the bone

1 cup Soffritto (page 40)

2 garlic cloves, lightly crushed with your fist

2 cups full-bodied red wine

About 4 cups Meat Broth (page 146)

1 cinnamon stick

2 sprigs fresh rosemary

3 bay leaves

1 bunch fresh thyme

A few fresh sage leaves

Salt

Pecorino cheese fonduta

2 cups milk

2 tablespoons unsalted butter

$^1\!/_4$ pound mixed Sicilian cheeses (such as pecorino, *primo sale, vastedda, piacentino, ragusano*, or *provola*), coarsely grated

1 egg yolk

Salt

To assemble

Pat of butter

Salt

1 FOR THE CHICCHE: Bring the potatoes to a boil in a large pot of salted water. Reduce the heat and cook for around 10 minutes, until the potatoes can be easily pierced with the tip of a knife. Drain, cool slightly, and then press the potatoes through a ricer.

2 In a mixing bowl, combine the potatoes, 1 teaspoon salt, the beaten egg, Parmesan, and flour. Form the dough into a ball and cut it into 8 smaller rounds of dough. Roll out each round separately to form long logs that are between $^1\!/_2$ and 1 inch thick. Using a knife, cut the logs into tiny pieces, about $^1\!/_2$ inch thick. Place the *chicche* on a baking sheet sprinkled with flour. Sprinkle more flour on top of the *chicche* and place the baking sheet in the refrigerator while you make the ragù. (You may prepare the *chicche* in advance up to this point: They will keep, covered with plastic wrap, in the refrigerator for up to 2 days or in the freezer for up to 1 week.)

3 FOR THE RAGÙ: Mix the cocoa powder with the olive oil, then rub the mixture all over the beef. Cover and refrigerate overnight.

continued ↓

4 Preheat the oven to 350°F. Heat a heavy-bottomed Dutch oven over high heat until hot. Add a touch of oil. In batches so as not to crowd the pan, add the pieces of beef and sear on all sides, turning with tongs. The meat should brown on the surface. (To sear correctly, make sure that the pot is very hot but is not smoking; smoking indicates that you need to lower the heat slightly. Do not sear all pieces of meat at the same time and make sure they are not too close together, or else they will steam instead of sear.) When all the pieces are seared, return all the beef to the pot, add the soffrito and garlic, and then the wine. Using a wooden spoon, scrape up all the tasty caramelized bits from the bottom of the pot. Add enough broth to cover the meat, along with the cinnamon stick, rosemary, bay leaves, thyme, and sage. Bring to a boil, then reduce the heat to low, cover, and transfer the Dutch oven to the oven. Bake for 1 hour.

5 Add about 1 tablespoon sea salt after 1 hour. You can always add more later to taste. Continue to cook until the meat is so soft it is literally falling off the bone, an additional 2 to 3 hours. At this point, most of the liquid will have reduced and evaporated, but the precise cook time will depend on the exact temperature of your oven.

6 Let the meat cool, then pull it off the bone. The best way to do so is with your hands (using cooking gloves, if you prefer), gently tearing the meat from the bone. Short ribs often contain a gelatinous outer layer, which should be removed and discarded. Add the pulled shreds of meat to the remaining braising liquid. Discard any bay leaves or herb stems that remain intact. (You may prepare the ragù in advance; it will keep, covered in the refrigerator, for up to 3 days.)

7 FOR THE FONDUTA: In a heavy-bottomed saucepan over medium heat, bring the milk and butter to a boil, then reduce the heat to low. Add the grated cheeses to the milk and let the cheeses melt and the liquid reduce by half. In a mixing bowl, whisk the egg yolk. Add a touch of the cheese mixture to the yolk and whisk well to temper the yolk. Whisk the yolk mixture into the sauce in the saucepan and add salt to taste. The amount of salt needed will vary depending on the type of cheeses you've used. Whisk well and remove from the stovetop. (You may prepare the fonduta in advance; it will keep in an airtight glass container in the refrigerator for up to 2 days.)

8 TO ASSEMBLE: In a sauté pan, warm up the ragù. If there's not much liquid, add some more meat broth or water.

9 Bring a pot of salted water to a boil. Add the *chicche* and cook until they float to the top, only a few minutes, then remove them gently with a slotted spoon or strainer.

10 Add the *chicche* to the ragù. Add a small pat of butter and let the contents of the pan coat the *chicche*.

11 Meanwhile, gently reheat the fonduta. (This is optional, but right before plating the pasta, I like to whip the fonduta with an electric mixer or immersion blender, which makes it airier and lighter.)

12 Spoon some of the fonduta on the bottom of each serving plate. Top with spoonfuls of the *chicche* and ragù and serve immediately.

HANDMADE COUSCOUS

{ *Couscous* }

CUSCUSU

*On the western coast of Sicily, in the province of Trapani and the surrounding islands such as Favignana, a territory with frequent social and historical ties to Tunisia and Libya, couscous (*cuscusu *in dialect), is one of the most iconic dishes.* Cuscusu *is simply semolina worked by hand with water so that the milled grain forms tiny clusters in a process known as the* incocciata. *The tiny semolina bunches are steamed in a special glazed clay pot, known as a* cuscussiera. *Unlike North African versions of couscous, Trapanese-style* cuscusu *is prepared with a fish broth and topped with an array of chunks of fish and prawns. It is a fun process to prepare couscous by hand, but if you're not excited to undertake the task, it's fine to use the store-bought version.*

In some parts of the province of Trapani, around the cities of Marsala and Mazara del Vallo, semolina is rolled with water and egg yolk into slightly larger balls, known as frascàtuli, *which are reminiscent of Sardinia's* fregula. Frascàtuli *are cooked with seafood or can be accompanied by a cauliflower soup with chickpeas, beans, carrots, and other vegetables.*

About 1 pound dried couscous

2 cups semolina (see page 86)	1 tablespoon extra-virgin olive oil
1¹/₂ teaspoons salt	

1 Pour the semolina onto a clean work surface or into a large bowl. Add about 1 teaspoon of the salt.

2 Dissolve the remaining ¹/₂ teaspoon salt in 4 cups water and drizzle the oil into the water. Sprinkle the semolina with the mixture.

3 Stir the semolina with your hands, collecting dry grains from the edges of the bowl, adding more water as needed, until the grains have swelled to about five times in size.

4 Spread out the moist semolina on a tablecloth. Let the couscous dry out for a few hours before cooking. It should be cooked within 1 day.

SEAFOOD COUSCOUS

{ Couscous di Pesce }

CUSCUSU RI PISCI

For this recipe, either prepare your own (see opposite) or purchase prepared couscous. If opting for the latter, I suggest a hand-rolled Tunisian couscous from Les Moulins Mahjoub (see Sources, page 326). Their couscous is made in the traditional Berber style in Tunisia, and although it is larger in cluster size than Sicily's typical couscous, it most resembles the taste of homemade. This recipe instructs how to cook couscous in a nontraditional style, without a classic clay pot, but rather by cooking the couscous directly on the stovetop. The best type of fish to use is monkfish tail, grouper, or scorpion fish.

Serves 4

2 pounds white-fleshed fish, filleted with bones carefully removed and cut into chunks

1 onion, cut in chunks

1 celery stalk, cut in chunks

1 carrot, cut in chunks

1 cup tomato sauce (page 172)

1 bunch fresh parsley

1 teaspoon whole black peppercorns

2 bay leaves

1 cinnamon stick

Salt

¾ pound couscous

1 tablespoon extra-virgin olive oil

1 teaspoon saffron threads

¼ cup slivered almonds, toasted

1 In a large stockpot, combine the fish, onion, celery, carrot, tomato sauce, parsley, peppercorns, bay leaves, and cinnamon stick. Add about 2 cups water to cover all the ingredients. Bring to a boil over high heat, then reduce the heat to low and simmer for 5 minutes, until the fish flakes easily when prodded with a fork. Use about 1 teaspoon of salt to season the broth to taste. Hold the fish in the broth while cooking the couscous.

2 Combine about 1 cup of the broth, the couscous, olive oil, and saffron in a heavy-bottomed saucepan and heat over medium heat. Simmer, briskly stirring with a wooden spoon and adding more hot broth as needed, until the couscous is fluffy and tender to the bite. The cooking time and amount of broth needed will depend on the size of the clusters. Regular commercial couscous will take about 5 minutes, but Tunisian couscous (see above) can take up to 10 minutes. When the couscous is cooked, taste and add more salt if needed. Since the broth is salted, the couscous should need little to no extra salt.

3 Spoon the couscous onto a platter and top with pieces of fish from the broth and additional broth. Finally, top with the almonds and serve immediately while hot.

Chapter 7

VEGETABLES

MULTIPLE VOLUMES could be written about the vegetable bounty of the island. Many vegetables are associated with specific geographical areas of Sicily. For example, cherry tomatoes are considered of the highest quality when they come from Pachino, even though they are grown all over the island. Purple cauliflower, on the other hand, is a specialty of Mount Etna. Tiny spiny artichokes hail from Menfi. While this chapter includes only recipes based on these sorts of cultivated vegetables (which are also available outside Sicily), I also want to underscore the importance of the wild herbs and greens that grow in abundance in the Sicilian countryside.

At Feudo Montoni, I've discovered that I could cook all year round with the greens that grow spontaneously on the property. When I first moved to Sicily, I spent my Saturdays in the countryside at the winery. I used to take long walks and observe the wild plants that were growing in the area. Every week I noticed that new plants would sprout up, creating new aromas in the fields. During my first fall and winter here, I discovered—all in the wild—purslane, chard, fennel, honeysuckle, wild broccoli (known most commonly in dialect as *cavuliceddi*), mustard greens, arugula, malva, and stinging nettles (which lose their sting when cooked). When spring rolled along, mint, celery, borage, cardoons, tall asparagus, and chamomile popped up. Luckily, I was able to recognize many of the less common plants because, back in New York, I used to purchase many of them from Blooming Hill Farm. Others I learned to recognize after chatting with elders from the area who traditionally ate these wild vegetables.

These elders would often instruct me to thoroughly boil the wild greens, but I found this leached away too much of their intense flavor. Instead, I like to cook them this way: First I lightly sauté some finely chopped onion with an abundant amount of extra-virgin olive oil, then I add a finely chopped mixture of about three different types of greens. I add just enough water to cover the greens, then let them cook until the water fully evaporates. I finish by sautéing everything in the pan for another 5 to 8 minutes. I enjoy eating this on its own or as a condiment for pasta. Occasionally, I even add some finely chopped pancetta for additional flavor, but the greens exude such an aroma that they really need no embellishment.

You could say that the wild plants became an obsession for me, and still are, along with the numerous varieties of vegetables in my garden that rotate throughout the year. Today at the winery, I lead guests into the garden and around the property, instructing them when vegetables are ready for harvest and which wild herbs to pick before we go back to the kitchen to cook with them.

The "Truncated" Cabbage

Kohlrabi, known as *cavolo trunzu* (literally "truncated cabbage") in Sicily, is highly prized in the cuisine of the province of Catania, and grows most commonly around the town of Acireale. This round, white root vegetable (part of the cabbage family) has an outer layer tinged with a violet hue and green leaves that grow above the ground. The root can be stuffed or eaten raw in salads. The greens are used along with the root to prepare pasta, most commonly with some garlic and tomato pulp. There is even a variation of pasta with sardines (page 181) that features kohlrabi. For a salad featuring kohlrabi, which is readily available outside Sicily nowadays, cut the root into small matchstick-sized pieces. Add some carrots and apple (also ingredients that grow in Sicily), cut in the same shape and size. Toss with a red wine vinaigrette and serve immediately.

TWICE-COOKED FAVA BEANS

{ *Fave Sbuciate Due Volte* }

FAVI PIZZICATI A DU VOTI

Last spring, friends invited me for dinner, mentioning beforehand that they had made la frittedda, *a classic Sicilian preparation incorporating stewed fava beans, artichokes, peas, spring onions, and wild fennel. My grandmother often prepared this dish when the ingredients came in season. But I was in for a surprise: When the pot came from the kitchen, it contained only fava beans—a reminder to me that often the name of a dish is irrelevant in Sicily, as preparations can undergo countless adaptations. This* la frittedda *was their family's* la frittedda, *which was, needless to say, completely different from my family's.*

Ultimately, I decided to include their luscious version here, which they also call favi pizzicati due volte, *"twice-peeled fava beans," to convey that the fava beans are first removed from their pods, cooked, and then removed from the shell encasing the beans. This is a dish that so elegantly expresses the simplicity of Sicilian cuisine, the abundance of the fruits of the land, and the clear ingenuity behind the country's peasant cooking. With some crusty bread on the side for sopping, this makes an excellent light supper.*

An important factor when purchasing fava beans for this dish is that they should not be too mature, as older beans become tough and dry. Young fava beans are much more tender and break down more easily during the cooking process, transforming into a creamy mash. However, the window for young fava beans is very short. To the untrained eye, identifying young versus older pods can be challenging, since the differences are subtle. It's best to buy them at a local farmers' market and ask the farmer to confirm what stage they are in.

Serves 4

4 pounds fresh fava beans
Salt

2 cups Vegetable Broth (page 147)
½ cup extra-virgin olive oil

1 The first step is to remove the fava beans, one by one, from their pods, collecting the beans in a bowl.

2 Place the shelled beans in a pot with about 1 teaspoon salt. Cover with cold water, then place the pot over high heat. When the water comes to a boil, remove the beans from the pot, using a slotted spoon, and put them in a bowl of cold water so that they cool quickly.

3 Using your thumb and pointer finger, gently squeeze each fava bean, one by one, releasing the inner segments from the shell. Discard the shells and place the inner segments in another pot, along with the broth and olive oil. Bring to a boil, reduce the heat, and simmer, stirring occasionally. Cook for about 15 minutes, until the fava beans become completely tender and start to fall apart. In the process, the oil and broth should emulsify with some of the beans to create a creamy base for the dish. Serve immediately.

CUCUMBER *and* TOMATO SALAD

{ Insalata di Pomodoro e Cocomero }

'NSALATA RI PUMADORU E CUCUMMERU

In Sicily, salads are served as side dishes to main courses rather than as appetizers. In restaurants, lettuce-based salads are commonly served plain, with the condiments for dressing the salad on the side.

When dressing a salad composed of lettuce greens, a lemon vinaigrette is most classic. Simply add lemon juice to your salad followed by salt to taste, which will dissolve into the lemon juice. Then drizzle with a fine extra-virgin olive oil. I like a one-to-one ratio of lemon to olive oil.

Bitter greens such as escarole, chicory, and dandelion make regular appearances on the Sicilian table, and can be sautéed or made into a salad. I find that these bitter leaves are better suited to a vinegar-based vinaigrette.

The following salad should be made without exact measurements. I like to use equal parts of cucumber and tomato. In Sicily, I use a variety of cucumber that is similar to a Persian cucumber and that has a strong floral aroma. You can add basil, mint, and/or parsley to the salad, depending on your taste. In Sicily, the vinegar I procure is strong, so a little goes a long way.

The best way to prepare a dressing for this salad is to add a touch of red wine vinegar and a pinch of salt and stir the salad, then taste it and add more vinegar or salt accordingly. Finally, add extra-virgin olive oil.

Cucumber, peeled and seeded

Ripe tomatoes, cut into bite-sized chunks

Vinegar

Salt

Extra-virgin olive oil

In a mixing bowl, toss the cucumber and tomatoes. Add the vinegar and salt to taste. Add olive oil and toss again. Serve immediately.

A TOUCH OF SMOKE

Many types of vegetables taste delicious when cooked over charcoal, because the grilling process concentrates the flavors while caramelizing the natural sugars and adding a touch of smoky flavor. Grilled vegetables are eaten as side dishes in Sicily, or they may be preserved in oil to enjoy later. Eggplants and zucchini are two vegetables that are commonly grilled and preserved in olive oil. Try serving grilled vegetables (either hot or at room temperature) with a drizzle of *salmoriglio* (page 41) or with Trapanese Pesto (page 39). Corn, which is not commonly associated with Sicilian cuisine, is grilled in Palermo as a street food in late summer when it's in season.

SQUASH BLOSSOMS STUFFED *with* RICOTTA

{ *Fiori di Zucca Ripieni con Ricotta* }

CIURI RI CUCUZZA RICHINI CÀ RICOTTA

During summer months, squash blossoms are ubiquitous in vegetable gardens. I've found they are best picked early in the morning when they are firm and open, as the hot Sicilian sun tends to dry them up as the day rolls along. To pick, gently remove them from the tip of the squash. Before cooking, they need to be cleaned with care. First, check inside for any insects (or animals—once I found a baby frog hiding in a flower), and then remove the thick inner pistil with your fingertips. Place the flowers in a colander and lightly rinse them with water. To dry, do not use a towel, but rather place the colander in a sunny spot of your kitchen or patio and let them air dry.

Sicilians traditionally prepare stuffed squash blossoms in two styles: They are coated in a batter then fried in olive oil. Or, as described here, they go into the oven, which I prefer because I find the delicate taste of the blossom comes through more. Stuffings abound as well. Another version I often prepare includes a piece of soft primo sale *cheese (see page 64) and a basil leaf.*

Serves 4

12 squash blossoms	1 large egg, beaten
1/2 pound ricotta	1 teaspoon salt
1/2 cup grated Parmesan cheese	Ground black pepper
2 tablespoons finely chopped fresh parsley	1 tablespoon olive oil

1 Preheat the oven to 300°F. Clean the squash blossoms delicately with a damp soft dishtowel, and remove the pistils with your fingertips.

2 In a mixing bowl, use a rubber spatula to fold together the ricotta, Parmesan, parsley, egg, salt, and pepper to taste.

3 Fill the inside of each blossom with about 2 tablespoons of the stuffing. The easiest way to do so is to place the stuffing inside a pastry bag without a pastry tip. Or place the filling in a resealable plastic bag and cut off one corner. Place the tip of the pastry bag or the corner of the plastic bag inside the blossom and squeeze the stuffing inside to fill. Make sure the petals completely enclose the stuffing.

4 Drizzle the olive oil on a baking sheet and place the stuffed blossoms on top. Turn them to coat with the oil, then bake for about 10 minutes, until the flowers are wilted around the hot filling. Serve immediately.

STUFFED VEGETABLES

{ Ripieni per Ortaggi }

CONZA RI ORTAGGI

Stuffed vegetables are a common main course in Sicily. It's a basic technique that is endlessly adaptable, a great trick to keep in your repertoire to turn to again and again depending on which vegetable is in season. Here I offer a few simple templates to get you started.

While there are countless recipes for stuffing, most fall into the category of a meat stuffing or a breadcrumb stuffing. Both types are delicious, but very different in texture as well as taste. The meat stuffing is more compact and spongier, but smoother in texture and sweeter in taste, due to the addition of raisins and onions. The breadcrumb stuffing is saltier due to the grated cheese, capers, and olives, and has a grainy and crunchy texture. Some cooks like to replace the anchovy paste in the breadcrumb stuffing with 2 tablespoons sausage meat (page 265).

Stuffed Bell Peppers

Serves 4

1 tablespoon extra-virgin olive oil

4 long pointed peppers or bell peppers (green, yellow, or red)

Meat or Breadcrumb Stuffing (page 224)

1 Preheat the oven to 350°F. Grease a large baking pan with the oil.

2 With the point of a paring knife, cut out the stem of each pepper and discard. Cut off the top 1 inch or so of each pepper and reserve. Clean out all the seeds from inside the peppers with the point of the paring knife. Rinse the peppers out with water if any seeds remain stuck inside.

3 Use either stuffing to stuff the peppers entirely. Place the top pieces back on the peppers and use a wooden or metal skewer to pierce each top and attach it to the stuffed body of the pepper. If using long pointed peppers, lay them down on their side in the baking pan. If using bell peppers, stand them up on the pan. (You can prepare the peppers up to this point several hours in advance and hold them in the refrigerator.)

4 Bake for about 30 minutes, until the peppers are soft and the skin starts to turn darker in color. Serve immediately.

Stuffed Artichokes

Serves 4

8 large artichokes

Breadcrumb Stuffing (page 224), prepared without the capers, dried tomatoes, or *provola* cheese)

Juice of 1 lemon

2 tablespoons extra-virgin olive oil

1 Preheat the oven to 350°F.

2 Remove the stems of the artichokes with a paring knife, creating a flat bottom for the vegetables to stand on. Hit the artichokes on each side on a countertop in order to loosen up the leaves. Using a sharp serrated knife, cut off the top inch of the artichokes and discard. Using a paring knife, remove the inner leaves and the choke from the inside of each artichoke.

3 Insert the breadcrumb stuffing inside the artichokes with a spoon.

continued ↓

4 Put $\frac{1}{2}$ inch of water and the lemon juice in a large baking pan. Place the stuffed artichokes in the pan and drizzle the olive oil on top of them. Cover with aluminum foil and bake for about 20 minutes. Remove the foil and continue baking for another 30 minutes, until the artichokes are soft to the touch. Not all of the water will have evaporated. Remove the artichokes from the baking pan, discarding the remaining water, and serve immediately.

Meat Stuffing

Makes about 6 cups (enough for 8 peppers, 8 small eggplants, or 8 zucchini)

2 cups caramelized onions (see page 103), finely chopped

2 cups Dried Tomatoes (homemade, page 73, or store-bought), roughly chopped

1 pound ground beef

$\frac{1}{4}$ cup golden raisins or dried currants, soaked in red or white wine for about 1 hour

$\frac{1}{4}$ cup pine nuts

$\frac{1}{2}$ cup coarse breadcrumbs (page 42)

$\frac{1}{4}$ cup finely chopped fresh parsley leaves

4 tablespoons extra-virgin olive oil

$\frac{1}{2}$ cup grated aged pecorino cheese

1 teaspoon salt, or more to taste

Ground black pepper

Combine all of the ingredients in a mixing bowl and mix well with a spatula to incorporate. To taste for salt, prepare a small patty, about the size of a quarter, and cook it in a small nonstick pan over medium heat until cooked through. Taste the stuffing for salt and add more accordingly.

Breadcrumb Stuffing

Makes about 6 cups (enough for 8 peppers, 8 small eggplants, 8 zucchini, 8 onions, or 8 artichokes)

3 cups coarse breadcrumbs (see page 42)

2 cups semi-dried tomatoes (page 73), roughly chopped

1 cup grated aged pecorino cheese

$\frac{1}{2}$ cup *provola* cheese cut into $\frac{1}{4}$-inch cubes

1 tablespoon Garlic Paste (page 40)

$\frac{1}{4}$ cup extra-virgin olive oil

$\frac{1}{4}$ cup finely chopped fresh parsley leaves

2 tablespoons dried Sicilian oregano

1 tablespoon salted capers, well rinsed of the salt

4 anchovies, well rinsed of the salt and chopped or ground into a paste

$\frac{1}{2}$ teaspoon salt, or more to taste

Ground black pepper

Combine all of the ingredients in a mixing bowl and mix will with a spatula to incorporate. Taste the stuffing for salt and add more if necessary.

CLOCKWISE FROM TOP LEFT: *Breadcrumb-stuffed artichokes (page 223); meat-stuffed peppers (page 223); Frittata (page 233) with spring vegetables*

SEMOLINA POLENTA

In Sicily's rich and vast cuisine, there exists a meager dish, *frascàtula*, which nowadays is almost forgotten to history. Similar to a corn polenta famous in other parts of Italy, *frascàtula* (not to be confused with the *frascàtuli trapanesi* discussed on page 212) is a dense semolina porridge that is cooked with vegetables. Ancient Romans cooked wheat flour to prepare soups known as *puls*, a precursor to polenta. In the province of Enna, *frascàtula* is widespread and varies from one household to another. Not surprisingly, some areas have different names for the dish. In Nicosia, semolina is mixed with dried beans and is called *picciotta*, while in Troina, the dish is prepared with chickpea and grass pea flour and is known as *piciocia*. In Agrigento and Caltanissetta, *frascàtula* is made with semolina, wild fennel, and pancetta, while in Modica it is cooked simply with olive oil and salt and topped with grated cheese.

To prepare a typical Ennese version of *frascàtula* for four people, start by boiling about 1/2 pound broccoli florets in about 1 gallon salted water until tender. Meanwhile, prepare a soffritto over low heat with about 2 tablespoons olive oil, 2 chopped garlic cloves, some dried spicy chile pepper, and about 1/2 cup diced pancetta. Add the cooked broccoli (do not discard the hot salted cooking water) to the soffritto and cook for an additional few minutes. Add the soffritto mixture to the pot of water and bring to a boil. Add 2 cups semolina flour in a slow and steady stream to the boiling water and stir constantly with a wooden spoon for about 10 minutes, until the mixture turns creamy. Taste to make sure that the sauce does not feel gritty in texture. When serving, drizzle with extra-virgin olive oil.

THE SPINY ARTICHOKES OF MENFI

On the western side of Sicily, around the city of Menfi, artichokes grow in abundance, and, happily, many of the varieties are hybrids with few thorns. For the last few hundred years, a spiny variety of artichoke, known as *carciofi spinosi di Menfi*, has grown in this area as well, but today cultivation is limited to twenty-five acres out of nearly fifteen hundred acres of artichokes. Slow Food has added this variety to its list of protected foods in order to find new markets and increase acreage. The thorns are undoubtedly obstacles for some people, as they require a little patience to remove, but this variety has many other fine qualities: It is aromatic, crisp, and delicate in flavor. Much sought after for grilling, these spiny artichokes are also great for preserving (page 67), or in an artichoke caponata.

For a light dinner, I cut these artichokes in half (after trimming the exterior leaves), then add them to a sauté pan with sautéed garlic, roughly chopped parsley, some extra-virgin olive oil, and water about half way up to the top of the artichokes. When the water evaporates, the artichokes will be cooked through, but let them brown in the sauté pan before serving. I find that a heavy nonstick pan works best for cooking the artichokes in this fashion, so that the leaves brown but do not stick to the pan.

STUFFED ESCAROLE *with* GROUND BEEF, PINE NUTS, *and* GOLDEN RAISINS

{ *Scarola Ripiena* }

SCAROLA AMMUTUNATA

This dish marries the slight bitterness of the escarole greens with the sweet and savory flavors of a beef filling. To prepare escarole for stuffing, it's important to wash the escarole thoroughly while keeping the heads intact. To wash away all dirt and grit, hold each head of escarole by the stem end and immerse the leaves upside down in a tub of water. Shake the escarole in the water until the leaves are free of dirt. There is no need to dry the escarole because the water remaining on the leaves helps in the cooking process.

Serves 4

4 tablespoons
extra-virgin olive oil

4 garlic cloves,
smashed into a paste

3 tablespoons sliced pitted
black or green olives

3 tablespoons golden raisins

2 tablespoons salted
capers, rinsed well

3 tablespoons
pine nuts, toasted

1 pound ground beef

$^{1}/_{2}$ cup coarse breadcrumbs
(page 42)

$^{1}/_{4}$ cup finely chopped
fresh flat-leaf parsley

$^{1}/_{2}$ teaspoon
ground cinnamon

Salt

Freshly ground black pepper

2 small heads escarole
(about 8 ounces each)

1 cup grated aged
pecorino cheese

1 Preheat the oven to 375°F.

2 Pour 2 tablespoons of the olive oil into a skillet over medium heat. Add the garlic and cook for 1 minute, until softened and aromatic. Stir in the olives, raisins, capers, and $1^{1}/_{2}$ tablespoons of the pine nuts and cook for 1 minute more. Stir in the beef and cook for 3 minutes, until the meat is cooked halfway through. Remove the skillet from the heat and mix in $^{1}/_{4}$ cup of the breadcrumbs, the parsley, and cinnamon. Season with $^{1}/_{2}$ teaspoon salt and a pinch or two of pepper.

3 Leaving the stem on, press the leaves down on each head of escarole to flatten. Place half of the ground beef filling in the center of each head. Gather the leaves together and press them closed. Using butcher's twine, secure each head closed by tying them crosswise about 6 times each.

4 Pour 1 tablespoon of the remaining oil into a 9 by 13-inch baking dish. Nestle the escarole into the baking dish, leaving space between the two heads, and pour in 2 cups water. Sprinkle the remaining $^{1}/_{4}$ cup breadcrumbs, the remaining $1^{1}/_{2}$ tablespoons pine nuts, and the pecorino on top of the escarole heads, pressing lightly to adhere, then drizzle the remaining 1 tablespoon oil over the top.

5 Cover the dish with aluminum foil and bake for 30 minutes. Remove the foil and bake for another 8 to 10 minutes, until the rolls are lightly caramelized, the water has evaporated, and the topping is crisp and golden brown. Before serving, cut away the butcher's twine.

THE GIANTS OF MOUNT ETNA

Mount Etna's huge purple cauliflowers, known as *violetta*, can weigh up to several pounds per head. Relatives will often divvy up a single cauliflower to share. These big beauties stand out for their vibrant purple color (which holds up during the cooking process) and a unique flavor, much bolder than that of a regular cauliflower. During the fall and winter, you will see *violetta* in markets around the island (although they're most commonly found in the Mount Etna area), along with green cauliflower (called *broccolo* in Sicilian dialect), white cauliflower, and romanesco.

My favorite way to cook a purple cauliflower is to braise the entire head slowly over low heat in a large pot filled about halfway with some broth, red wine, seared garlic, onion, black olives, and anchovies. After about 45 minutes, when the cauliflower is cooked through (test by placing a paring knife in the core, which should slide in smoothly), I remove it from the pot and top with grated aged pecorino cheese and coarse breadcrumbs. This traditional recipe, prepared during Christmastime, is known as *brocculi affucati*. This recipe can be prepared with green or white cauliflower as well.

Cauliflower is also commonly combined with sausage in Sicily, such as in a baked casserole prepared with layers of boiled cauliflower, sausage, and béchamel—a dish most commonly called *broccolo al fornu*.

CAULIFLOWER FRITTERS

{ *Frittelle di Broccoli* }

FRITTEDDI RI VROCCULI

In some parts of Sicily these fritters are made for Saint Martin's Day (see page 325). This batter can also be used to coat artichoke chunks, leeks stuffed with anchovies, and other vegetables before frying. The wild fennel seeds are sometimes replaced with a pinch of nutmeg and cinnamon. You can also fry the dough alone, or coat pieces of ricotta salata or salted anchovies with the batter and fry them.

Cardoons, a bitter vegetable with a taste reminiscent of artichokes, are ubiquitous in Sicily, and cardoon fritters are traditionally eaten during Christmastime, though they are typically fried with a simple yeast-free flour and water batter called a pastella.

Serves 4

Frittelle batter

1 teaspoon active dry yeast

1 cup warm water

1 cup all-purpose flour

1 large egg, beaten

1 teaspoon salt

1 tablespoon wild
fennel seeds

Cauliflower fritters

1 head cauliflower,
cut into bite-size florets

Vegetable oil, for frying

Salt

1 FOR THE *FRITTELLE* BATTER: Combine the yeast and 3 table-spoons of the warm water in a mixing bowl and let it sit. After 10 minutes, the yeast should be foamy. Add the flour, beaten egg, and the remaining water. Whisk to mix well, then whisk in the salt and wild fennel seeds. Let the batter sit for about 30 minutes before using.

2 FOR THE CAULIFLOWER FRITTERS: In a pot of salted boiling water, cook the cauliflower florets for about 8 minutes, until a paring knife easily slides into a floret. Remove them from the water and let dry on a clean kitchen towel.

3 Heat about 3 inches of vegetable oil in a heavy-bottomed pot over medium to high heat. When the oil reaches 350°F on a deep-fry thermometer, it is ready.

4 Working in batches, place the cauliflower florets in the batter. With a slotted spoon, transfer each floret to the hot oil, shaking off excess batter. Deep-fry until golden brown, 4 to 5 minutes. Remove the fritters from the oil, sprinkle with salt, and place on paper towels to drain off excess oil before serving.

Fritters with Anchovy-Stuffed Leeks

Trim leeks by cutting off the roots, making sure not to cut into the stem. Cut off the green part on the top of the leeks, then slice them in half lengthwise. (The green part can be reserved for making broth.) Place a mixing bowl in the sink and fill it with water. Add the leek halves, top side down, and swish to remove any sand that might be stuck inside the leeks. Bring a large pot of water to a boil. Add the leeks and cook for about 10 minutes, until they are cooked through. Remove from the boiling water and let them dry on a clean kitchen towel. Place one salted anchovy inside each leek slice. Drop in the frittelle batter to coat and deep-fry until golden brown, about 5 minutes.

THE MEAT OF THE EARTH

In Sicily, eggplants are considered "the meat of the earth," and one could argue that they are the most important vegetable in Sicilian cuisine. They are in season in the summer months and are found in multiple varieties. The most common variety found at local markets is called a *violetta nana*, and is round in shape and violet in color. Most Sicilian cooks are familiar with countless recipes that use eggplants. When in season, they are prepared fried, stewed, baked, roasted, stuffed, or grilled. The *ragusano* cream recipe that's paired with the *tenerumi sformato* (page 125) also combines well with the flavor of eggplant. But the absolute simplest way to prepare eggplant is to cut them in cubes or slices, sauté with a bit of olive oil, then spoon over pasta that is tossed with tomato sauce (page 172). They are also delicious when preserved in oil (page 68) and made into caponata (page 74) or savory marmalade for enjoyment all year round.

EGGPLANT "MEATBALLS"

{ *Polpette di Melanzane* }

PURPETTI RI MILINICIANI

In English we translate polpette *as "meatballs," but in Italy* polpette *are prepared with numerous ingredients, not just meat. Here eggplant takes the central role. Another popular* polpetta *is prepared with a base of sardines, either fresh or canned.*

Variations of these eggplant "meatballs" include raisins and pine nuts or a soft cheese filling, such as a chunk of provola *or* primo sale *cheese, which oozes out magnificently when the* polpette *are served hot.*

Serves 4 as an appetizer

1 to 2 whole roasted eggplant, about 1 pound (see page 98)

2 cups fine or coarse breadcrumbs (page 42)

2 tablespoons minced fresh mint or basil (one or the other)

1 egg yolk

$1/2$ cup grated aged pecorino cheese

1 teaspoon Garlic Paste (page 40)

Vegetable oil, for frying

1 Scoop the pulp from the eggplant into a bowl. Add $1/2$ cup of the breadcrumbs, the mint, egg yolk, cheese, and garlic paste and mix well to combine.

2 Using an ice cream scooper, portion out the eggplant mixture into about 20 equal-sized balls. Put the remaining breadcrumbs in a shallow dish and roll the balls in the crumbs to coat.

3 Pour about 3 inches of oil into a skillet and heat over medium to high heat until the oil reaches 350°F on a deep-fry thermometer. Fry the "meatballs," in batches, for about 4 minutes, until golden brown on all sides. Serve immediately.

MARIA'S EGGPLANT CUTLETS

{ *Cotolette di Melanzane di Maria* }

CUTULETTI RI MILINCIANI RI MARIA

It's hard to believe that as a child I didn't enjoy eggplant. I was disturbed by the way the hot flesh burned my tongue, so I refused to eat them or even touch them. In our Sicilian-American household, however, they kept appearing on our table, despite my requests to keep them afar. One summer in my early teens, while feasting in my cousin Maria's kitchen in Sicily, I found something on my dish that resembled a fried chicken cutlet. This golden, breaded patty was oval in shape, nearly 2 inches thick, and smelled toasty and delicious. Grabbing a steak knife, I cut into the flesh of the cutlet and, without looking, I devoured the first bite. As I did so, melted soft cheese came oozing out. Then, I noticed the saltiness of baked ham, which was encased between layers of something sweet and pungent that I had never tasted before. Within moments, I had finished the food on my plate and was requesting another serving. As Maria placed another cutlet on my dish, she smiled and said in Sicilian dialect, "Eggplants, they are the meat of this earth." And so began my fascination with this noble fruit.

Serves 8

2 or 3 eggplants, sliced crosswise in 3/4-inch segments to make 16 slices

8 slices prosciutto cotto (Italian ham)

8 thin slices *primo sale* cheese (or fontina or any other soft, mild cheese)

8 fresh basil leaves

Ground black pepper

2 large eggs

Salt

2 cups fine breadcrumbs (page 42)

Olive oil, for frying

1 On one slice of eggplant, layer a slice of ham, a slice of cheese, and a basil leaf, then sprinkle with black pepper. Top with another slice of eggplant. Continue with the remaining eggplant, ham, and cheese to make 8 eggplant "sandwiches."

2 Beat the eggs in a shallow bowl with a pinch of salt. Place the breadcrumbs on a plate. Dip the stuffed eggplant patties in the egg, then dredge them in the breadcrumbs, covering them completely and being careful to seal the edges together.

3 Pour enough of the oil in a flat heavy-bottomed frying pan to reach a depth of 1/2 inch. Heat the oil over medium to high heat until it reaches 350°F on a deep-fry thermometer. Using a spatula and working in batches, place the breaded eggplant in the oil and fry, turning once, until golden brown, 5 to 7 minutes. Remove from the hot oil and drain on paper towels. Serve immediately.

FRITTATA

{ *Frittata* }

FRITTATA

In Sicily, a frittata is a vegetable dish that is held together with beaten egg so that it resembles a cake. There are several types of frittata that I make with the eggs from my hens (who feed off the vegetable scraps from my kitchen). For the best flavor, seek out eggs from hens that have been raised with access to roam and peck, and avoid the industrially produced ones. One frittata I love is prepared with fresh mint, breadcrumbs, pecorino, and sautéed onion. It is delicious cooked very thin, then rolled and sliced into rings before serving. I serve it in the spring and summer, when mint grows in the wild.

Another favorite is a frittata prepared with thin slices of fried potato. Often, I will fry an extra portion of potatoes with dinner and save them to make a frittata for lunch the next day. (Refrain from rinsing the potatoes after they are sliced, so the starches stay intact and allow them to stick together in the frittata.) Yet another favorite type of frittata features wild vegetables, such as asparagus or broccoli leaves and florets (which can be substituted with broccoli rabe), and sautéed onions.

Unlike the American custom of limiting egg dishes to breakfast time, in Sicily we will eat a frittata as a light lunch or dinner. My grandmother in New York, on the other hand, split the difference: She would often prepare frittata in the mornings, but they were always full of Sicilian flavors. In the spring, after a meal rich in stewed artichoke hearts, fava beans, peas, or spring onions, she would whip the leftovers into a frittata the next day.

You can use any vegetable you choose, but make sure that it is cooked and cut up prior to mixing it with the eggs. The ratio of egg to vegetable is also important. A frittata is not an omelet, meaning that it is not heavy on the egg. For 2 cups cooked vegetables, I use only 4 eggs. For any frittata, a generous amount of freshly grated aged pecorino cheese is highly recommended.

Serves 4 to 6

1 to 2 tablespoons olive oil

8 pasture-raised eggs

1½ teaspoons salt, or less if adding the cheese

4 cups chopped cooked vegetables or 2 cups chopped herbs of your choice

½ cup grated aged pecorino cheese (optional)

1 With a paper towel, rub the olive oil around the bottom and sides of a 6-inch nonstick pan or well-seasoned cast-iron skillet.

2 In a mixing bowl, vigorously whisk together the eggs with the salt. Keep in mind that if you are using the aged cheese, you should go light on the salt. Mix in the vegetables or herbs, stirring to incorporate.

3 Place the prepared pan over low to medium heat and add the egg mixture. Stir rapidly with a spatula or wooden spoon, making sure that none of the egg mixture sticks to the sides of the pan. Do not let the egg mixture brown. When the mixture firms up, turn it over to cook on the other side by flipping it in the pan. If you're concerned about breaking the frittata, follow this procedure: Place a plate on top of the pan, turn the pan upside down, letting the frittata fall out onto the plate, then slide it back in the pan with the cooked side up.

4 Continue cooking for a few minutes on the other side. It is important that the frittata remain custardy and the edges not turn brown. Make sure it does not overcook, which would leave it dry and unpleasant. To test for doneness, press the frittata surface with your fingertips: It should bounce slightly like a drum. Remove from the pan and serve immediately, or let cool and serve at room temperature.

Chapter 8

SEAFOOD

LOOKING OUT from the border of Sant'Anna, my ancestral village, I gaze at hills that resemble a camel's back dotted with a cornucopia of prickly pear bushes, citrus groves, and grayish green olive trees situated in what seem like neverending rows. Nestled in the pastures are winding country roads connecting clusters of limestone structures that form towns. The deep blue Mediterranean Sea melds into the sky during the daytime, making it nearly impossible to locate the horizon. At dusk, the setting sun reflects against the body of water, causing it to appear like a lake of liquid silver.

Framing the landscape, the immense body of water appears so close to Sant'Anna, but in the past, before automobiles were used, such a distance may as well have been worlds apart. Although Sicily is surrounded by the sea, only the seaside port cities historically have a deep-rooted fish-eating culture. Towns such as Sant'Anna in the interior parts of the island had very limited access to seafood, and as tradition would have it, most dishes there are vegetable and meat based.

During summers in Sant'Anna, my exposure to seafood came through visits to Sciacca, the nearby fishing port city. I found the port approachable (although it appears chaotic due to the negotiations in Sicilian dialect between the fishermen and the wholesalers), and I learned a lot about the varieties of fish in the Mediterranean Sea through simple conversations with fishmongers and wholesalers. The scene at the dock is vibrant as the fish come off the boats. As the fishermen scurry to clean and weigh their bounty, wholesalers await boatside to bid.

The fishing industry in Sicily can be traced back to ancient times. With three seas surrounding the country, there are an array of varieties to try. A walk through fish markets in cities on the opposite sides of the island will illuminate both similarities and differences in seafood types. For instance, at markets in Catania, you'll find a type of shellfish that resembles a little oyster in the shape of a bull's eye, known as *occhi di bue*. In Mazara del Vallo are sold a type of sweet red shrimp that are caught only by boats that stay at sea for long periods, plying the waters close to Africa.

Although most ports house day boats, which leave for sea in the night and return the next day in the early afternoon, some house larger boats that carry the fishermen to sea for weeks at a time.

Different types of fish are available throughout the year, depending on the season. For instance, sardines are iconic in the early spring, although they can be found during most of the year. Bluefin tuna are at their peak in May and June.

MUSSELS *in* TOMATO BROTH

{ *Pepata di Cozze* }

'MPIPATA RI COZZI

Near Messina, on Sicily's northeast point, sits the village of Ganzirri, *with its two saltwater lakes: Lake Ganzirri and Lake Faro. The former is connected to the Ionian Sea, the latter to the Tyrrhenian Sea. While the name* Ganzirri *derives from the Arabic word* khanzir, *or "pig," which are found in abundance in this area of Sicily, the lakes are historically famous for their mussel farming, which is unfortunately diminishing in production. However, in any fishing port, mussels from the sea can be found. There are many ways Sicilians prepare mussels, but this is one of the simplest and most delicious.*

Serves 4

3 garlic cloves, peeled

¹/₂ cup extra-virgin olive oil

¹/₂ pound ripe tomatoes, peeled and seeded (see page 91) and cut into chunks

¹/₄ cup finely chopped fresh parsley leaves

Sea salt and cracked black pepper

3 pounds mussels, scrubbed and debearded

1 cup white wine

8 slices toasted day-old bread, for serving

1 Sauté the whole garlic cloves in the olive oil in a pot over low heat. Add the tomatoes, a splash of water, the parsley, and salt and pepper to taste and increase the heat to medium. Cook the tomatoes for less than 10 minutes, until the water evaporates and the tomatoes thicken into a sauce.

2 Add the mussels and the white wine and cover the pot. The mussels should take about 5 minutes to open (which indicates that they are cooked) over medium heat. Discard any mussels that do not open. Taste the sauce for salt and add more if necessary. Serve the mussels in their sauce with some toasted day-old bread.

BAKED MUSSELS

{ *Cozze Gratinate* }

COZZI CÀ MUDDICA

Baked mussels make a delicious finger food or can be served as an appetizer.

Before cooking any mollusks—mussels, oysters, or clams—make sure their shells are closed, which indicates they are still alive and fresh. If any shells are open, discard them as they could contain harmful microbes.

Serves 4

3 tablespoons olive oil

2 garlic cloves, crushed

2 tablespoons roughly chopped fresh parsley leaves

1 tablespoon fresh thyme leaves

4 pounds large mussels, scrubbed and debearded

¹/₂ cup white wine

Breadcrumb stuffing

³/₄ cup fine breadcrumbs (page 42)

³/₄ cup peeled chopped tomato (see page 91)

¹/₄ cup finely chopped fresh parsley leaves

¹/₄ cup grated aged pecorino cheese

About ¹/₂ tablespoon salt

Ground black pepper to taste

¹/₄ cup extra-virgin olive oil

1 Heat a sauté pan over medium heat and add the olive oil, garlic, parsley, and thyme. After simmering for a minute or two (before the garlic browns), add the mussels and the white wine, cover the pan, and cook until the shells open, about 5 minutes. Remove the mussels from the pan and let them cool slightly until they are not too hot to touch. (Discard the shell of each mussel that does not contain the mollusk.) Strain and reserve the cooking liquid for later use.

2 FOR THE BREADCRUMB STUFFING: In a mixing bowl, combine the breadcrumbs, tomato, parsley, cheese, salt, pepper, olive oil and about ¹/₂ cup of the reserved cooking liquid. The stuffing should feel like moist sand in texture, but should not be overly soaked in liquid.

(The stuffing can be prepared up to 1 day in advance and held in a container in the refrigerator.) Fill the mussels with the breadcrumb mixture and slightly press down the stuffing into the shell.

3 Preheat the oven to 350°F. Place the stuffed shells, open sides facing up, on a baking pan and bake for about 15 minutes, or until the breadcrumbs are golden brown in color. Serve immediately.

GRILLED SHRIMP *in* MARSALA SAUCE

{ *Gamberoni alla Griglia Marsalati* }

AMMARUNA ARRUSTUTI CU MARSALA

In Sciacca, day boat fishermen catch white shrimp of all sizes. In Mazara del Vallo, a larger port on the southwest point of the island, fishermen go to sea for weeks at a time. Their voyages lead them to distant parts of the Mediterranean, areas that are too far for day boats to reach. Thus, the port of Mazara is famous for its red shrimp (gambero rosso), which hail from deep waters found closer to Tunisia than Sicily. The gambero rosso *is considered the most valuable type of shrimp species in Sicily, and for some, in all of Italy. Excellent when raw and almost buttery in texture, these shellfish can be found in upscale restaurants throughout the island.*

In the following recipe, prawns, or jumbo shrimp, are used, which range in size from 6 to 8 inches with the shell on. In Sicily, this dish is optimal when prepared with red shrimp, but white jumbo shrimp make a good substitution. When purchasing any type of shrimp, make sure they smell like the ocean, are firm in texture, and have shells that are not yellowish in color and do not contain any black spots. When cooking with prawns, make sure to remove the intestine, the dark vein along the back of the body. To do so, use a paring knife to cut a fine slit along the dark vein, which can then be removed with the tip of the knife.

Serves 4

Juice of 1 lemon

¹⁄₂ cup sweet Marsala

1 teaspoon honey

1 teaspoon white wine vinegar

¹⁄₂ teaspoon cornstarch

¹⁄₂ teaspoon salt

Ground black pepper

12 prawns or jumbo shrimp, heads on (if available), shelled and deveined

1 Heat a charcoal or gas grill to medium heat, or heat a grill pan on the stovetop over high heat.

2 In a saucepan, whisk together the lemon juice, Marsala, honey, vinegar, cornstarch, salt, and pepper to taste. Over low heat, cook, whisking to prevent lumps, for about 3 minutes, until slightly thickened. Set aside.

3 Thread the prawns onto skewers. Grill over medium heat for 1 minute. Remove and toss with the Marsala sauce. Return to the grill and cook for another 2 to 3 minutes, until the sauce has caramelized around the shrimp and the shrimp are pink and firm but before the shells begin to char.

SEAFOOD FOR THE GRILL

In Sicily, grilled fish is commonly drizzled with lemon and olive oil after coming off the grill. However, many sauces also complement grilled seafood. *Salsa verde* (page 44), Caper Pesto (page 44), Parsley-Mint Oil (page 43), and *salmoriglio* (page 41) all make perfect accompaniments to grilled fish. Here are some general guidelines for grilling seafood.

To grill a whole round fish such as fresh sardines, red mullet, or bass: Remove the guts and then scale the fish, or have your fishmonger do so. Brush or rub the outside with olive oil and sprinkle the cavity and outside with salt and pepper. Insert herb sprigs in the cavity. Place the fish in a grill basket and place the basket on a grill over low heat. Grill, turning once, until the skin is slightly charred and has visible grill marks, and the flesh is firm to touch. Depending on the size of the fish, the cooking time will range from 10 to 30 minutes.

To grill a fish fillet: Marinate the fillets for about 30 minutes in olive oil, lemon juice, Garlic Paste (page 40), salt, and pepper. If grilling a delicate fillet of white fish (such as bass, John Dory, or red mullet) with its skin on, place the fillet inside a grill basket so that it does not stick to the grill. A thick fillet of swordfish or tuna steak can be placed directly on the grill. Whether the fillet is thick or thin, grill over medium heat. The best method to test if a fillet is cooked through is by touching it. If the fillet feels rubbery, it is not yet cooked. As soon as the fillet feels firm to touch, it is ready to be removed from the grill.

To grill squid: Marinate the whole squid overnight in lemon, Garlic Paste (page 40), herbs, olive oil, salt, and pepper. Place the squid on a hot grill. The flesh of the squid will tighten as moisture exudes from it. When the squid has reduced in size by one-third and the squid is lightly charred, 5 to 8 minutes, remove from the grill and serve while hot.

CLOCKWISE FROM TOP LEFT:
Spatola (ribbonfish), triglie (red mullet), scorfano (scorpion fish), cernia (grouper), gamberetti (pink shrimp), sgombro (mackerel), scampi (langoustines), acciughe (anchovies)

TUNA SAUSAGES

{ Salsiccia di Tonno }

SASIZZA RI TONNU

Grill these spicy tuna sausages and serve them with toasted bread and Onion Marmalade (page 41). Or simmer them in a tomato sauce with onions and white wine. If you don't have casings, form the tuna mixture into small patties and just sear them in a pan.

Makes 1¹/₂ pounds sausages (serves 4 as an appetizer)

1 pound tuna loin,
finely chopped

1 cup fine breadcrumbs
(page 42)

1 cup loosely packed
fresh parsley leaves,
finely chopped

¹/₂ cup grated aged
pecorino cheese

¹/₂ cup red wine

1 teaspoon salt

1 teaspoon cracked
black pepper

1 teaspoon spicy chile
pepper flakes

3 feet pork sausage casing,
or 4 feet lamb casing

2 tablespoons olive oil

1 In a bowl, mix together the tuna, breadcrumbs, parsley, cheese, wine, salt, black pepper, and pepper flakes. Cover and refrigerate for a few hours before stuffing into the casings.

2 Fill the casings with the tuna mixture, following the sausage-making steps on page 265.

3 Heat a charcoal or gas grill to medium heat, or heat a grill pan on the stovetop over high heat.

4 Toss the sausages with the olive oil. Transfer to the hot charcoal grill or grill pan and grill for 3 to 5 minutes, turning over halfway through the cooking time. Keep in mind that these sausages cook fast and when overcooked, they tend to be dry. To check if they are ready, pierce the casing with the point of a sharp paring knife. The liquid that exudes from the casing should be pink in color.

SALT-BAKED SEA BASS

{ Spigola Cotta sotto il Sale }

SPIGULA SUTTA SALI

Whole fish is luscious when baked inside a salt crust. The salt encases the fish, as if in a vacuum-sealed pack, allowing it to bake in its own juices. The fish does not end up too salty because the skin protects the flesh from absorbing too much salt. Any of the whole fish mentioned in the next recipe—with the exception of the red mullet—can be baked in salt. I like to serve with a simple salad of fennel and orange slices dressed with olive oil and garnished with pomegranate seeds.

Serves 2

1 (2-pound) whole fish,
cleaned, gutted, and scaled

1 lemon, thinly sliced

2 garlic cloves, thinly sliced

5 sprigs fresh mint
and parsley

3 cups coarse sea salt

2 egg whites

¹/₂ cup white wine

1 Preheat the oven to 350°F.

2 Stuff the cavity of the whole fish with the lemon slices, garlic slices, and mint and parsley sprigs.

3 In a mixing bowl, stir together the salt, egg whites, and wine. Place half of the salt mixture in a 12-inch baking dish with at least 3-inch-high sides.

4 Place the fish on its side in the baking pan. Cover the fish with the remaining salt mixture. Bake for about 15 minutes. Using the back of a spoon, crack the salt crust and pierce the meat of the fish with a paring knife to make sure that the fish is fully cooked. The flesh should be opaque and flake easily.

OVEN-BAKED BREAM

{ Orata al Forno }

ORATA 'NFURNATA

The difference between grilled and baked fish can be detected in the texture of the cooked fish. Smoky and flavorful grilled fish can be dry and often needs something drizzled on it just before serving, while baked fish should contain enough moisture and flavor that it doesn't need additional adornment.

The best whole fish to bake in this style are sea bass, gilt-head bream (pictured on page 246), bream, John Dory, striped bass, and red mullet. The smaller fish, such as the red mullet, cook faster than the others. For this recipe, either use two 1-pound fish, or four ½-pounders.

Serves 2

3 tablespoons extra-virgin olive oil

1 onion, finely minced

1 large tomato, diced

1 teaspoon Garlic Paste (page 40)

5 fresh basil leaves

1 teaspoon salt

2 pounds whole fish, cleaned, gutted, and scaled

½ teaspoon freshly chopped spicy chile pepper (optional)

1 cup white wine

¼ cup pitted black olives

½ teaspoon cracked black pepper

1 Preheat the oven to 350°F.

2 Heat the olive oil in a sauté pan over low heat. Add the onion and sauté for a few minutes, until translucent. Add the tomato, garlic paste, and basil and cook for about 1 minute, until the ingredients incorporate and the tomatoes soften. Remove the pan from the heat.

3 Salt the insides of the fish and the skin. Using a small rubber spatula, spread the onion-tomato mixture inside the cavities of the fish.

4 Place the fish in a baking pan, along with the spicy pepper (if using), the wine, olives, and black pepper. Bake for about 20 minutes, until the fish is cooked through. To check if the fish is done, use a fork and lift up a piece of the fillet. The meat should be opaque and flake easily. Remove from the oven and serve immediately.

Variation: Baked Bream with Potatoes

Toss 1-inch cubes of blanched potatoes, chunks of onions, and cherry tomatoes with olive oil, garlic cloves, rosemary sprigs, and salt. Spread out in the baking pan and top with the fish. Bake as directed, until the fish is cooked through and the potatoes are tender.

STUFFED BABY CUTTLEFISH

{ *Seppie Farcite* }

SICCI RICHINI

Baby cuttlefish are very tender and cook quickly. Here, they are filled and baked with the same breadcrumb stuffing used to stuff vegetables. While cuttlefish are not native to the Americas, they are imported and sold, usually already cleaned, by fishmongers. If, however, you have trouble finding cuttlefish, replace them with large squid.

Serves 4

10 whole cleaned baby cuttlefish

4 cups milk

2 cups Breadcrumb Stuffing (page 224)

1 tablespoon olive oil

½ cup *salmoriglio* (page 41)

1 Place the fish in a nonreactive bowl and cover with the milk. Cover the bowl and marinate the fish in the refrigerator overnight. Discard the milk and rinse the cuttlefish.

2 Preheat the oven to 350°F.

3 By hand or in a food processor, finely chop 2 of the cuttlefish. In a large bowl, combine the chopped fish with the breadcrumb stuffing and mix well.

4 Stuff the mixture inside the cavities of the 8 remaining cuttlefish. Close the openings of the cuttlefish cavities with toothpicks. Arrange them in a small baking pan, packed tightly, and drizzle lightly with the olive oil.

5 Bake for about 20 minutes, until the cuttlefish are firm to touch. Serve immediately, drizzled with the *salmoriglio*.

SCORPION FISH *in* PARCHMENT

{ *Scorfano in Cartoccio* }

SCORFANU 'NCARTOCCIU

A perfect way to bake delicate fillets of white fish is to season them and wrap them in parchment paper with tomatoes, nuts, and fresh herbs. The fish will steam while absorbing the added flavors. Experiment with your favorite herbs and flavor enhancers; each will impart a different flavor to the fish—olives and capers are good options. You can prepare the packets in advance and slip them into the oven just as guests arrive. Everyone will be pleased at the intense aromas that escape when the parchment is opened at the table.

Serves 4

4 (8-ounce) fillets white fish (such as scorpion fish, amberjack, codfish, or black bass), about 1 inch thick

4 teaspoons olive oil

1 teaspoon Garlic Paste (page 40)

1 large ripe tomato, diced

8 sprigs fresh thyme

2 tablespoons pine nuts

Salt

1 Preheat the oven to 350°F.

2 Place a piece of parchment paper on your work surface. Place a piece of fish on the parchment and drizzle with olive oil. Top with a quarter of the garlic paste, diced tomatoes, thyme, and pine nuts, and season with salt. Close the parchment by folding the top pieces together and twisting or folding the sides. Repeat to make 4 packets of fish.

3 Bake for about 15 minutes and serve immediately.

CLOCKWISE FROM BOTTOM LEFT:
*Scorpion Fish in Parchment (page 245);
Oven-Baked Bream (page 244) and red
mullet; Pistachio-Crusted Monkfish
(page 248); Skate with Sweet-and-Sour
Onions (page 253); Sweet-and-Sour
Swordfish with Mint Sauce (page 254);
Stuffed Baby Cuttlefish (page 245)*

PISTACHIO-CRUSTED MONKFISH

{ *Rana Pescatrice in Crosta di Pistacchi* }

RANA PISCATRICI IN CRUSTA RI FASTUCHI

The meat of the monkfish comes from its tail. Ask your fishmonger to remove the skin, which can otherwise be challenging to remove. The orange sauce pairs nicely with the pistachios in this dish, but it can also be drizzled on fillets of simply seared or grilled fish.

Serves 4

Monkfish

1 pound monkfish, cut into 4 pieces

2 tablespoons olive oil

1/2 cup peeled pistachios, finely ground

1/4 cup fine breadcrumbs (page 42)

1 tablespoon Garlic Paste (page 40)

1/2 teaspoon salt

Orange sauce

2 cups fresh orange juice

1/2 cup white wine

2 tablespoons fresh lemon juice

2 tablespoons honey

2 sprigs fresh thyme

1/8 teaspoon salt

1 FOR THE MONKFISH: Preheat the oven to 350°F. Grease a medium-size baking pan. Rinse the fish under running water, pat it dry, then rub with 1 tablespoon of the olive oil.

2 In a shallow bowl, mix the pistachios, breadcrumbs, garlic paste, and salt. Press the fish into the pistachio-breadcrumb mixture, coating each piece on all sides. Bake for about 10 minutes, then using kitchen tongs, turn the fish over. Bake for another 5 minutes, until the fish is firm to touch.

3 MEANWHILE, FOR THE ORANGE SAUCE: Mix together all of the sauce ingredients in a saucepan and bring to a boil over high heat. Reduce the heat to low and cook until the sauce is reduced to a glaze and coats the back of a spoon, about 10 minutes. Remove and discard the thyme sprigs. (The sauce can be prepared in advance, held in the refrigerator in a container, and reheated with a splash of water when serving.)

4 To serve, place a dollop of the orange sauce in the centers of individual plates or 4 dollops on a serving platter, and top with the monkfish fillets. Serve immediately.

THE FISH THAT CAN SING

A classic Sicilian preparation, *sarde a beccafico* is the peasant version of an aristocratic dish. Songbirds, known in Italian as *beccafico*, were once in high culinary demand by noble families. They were stuffed with breadcrumbs, pine nuts, and raisins, then rolled and cooked with their tails facing up. Peasant cooks reinvented the specialty by replacing the birds with inexpensive and readily available sardines, which also had a pronounced tail. The new dish became known as *sarde a beccafico*, or sardines prepared in the style of songbirds.

There are two decisively different ways to prepare this dish. In Palermo and throughout the western side of Sicily, *sarde a beccafico* indicates sardines that are cleaned and butterflied, then covered with breadcrumbs mixed with pine nuts and raisins before they are rolled with their tails facing up. They are then placed on skewers or in a baking pan and roasted.

In Catania, on Sicily's east coast, *sarde a beccafico* is a fried dish. The sardines are cleaned, butterflied, and covered with the same breadcrumb mixture, with the addition of a slice of caciocavallo cheese. They are then topped with another butterflied sardine to form a sandwich, which is dipped in egg, flour, and breadcrumbs and pan-fried.

FRIED MIXED FISH

{ *Fritto Misto di Pesce* }

À FRITTURA RI PISCI

Although fritto misto is prepared all over Italy, it is a classic Sicilian preparation made with a wide range of small fish, shellfish, and mollusks. This is a perfect summer dish to eat on your patio, as it tends to be messy. Be ready to use your fingers.

The key to a stellar fish fry is trifold: First, procure the freshest seafood possible. Second, use hard-wheat remilled semola flour to lightly dredge the seafood (as opposed to soft-wheat white flour), which adds a nice crunchy texture. Lastly, make sure that the oil has reached 350°F before frying. This ensures that the seafood cooks quickly and doesn't get soggy. Some cooks also cut zucchini into little matchstick shapes and serve them, breaded and fried, along with the seafood.

If you're using white bait, which are small, young fish with tender bones, leave the heads attached and the bones in.

Serves 4

Olive oil or vegetable oil, for frying	**1 cup hard-wheat remilled semola flour**
1 pound mixed seafood: squid (cleaned as per the directions on page 129 and cut into small segments), shrimp (with their shells on), and/or white bait	**Salt**
	Lemon wedges, for serving

1 Fill a heavy-bottomed pot or a deep fryer about two-thirds full with oil, making sure not to overfill or the hot oil might overflow when the seafood is added. Over medium to high heat, preheat to 350°F.

2 Meanwhile, dredge the seafood (keeping each type of seafood separate) in the flour, then transfer to a dry strainer or colander and sift the seafood back and forth to remove any excess flour. A key to a good fish fry is not to use too much flour.

3 When the oil reaches 350°F, fry each type of seafood separately, in batches, until the coating turns golden in color and the seafood is cooked through, about 3 minutes. Quickly remove from the oil and place in a bowl lined with paper towels to absorb any excess oil. Salt the fish to taste and toss well. Serve immediately with lemon wedges for drizzling.

FRIED SALTED CODFISH

{ Baccalà in Pastella di Farina di Ceci }

BACCALÀ IN PASTEDDA RI FARINA RI CICIRI

Tucked in the hills of Salina, one of the Aeolian Islands, Signum is a resort with the perfect mélange of rustic and modern, which is evident in its architecture, gardens, and the food served at its upscale restaurant. Although salt-cured codfish is classically served during winter months, the chef Martina Caruso developed this dish to highlight the baccalà *during the summer months at her family's resort. She fries the cod in a chickpea batter, serving it with a roasted pepper sauce and lightly sautéed, finely julienned celery and carrots,* as pictured. *The crunchiness of the vegetables works well with the soft flaky fish. The juxtaposition of the nutty chickpea flour with the saltiness of the fish and the sweetness of peppers is heavenly.*

Serves 4

Vegetable oil, for frying

1 cup chickpea flour

1 teaspoon salt

1 cup light beer

1 pound salted codfish fillets, rehydrated (see page 54) and patted dry with paper towels, or 1 pound fresh codfish or halibut

Sauce of choice, such as roasted pepper sauce (optional)

Lightly sautéed vegetable strips such as carrots, peppers, or celery, for serving (optional)

1 Fill a heavy-bottomed cooking vessel, ideally a cast-iron pan, about halfway full with vegetable oil. Over medium heat, preheat until the oil reaches 350°F.

2 In a mixing bowl, combine the chickpea flour and salt. Slowly pour in the beer and gently whisk together.

3 When the oil is hot, dredge each piece of fish in the batter and transfer immediately to the hot oil. Fry, using a fish spatula to gently turn the fillet of fish over in the pan so that all sides cook evenly. (Make sure not to spill any of the oil on the stovetop.) The fish is done when the batter turns golden brown and the flesh is cooked through, just a few minutes. Transfer the fillets to a plate lined with paper towels to drain excess oil.

4 To serve, place a dollop of sauce, if using, in the centers of individual plates. Top with the fried fish and sautéed vegetables of your choice. Serve immediately.

SKATE *with* SWEET-AND-SOUR ONIONS

{ *Razza con la Cipollata* }

RAIA CÀ CIPUDDATA

Cipollata is a condiment of onions stewed in vinegar and bay leaves. Classically it is prepared with slivers of large onions, but I like this less-classic version using halves of small cipollini onions because it better highlights the sweetness of the onion. Some prepare the condiment with red wine vinegar, giving the onions a pink hue, while others use white wine vinegar. I like to add a touch of balsamic vinegar, which imparts a richer flavor. Cipollata *can be served cold on its own as a side dish. But it is traditionally served with seared tuna or skate, as here.*

Serves 4

Cipollata

12 cipollini onions, cut in half; or 1 large onion, thinly sliced

1 teaspoon salt

2 tablespoons olive oil

½ cup white wine vinegar

1 tablespoon balsamic vinegar (optional)

1 tablespoon sugar

4 bay leaves

Skate

2 tablespoons vegetable oil

4 skate wings (about 1 pound), cleaned and skin removed

Salt

1 FOR THE *CIPOLLATA*: In a saucepan over medium heat, simmer the onions, 1 cup water, and the salt. As soon as the water evaporates, add the oil and sauté until the onions start to brown. Add the red wine vinegar, balsamic vinegar (if using), sugar, and bay leaves. Cook until the vinegar evaporates, then remove from the heat. The *cipollata* can be prepared up to 2 days in advance and held in an airtight container in the refrigerator. To serve, reheat in a sauté pan over low heat.

2 For the skate, heat a heavy-bottomed sauté pan over high heat for 1 minute, or until very hot. Add the vegetable oil and let it heat up. Add the skate, lower the heat to medium so that the fish sears but doesn't burn, and press down on each fillet with a fish spatula so that the fish sears evenly. Cook almost entirely on one side, shaking the pan slightly so that the fish doesn't stick to the bottom of the pan, until the fish is firm, about 4 minutes. Using the spatula, flip the skate to the other side to finish the cooking process, another minute. Top with the warm *cipollata* and serve immediately.

SWEET-AND-SOUR SWORDFISH *with* MINT SAUCE

{ *Pesce Spada alla Stimpirata* }

PISCI SPATA A LA STIMPIRATA

Stimpirata, *the Sicilian version of the Italian word* temperare, *which means "to soften" or "to transform," is a classic technique for cooking white meat and oily fish with sweet and sour ingredients that is popular in southeastern Sicily. The combination of vinegar and sugar serves to transform the flavor and texture of the dish's main ingredient, in this case swordfish.*

A swordfish steak is a piece of the fish still attached to the thick and rubbery skin. The skin does not get crispy when seared and is typically removed in upscale restaurants for aesthetic reasons, but I prefer to leave it on at home. Some enjoy swordfish lightly cooked, but it is most popularly prepared cooked through.

Serves 4

Swordfish

Salt

4 swordfish steaks, about 1 inch thick (about 1 pound), skin on

1 cup all-purpose flour

2 tablespoons olive oil

Stimpirata

1 tablespoon olive oil

1 onion, finely chopped

2 celery stalks, with leaves, finely chopped

1 cup Dried Tomatoes (page 73)

1 cup pitted green olives

2 tablespoons salted capers, rinsed well

3 tablespoons white wine vinegar

Salt and ground black pepper

Mint sauce

1 cup loosely packed fresh mint leaves

1/4 cup blanched almonds or pine nuts

4 tablespoons extra-virgin olive oil

1/2 teaspoon salt

1 teaspoon fresh lemon juice

1 FOR THE SWORDFISH: Salt the swordfish steaks. Spread the flour on a plate. Dredge each swordfish steak in the flour to coat, then holding one end of the fish, shake off any excess flour. The fish should only be lightly coated with flour.

2 Heat a heavy-bottomed pan over high heat for 1 minute, until very hot. Add the olive oil and let it heat up. Add the fish, lower the heat to medium so that the fish sears but doesn't burn, and press down each fillet with a fish spatula so that it sears evenly. Cook almost entirely on one side, shaking the pan slightly so that the fish doesn't stick to the bottom of the pan, until the fish is firm, about 5 minutes. Using the spatula, flip the steaks to the other side to finish the cooking process, another minute. Transfer the fish to a plate and keep warm while you prepare the *stimpirata*.

3 FOR THE *STIMPIRATA*: Heat the olive oil in the same pan over medium-high heat. Add the onion and celery and cook, stirring the vegetables to remove any stuck pieces of fish from the pan, until the vegetables are soft. Add the dried tomatoes, olives, and capers and mix well. After a few minutes of cooking, return the swordfish steaks to the pan and add the vinegar. Cover and cook until the vinegar evaporates, about 2 minutes. Season with salt and pepper to taste.

4 FOR THE MINT SAUCE: In a food processor, combine the mint, almonds, 2 tablespoons of the olive oil, and the salt. Mix on high speed, then add the remaining 2 tablespoons olive oil and the lemon juice.

5 Drizzle the swordfish steaks with the mint sauce and serve immediately with the *stimpirata*.

Variation: Swordfish with *Peperonata*

Prepare the swordfish through step 2, adding the *peperonata* (at right) to the steaks a few minutes before they are fully cooked. Serve while hot.

Peperonata

Peperonata is a side dish or a sauce that pairs well with seafood. Different versions of peperonata *include* agrodolce *(page 46), a sweet and acidic mixture of sugar and vinegar, or incorporate either capers and olives, or raisins and pine nuts. Heavier versions include eggplant and/or potatoes, and when served as a side dish,* peperonata *often is sprinkled with breadcrumbs. This simple onion-pepper* peperonata *works well with oily fish, or any fish with a strong defined flavor, especially swordfish.*

1 cup caramelized onions (see page 103)	**¹/₂ teaspoon Garlic Paste** (page 40)
2 tablespoons extra-virgin olive oil	**Salt and ground black pepper**
2 red bell peppers, cut into thin strips	**About ¹/₄ cup *agrodolce*** (page 46)
1 cup Tomato Pulp (homemade, page 70, or store-bought)	

Heat the caramelized onions in a sauté pan with the olive oil. Add the red peppers and a splash of water and cook until they are soft and the water evaporates. Add the tomato pulp, 1 cup water, and the garlic paste. Let cook until the water evaporates, then add the *agrodolce* with salt and pepper to taste.

GROUPER *in* TOMATO BROTH *with* OLIVES *and* CAPERS

{ *Cernia in Brodo di Pomodoro con Olive e Capperi* }

CERNIA AGGHIOTTA

Agghiotta *is a style of cooking, traditional to Messina, in which seafood is submerged in a tomato-based brothy sauce and slow-cooked.* Agghiotta *almost always contains olives and capers. Grouper is a popular fish in the Mediterranean and readily available in the United States. Its flavor is delicate and, when cooked, its meat stays moist and firm with big flakes. The same dish can be prepared with most nonoily white fish, such as monkfish or hake. In Messina, the dish is often prepared in winter months with salt-cured codfish (*baccalà*) or air-dried codfish (*stoccafisso*). If substituting either type of dried codfish, be sure to first rehydrate the fish for a few days; see the instructions on page 54.*

Serves 4

1 cup all-purpose flour

1 pound grouper fillets, cut into 4 equal pieces

1 onion, thinly sliced

2 tablespoons extra-virgin olive oil

3 garlic cloves, peeled

2 cups Tomato Pulp (homemade, page 70, or store-bought)

2 cups Fish Broth (page 147)

½ cup white wine

½ cup pitted green Sicilian olives

2 tablespoons salted capers, well rinsed

1 Spread the flour on a plate. Dredge each fillet in the flour to coat, then, holding one end of the fish, shake off any excess flour. The fillets should only be lightly coated with flour.

2 In a saucepan over medium heat, sauté the onion in the olive oil until soft and slightly translucent. Add the garlic and floured grouper, then the tomato pulp, broth, wine, olives, and capers. Reduce the heat to low and cook the fish for about 15 minutes. The fish is ready when the flesh becomes opaque and flakes when touched with a fork.

3 Remove the garlic cloves. Serve immediately.

An Evanescent Spring Delicacy

A delicacy in Sicily, *neonati di pesce* are newly born fish, just past the larval stage. For centuries, these little fish have been a seasonal part of Sicilian culinary culture, enjoyed in the spring months. But today they are difficult to find because of recently established fishing laws. In Italian, these tiny fish are called *novellame di pesce,* but throughout Italy, they are referred to by several different names in regional dialects, most commonly known in Liguria as *bianchetti,* for example. Depending on the time of year, various species of newborn fish can be found in waters around Sicily, but are most commonly of the sardine, anchovy, and shad species.

The length of a sewing needle, the fish are even smaller than white bait, and are white in color, but translucent. They are delicious raw and simply garnished with a touch of olive oil, but also commonly used as a sauce for pasta when tossed with garlic sautéed in olive oil. In addition, *neonati di pesce* are commonly made into patties, mixed with flour, egg, pecorino, parsley, and salt, then pan-fried.

GRILLED SWORDFISH BRACIOLE

{ Involtino di Pesce Spada }

'NVOLTINU RI PISCI SPATA

Involtino *and* braciole *are synonymous Italian-American terms for stuffed and rolled foods. Vegetables, fish, and meat can all be prepared in this style. This is a classic recipe for swordfish, stuffed with a breadcrumb and cheese mixture, rolled, placed on skewers, and then grilled (see a similar one for beef on page 264).*

There are three keys to preparing a swordfish involtino without letting the fish dry out: First, the swordfish should be marinated after it is pounded out, but before it is stuffed. (Marinating is my own touch, not so traditional, but I find it to be an essential factor in making the rolls come out moist.) Second, the stuffing should contain some moisture, in the form of orange juice and olive oil. Third, you should stand next to the grill and monitor the fish rolls closely so that they do not overcook. Serve them straight from the grill. Note that the wooden skewers should be soaked in water for an hour prior to use so that they don't burn on the grill.

Serves 6

Swordfish

6 pieces swordfish loin (3.5 ounces each), without the bone or blood lines

Juice of 2 lemons

½ cup olive oil

1 tablespoon dried Sicilian oregano

Filling

½ cup plus 3 tablespoons extra-virgin olive oil

1 onion, finely minced

2 tablespoons golden raisins, soaked for at least 1 hour in water and drained

2 tablespoons pine nuts

Filling, **continued**

2 salted anchovies, rinsed well and made into a paste

2 organic oranges

1 cup fine breadcrumbs (page 42)

½ cup grated pecorino *primo sale* cheese

1 teaspoon salt

½ teaspoon cracked black pepper

For grilling

12 bay leaves

½ onion, cut into 2-inch-wide slices

Salt

1 FOR THE SWORDFISH: Place one piece of swordfish loin on a cutting board. Using a meat tenderizer, pound out the fish until it is about ⅛ inch thick. Repeat with the remaining pieces. Place the swordfish in a nonreactive bowl with the lemon juice, olive oil, and oregano. Cover and marinate in the refrigerator for about 1 hour.

2 MEANWHILE, FOR THE FILLING: Heat ½ cup of the olive oil in a sauté pan over low heat. Add the minced onion and gently cook, making sure not to brown the pieces, until soft, about 5 minutes. Add the raisins, pine nuts, and anchovy paste, mix well, and sauté for a few minutes. Remove the pan from the heat and let the contents cool to room temperature.

3 Heat a charcoal or gas grill to medium heat, or heat a grill pan on the stovetop over high heat.

4 Grate the zest from one of the oranges, and juice both of them. In a mixing bowl, combine the sautéed onion mixture, orange zest and juice, breadcrumbs, cheese, the remaining 3 tablespoons olive oil, salt, and pepper.

5 Remove the swordfish from the marinade. Spread the breadcrumb mixture thinly on one side of each piece of fish. Roll up each piece, wiping away any breadcrumbs that remain on the outer part of the swordfish roll. Cut each roll in half. Thread three rolls onto a wood or metal skewer, separated and surrounded by a bay leaf and a slice of onion. Repeat to make 4 skewers. Lightly salt the outside of each roll.

6 Grill the skewered rolls for 5 to 8 minutes. Using a paring knife, cut a small incision in one of the rolls to make sure that it is cooked through; if not, grill for a few more minutes. Serve immediately.

OLIVE OIL–POACHED HAKE

{ *Nasello Cotto nell'Olio d'Oliva* }

NASEDDU COTTU NÀ L'OGGHIU R'ALIVA

When firm white fish fillets, such as hake or monkfish, are seared or grilled, they tend to be dry in texture, and are usually best when served with a sauce. In this recipe, hake is poached in olive oil at a low temperature, which is an easy and quite delicious way to prepare fillets of fish. Not only do the fillets stay moist, but they gain a silky texture. Feel free to swap in monkfish, codfish, halibut, or salmon for the hake, although the latter three do not live in the waters around Sicily.

Use extra-virgin olive oil because its nuanced flavor will add an excellent taste to the fish. Granted, there is a lot of olive oil called for in this recipe. However, consider that the olive oil can be strained in a sieve after it cools down, and stored for reuse to cook other seafood dishes. When straining, make sure to discard the oil at the bottom of the pan, where liquid released from the seafood will have settled.

In this recipe, the olive oil–poached hake is served with black Sicilian lentils, which have a pleasant crunchiness, and a mash of cauliflower.

Serves 4

Green cauliflower

2 tablespoons extra-virgin olive oil

2 garlic cloves, crushed with the palm of your hand

1 head green cauliflower, stems removed, cut into individual florets

2 cups Vegetable Broth (page 147), warmed

½ teaspoon salt, plus more if needed

Black lentils

½ pound black lentils

1 spring onion, finely chopped

1 stalk celery, finely chopped

2 tablespoons extra-virgin olive oil

Salt and ground black pepper

Hake

4 cups extra-virgin olive oil

10 sprigs fresh thyme, oregano, rosemary, and/or parsley

Salt

1 pound hake fillets, cut into 4 equal pieces

1 FOR THE GREEN CAULIFLOWER: Heat the olive oil in a tall pot over medium heat. Add the garlic cloves and cook for under 1 minute, until they start to turn a light golden color. Add the cauliflower florets and let sear for a few minutes before adding the warm broth. Stir the contents of the pot, add the salt, and cover. Cook for at least 15 minutes, until the cauliflower is easily pierced with a paring knife.

2 Remove the garlic cloves, if they are still intact. Using a hand-held potato masher, mash the cauliflower. (Alternatively, for a smoother mash, place the cooked cauliflower in a food processor and mix until the cauliflower is pureed.) Taste for salt and add more accordingly.

3 FOR THE BLACK LENTILS: Place the lentils in a pot of cold water and bring to boil over high heat. Add the onion and celery, lower the heat to medium, and cook for about 45 minutes, until the lentils are cooked through. To test if the lentils are done, remove one from the pot and let cool for a few seconds; squeeze between your fingers—if it softly crushes, the lentils are ready. Using a slotted spoon, transfer the lentils to a mixing bowl. Drizzle them with the extra-virgin olive oil, and add salt and pepper to taste.

4 FOR THE HAKE: Remove the fish from the refrigerator about 30 minutes before cooking, so that it is not cold when placing it in the pot of hot oil.

5 Combine the olive oil and the herb sprigs in a straight-sided, heavy-bottomed pan (about 8 inches in diameter). Heat over low heat until the oil reaches around 120°F, about 5 minutes. Salt the pieces of fish and place them gently in the oil, making sure not to splatter oil on the stovetop. Do not worry if the pieces of fish are tightly packed in the pan, but make sure they are completely covered with the oil. Cook the fish for about 20 minutes, then test to see if they are done: Poke a paring knife into the interior part of a fillet and, if the flesh is firm, it is cooked through.

6 Remove the fish from the oil and serve immediately on top of the mashed cauliflower with the black lentils alongside.

Chapter 9

MEAT

A DRIVE THROUGH COUNTRY BACK ROADS in the interior parts of the island reveals the abundance of livestock. Like most islands, Sicily is famous for its abundant fresh seafood. However, the island's production of meat is just as robust. In interior parts of the island, meat is more commonly consumed than seafood. Pork and lamb are the most popular, but beef, veal, rabbit, hare, and goat meat are also seen on menus and cooked in home kitchens.

Pigs of numerous breeds are raised, but nowadays the most prized type of pig is the black pig, which is native to the Nebrodi mountain range in northeast Sicily (see page 56). Wild boar is also popular, although not as much as in other regions of Italy. It's actually illegal to catch boar in the wild in Sicily, so any wild boar you enjoy here is either imported from other regions of Italy or is cultivated on farms. Lamb has subcategories: *Castrato* is mutton, or male lamb that has been castrated. Baby lamb, which is available in the spring, has a more delicate flavor.

As for birds, in rural areas it's still common for villagers to raise their own chickens and roosters. Duck, goose, pheasant, and squab are more expensive birds, usually found only in restaurants, or in homes only on special feast days.

Living in Sicily, I came to understand the importance of establishing a good relationship with my local butcher. In the past, if I needed a deboned chicken or pounded veal cutlets or a whole goat butchered into morsels, I used to undertake such time-consuming tasks in my own kitchen. When I wanted to cook sausage laced with wild fennel and black peppercorn, I usually had to prepare the sausage myself (as in the recipe on page 265). In Sicily, I've found that I'm able to save precious amounts of time, simply by knowing a butcher whom I can trust and who always makes sure to provide me with the freshest meat in the shop.

Our Barbecues on the Beach

One of my fondest food memories in Sicily is eating grilled meat with friends and relatives on Ferragosto, the holiday on August 15 that marks the Assumption of Mother Mary. On the eve of the feast day, families and friends traditionally set up camp on the beach for the night and meat is grilled over bonfires for dinner. Large holes are dug in the sand, loaded with firewood, and lit into bonfires. Sausage, as well as pork, lamb, and veal chops, are all grilled over the flames. After the big meal, a midnight dip in the ocean is part of the tradition.

To grill meat that is juicy and flavorful, start with fresh, not frozen, meat. The cut of meat is important.

Chops are the best cut of meat to grill, especially when some fat is left on the edge, which keeps the meat from drying out. To add flavor, first toss the meat with *salmoriglio* (page 41) before grilling. During the cooking, continue to add *salmoriglio* to the meat with a brush.

It's uncommon in Sicilian homes to eat meat that is still red at the center. However, in restaurants, rare or medium-rare meat is all the trend. For rare meat, remove from the grill when an instant meat thermometer inserted into the flesh reads 135°F; for medium-rare, 140°F; for medium, 145°F; and for well done, 150°F.

GRILLED BEEF BRACIOLE

{ *Involtini di Carne* }

SASIZZEDDI

Meat involtini come in many forms, and are prepared with beef, veal, pork, or chicken. I prefer those made with veal thigh. The names and stuffings of these meat rolls also differ widely throughout the island. This recipe uses a stuffing popular in Catania, in which the breadcrumbs are laced with spicy salame. They are known as sasizzeddi. *In Palermo, these involtini (called* spiedini*) are rolled in fine breadcrumbs, and stuffed with prosciutto cotto and can be prepared in the oven or seared with olive oil on the stovetop. The meat used in* spiedini *tends to be pounded thinner than in other recipes. Other versions omit the breadcrumbs, and stuff the meat with tomato, caciocavallo, and herbs.*

Note that the wooden skewers should be soaked in water for an hour prior to use so that they don't burn on the grill.

Serves 4

Beef

1 pound veal thigh or beef tenderloin

2 tablespoons balsamic vinegar

¹/₂ cup olive oil

1 tablespoon dried Sicilian oregano

Filling

5 tablespoons extra-virgin olive oil

1 onion, minced

¹/₄ cup finely chopped spicy salame

2 tablespoons golden raisins, soaked for at least 1 hour in water and drained

2 tablespoons pine nuts

Filling, continued

1 cup fine breadcrumbs (page 42)

¹/₂ cup grated pecorino *primo sale* cheese

1 teaspoon salt

¹/₂ teaspoon cracked black pepper

For grilling

12 bay leaves

¹/₂ onion, cut into 2-inch-wide slices

Salt

1 FOR THE MEAT: Place the veal thigh on a cutting board. Using a meat tenderizer, pound out until ¹/₈ inch in thickness. Slice against the grain into 6 roughly equal-sized strips, each about 6 inches wide Place the meat strips in a nonreactive bowl with the vinegar, olive oil, and oregano. Toss to coat the meat and cover. Let marinate in the refrigerator for about 1 hour.

2 MEANWHILE, FOR THE FILLING: Heat 1 tablespoon of the oil in a sauté pan over low heat. Add the minced onion and gently cook, making sure not to brown it, until soft, about 5 minutes. Add the salame, raisins, and pine nuts, mix well, and sauté for a few minutes. Remove the pan from the heat and let the contents cool to room temperature.

3 Heat a charcoal or gas grill to medium heat, or heat a grill pan on the stovetop over high heat.

4 Meanwhile, in a mixing bowl, combine the sautéed onion mixture, breadcrumbs, cheese, the remaining 4 tablespoons olive oil, the salt, and pepper.

5 Remove the meat from the marinade. Spread the breadcrumb mixture thinly on one side of each strip of meat. Roll up each piece, wiping away any breadcrumbs that remain on the outer part of the roll. Cut each roll in half. Thread three rolls onto a wood or metal skewer, separated and surrounded by a bay leaf and a slice of onion. Repeat to make 4 skewers. Lightly salt the outside of each roll.

6 Grill the skewered rolls for about 10 minutes, turning once halfway through cooking, until the meat is firm. Serve immediately.

GRILLED SAUSAGE

{ Salsiccia }

SASIZZA

Sausage was born as a way to use all parts of the pig, so that there would be no waste. There are many different sausage styles throughout Italy. In Sicily, the most popular flavoring for sausage is wild fennel seeds and black pepper. Another variation is prepared with pecorino stagionato *cheese, spring onion, and parsley. In the latter, the cheese gives the pleasant taste of milk to the sausage. No matter the flavoring, sausage can be grilled, roasted, cooked in tomato sauce, or used as a stuffing.*

To make your own sausage at home, you will need a machine to stuff the sausage meat into the casings. I use the LEM manual sausage stuffer, but the food grinder attachment to a KitchenAid mixer also works well. If you don't want to track down casings, you can form the sausage meat into patties instead. You can also purchase authentic Italian sausage (see Sources, page 326). If you use store-bought for this recipe, look for a fresh Italian-style sausage of a small diameter that can be formed into a coil (not links).

Two sizes of natural casings are used to prepare sausage. The larger casing, which is slightly over 1 inch in diameter when filled, is made from pig intestines. Smaller casing, almost half the size, is made from lamb intestines, and is more popularly used in Sicilian sausage making. You can use either to prepare sausages; however, for grilling, lamb casing is optimal because the sausage is less thick and cooks through before the outside of the sausages can burn. Synthetic sausage casings are also available, but I prefer the natural kind.

Makes 2 pounds sausage (serves 8)

Sausage

2 pounds boneless pork meat from the cheek, belly, and shoulder, ground (or purchase ground fatty pork meat from your butcher)

2 tablespoons salt

1 cup white wine

2 tablespoons fennel seeds

2 teaspoons finely ground black pepper

4 feet of pork casing, or 8 feet of lamb casing

Peppers and onions

6 bell peppers (mixed colors), stems removed, cut in half and seeded

1/2 pound small onions, cut in half

1/2 cup *salmoriglio* (page 41)

1 FOR THE SAUSAGE: Put the ground meat in a mixing bowl with the salt, wine, fennel seeds, and black pepper and mix to incorporate. It's easiest to mix the meat with your hands, but you also can use a rubber spatula. Cover and refrigerate overnight, or at least 8 hours to allow time for the flavors to combine.

2 The next day, soak four wooden skewers in water for about 1 hour before you plan to grill. Wash the sausage casings under running water. Mix the meat filling again. Oil the tip of the sausage maker. Tie off the end of the casing and fit the non-tied end on the tip. Stuff the casing, following the manufacturer's instructions. After you have filled the full length of the casing, tie off the other end.

3 To grill the sausage and peppers and onions, heat a charcoal or gas grill to medium heat.

continued ↓

4 Coil the sausage in a circular shape, as in the photograph opposite. To secure the sausage in place, insert the skewers gently through the sides of the sausage coil. The skewers should run from top to bottom and from left to right. All four skewers should meet in the center of the coil.

5 Toss the peppers and onions with the *salmoriglio* and spread them out on half of the grill, with the sausage coil alongside. Grill, turning the vegetables and sausage, for about 20 minutes, until the vegetables are slightly charred and the sausage is cooked through. To test that the meat is fully cooked, gently pierce the sausage with a sharp paring knife; if the meat is still pink, return it to the grill to finish cooking.

Breaded Sausage

Cut the sausage into individual pieces about 8 inches in length and place them in pan covered with water over high heat. When the water boils, remove the pan from the heat, discard the water and add fresh water. Return the pan to the stove over high heat. Using a fork, gently pierce the skin of the sausage to allow some of the fat to render out of the sausage. When the water boils, remove the pan again from the stove and discard the water. Let the sausage cool and dry slightly. Then, roll them in a mixture of fine, untoasted breadcrumbs (page 42), laced with a pinch of salt and some dried Sicilian oregano. Place the sausage in a pan (ideally a nonstick pan) with a thin layer of olive oil. When the breading begins to turn brown, add a touch of white wine. (If preparing 8 pieces of sausage, add about $1/2$ cup white wine.) When the wine evaporates, let the breadcrumbs continue to cook and become crispy. Serve immediately.

Roasted Sausages with Potatoes

Cut the sausages into individual pieces. Peel and cube $1/2$ pound Yukon gold potatoes and toss them with about 3 tablespoons olive oil, 2 or 3 unpeeled cloves of garlic, fresh rosemary, and salt. Transfer the potatoes to a baking pan and top with the raw sausage pieces. Roast in a preheated 375°F oven for about 1 hour, until the sausage is cooked through and the potatoes are easily pierced with a paring knife.

Panino with Sausages and Sautéed Greens

In the autumn on Mount Etna, in the town of Linguaglossa, sausages are grilled or pan-fried with foraged wild cabbage leaves, known as *caliceddi*. To pan-fry, place the sausage in a heavy-bottomed pan filled halfway with water and cover. Bring to a boil, then uncover and cook over medium heat until the water evaporates, 10 to 15 minutes. Continue to cook until the sausage is browned on each side and cooked through. Slice the sausage into sections about 4 inches in length. To cook the leafy greens (you could use mustard greens, kale, or broccoli rabe), blanch for 5 minutes in boiling, salted water and drain. Cook some slivered garlic in olive oil in a large skillet. Before the garlic browns, add the boiled greens to the pan and cook for another 5 minutes, until they are soft. Then, stuff the cooked sausages and leafy greens inside a Soft Roll (page 90) and enjoy.

ROAST SUCKLING PIG

{ *Porchetta* }

PORCHETTA

Roasting a whole piglet might sound like a colossal task in the home kitchen, but it's quite easy to cook and the result is a succulent and impressive dish to feed a crowd. This slow-cooked piglet is ideal for those who enjoy their pork soft and tender. You will most likely need to call ahead to order a small piglet, gutted and cleaned, from your butcher. The exact amount of rosemary, oil, salt, and garlic needed will depend on the size of the piglet. Just make sure to prepare enough to coat the entire inner cavity well.

Serves 8 to 10

About 2 cups fresh
rosemary leaves

4 to 6 garlic cloves, smashed

1 cup olive oil

2 tablespoons salt

1 small piglet (12 to
18 pounds), cleaned by
your butcher

1 Preheat the oven to 350°F.

2 Whisk together the rosemary, garlic, olive oil, and salt in a bowl. Rub the marinade into the interior cavity of the pig. Use butcher's twine to tie the pig together. Cover the pig completely with aluminum foil. Place the pig in a roasting pan (belly down).

3 Roast for about 30 minutes for every pound. The pig is done when the meat starts to fall off the bone when prodded gently with a fork at the hip area.

4 Take the pig out of the oven, remove the foil, and leave to rest for 20 to 30 minutes before serving. To carve the piglet, place it belly side down on a large platter. Cut a slit in the back, running from the bottom of the head to the rear end. Then cut slices crosswise down the side of the pig, freeing up chunks of meat.

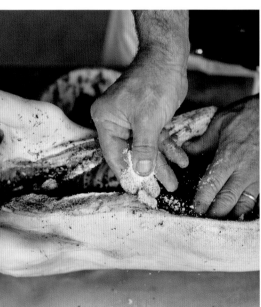
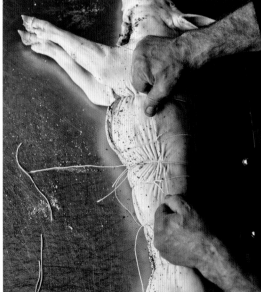

ROAST CHICKEN *with* SAUSAGE STUFFING

{ *Pollo Ripieno con Riso e Salsiccia* }

POLLU RIPIENU CU RISU E SASIZZA

Stuffing birds with a heady mix of sausage and rice is a typical Sicilian preparation. Ask your butcher to debone the chicken for you. In addition to chicken, the stuffing can be roasted in a deboned turkey. While chicken cutlets and roasted chicken pieces are popularly prepared for everyday meals in Sicily, this stuffed chicken is an ideal dish for a holiday celebration. The juxtaposition of the lean, delicate chicken meat and the rich fennel-laced sausage makes the bird irresistible. Ask your butcher to debone the chicken for you if you like.

Serves 4

1 cup arborio rice

Salt

2 tablespoons olive oil

1 onion, finely chopped

1 cup sausage meat
(see Grilled Sausage recipe, page 265)

1 large egg, beaten

About 10 sprigs
fresh rosemary

1 whole deboned chicken
(about 2 pounds), skin on

Finely ground black pepper

1 Preheat the oven to 425°F.

2 Combine the rice, 2 cups water, and 1 teaspoon salt in a pot over low heat and bring to a simmer. Cook until the water is absorbed and the rice is al dente, about 15 minutes.

3 Meanwhile, heat the olive oil in a sauté pan over medium heat. Add the onion and cook until translucent. Add the sausage meat, raise the heat slightly, and cook, stirring, to brown the meat. In a large bowl, combine the cooked rice, sausage mixture, and egg and mix to incorporate all the ingredients well. Remove the leaves from a few sprigs of the rosemary and add to the stuffing, then taste for salt and add more to taste, keeping in mind that the chicken cavity and skin will also be salted.

4 Lightly salt and pepper the interior of the chicken and place flat on a cutting board, with the skin side facing down. Form a mounded row of stuffing in the center cavity of the deboned chicken, placing more stuffing in the middle and less at the ends. Wrap the chicken around the stuffing, being careful not to rip the skin. Using butcher's twine, tie up the chicken so that it holds together: Make a slip knot and place it over the neck end of the bird. Tighten snugly. Loop the twine around the chicken, and cross over the top string to form a knot. Continue down the bird with the twine, keeping the package together and tight. Tie the twine off on the last turn. Alternatively, you can use a cooking needle and twine to sew together the open cut of the chicken. Lightly salt and pepper the exterior of the stuffed chicken.

5 Place the remaining rosemary springs in a medium-size baking pan and top with the chicken, cut side down. Roast for 10 minutes. Reduce the heat of the oven to 325°F and continue roasting for about 40 minutes, until the chicken is cooked through, with an internal temperature of 165°F. While roasting, baste the stuffed bird with drippings from the pan every 10 minutes.

QUAIL STUFFED *with* CHICORY

{ *Quaglia Ripiena con la Cicoria* }

QUAGGHIA AMMUTUNATA CÀ CICORIA

This dish is adapted from a creation of Chef Angelo Treno. An ingredient in the recipe is 'nduja Calabrese, which is a spicy spreadable pork sausage, a specialty of Calabria. It's not a typical ingredient in Sicily, but because of the close proximity of Calabria, there is a flow of ingredients between the two regions, including also bergamot oranges and red onions from Tropea.

In his version, the quail are lightly cold-smoked with eucalyptus branches before they are roasted. Rather than grill the onions in the first step of the recipe, Chef Angelo cooks them under hot ashes and then infuses the olive oil with the burnt onion skins. He also adds foie gras to the stuffing and serves the finished dish with a prickly pear granita. I've simplified the recipe, making it more approachable for the home cook. Ask your butcher to debone the quail for you. Chicory is a bitter leafy green that is delicious both raw and cooked. You can substitute escarole; the bitterness of either vegetable mixes well with the sweet onion and spicy 'nduja. Licorice powder adds an interesting depth to this dish, with its earthy sweetness.

Serves 4

1 large onion, unpeeled

8 quail, deboned

¹/₄ cup olive oil

1 head chicory, cleaned and finely chopped

15 cured black olives, pitted and finely chopped

1 tablespoon finely slivered Dried Tomatoes (homemade, page 73, or store-bought)

1 teaspoon 'nduja Calabrese (spicy spreadable pork sausage; see Sources, page 326)

Salt

¹/₂ teaspoon licorice powder (optional)

8 thin slices pancetta or guanciale

Garnish (optional)

1 teaspoon licorice powder

1 teaspoon sparkling water

1 Heat a charcoal or gas grill to medium heat. Grill the whole onion, turning multiple times, until the skin is charred, 8 to 10 minutes. Let cool. Remove the skin and thinly slice the onion.

2 To make the stuffing, heat the olive oil in a sauté pan over medium heat. Add the onion, chicory, olives, dried tomatoes, 'nduja, and ¹/₄ cup water. Cook until the water has evaporated and the chicory is soft and tender, about 10 minutes. If the chicory is cooked but water remains in the pot, place the mixture in a strainer and press on it with the bottom of a ladle to drain off the excess moisture. Taste the stuffing for salt and add more to taste. Due to the saltiness of the 'nduja and olives, you might not need to add any.

3 Preheat the oven to 375°F.

4 Gently add some salt and, if you like, a very small amount of licorice powder to the inside cavity of each quail. Place 1 tablespoon of the stuffing inside each cavity. Wrap the side of each quail around the stuffing and secure the birds with toothpicks. Three toothpicks will hold each bird closed. Wrap each bird with a slice of pancetta, which will keep the quail moist during the roasting process.

5 Place the quails in a roasting pan. Roast for about 15 minutes, until they turn a toasty brown color. The birds cook quickly since they are so small.

6 Remove the pancetta and toothpicks before serving. If you want to add the additional garnish, whisk the licorice powder into the sparkling water. Drizzle small drops of the licorice water around each quail and serve. (Since the licorice flavor is intense, a little goes a long way.)

ROASTED RABBIT *with* POMEGRANATE

{ *Coniglio Arrostito con Melograno* }

CUNIGGHIU ARRUSTUTU CU GRANATU

In Sicily, rabbit as well as wild hare are popular meat staples of the cuisine. Although they are from the same family, the meat of rabbit and hare have different flavor profiles. Hare tends be gamey, while rabbit meat is much more subtle. You can choose either for this recipe, although it is much easier to source rabbit. Note the importance of procuring fresh, as opposed to frozen, rabbit. Serve with a Winter Squash Caponata (page 77).

Serves 4

¹/₂ cup red wine

2 tablespoons red wine vinegar

1 garlic head, cut in half horizontally

3 sprigs fresh rosemary

1 whole rabbit, quartered

Seeds of 1 pomegranate

¹/₂ cup chopped skinned almonds

1 In a glass or stainless steel mixing bowl, combine the wine, vinegar, garlic, and rosemary. Add the rabbit, cover, and marinate in the refrigerator overnight or for up to 8 hours.

2 The following day, preheat the oven to 375°F.

3 Remove the rabbit from the marinade and place it in a baking pan along with the garlic head and rosemary. Strain the marinade into a thick-bottomed sauté pan over medium heat. Let it reduce by half and hold for drizzling on top of the roasted rabbit for serving.

4 Roast the rabbit for 30 minutes, until a meat thermometer inserted deep into a rabbit leg registers at least 160°F, but no more than 180°F. Top with the pomegranate seeds and almonds. Drizzle the reduced marinade on the rabbit and serve.

FINDING KISSES IN SHELLS

"Ziti a vasari e babbaluci a sucari, su' cosi chi nun ponnu mai saziari." (Kisses from one's lover and snails to suck, are things that one can never be full of.) There are several varieties of snails that grow in the wild, but four different sizes recognized by Sicilians. The most commonly prepared, called *babbaluci* in Sicilian dialect, have a white shell with brown stripes and measure about 1 inch in diameter.

Before cooking with snails picked in the wild, they need to be purged of any food that may be harmful to humans. However, farm-raised snails are sold ready to cook.

In Palermo, this dish is traditionally prepared for the Feast of Saint Rosalia, the city's patron saint. When in Palermo for this grand festival, look for the numerous *babbaluciari* who sell the snails at street food stands. My cousin Maria prepares snails in the summer, collecting them on her farmland after the occasional bout of rain. She only prepares the snails in one way, known as *picchi pacchi,* "fast and quick": with a sauce of onions and fresh tomatoes.

CLOCKWISE FROM TOP LEFT:
*Braised and Glazed Lamb Shanks
(page 281), Sicilian Beef Stew
(page 280), filet mignon with Olive
Oil Mashed Potatoes (page 275)
and a Nero d'Avola reduction; Roast
Chicken with Sausage Stuffing
(page 269); Grilled Beef Braciole
(page 264); Quail Stuffed with
Chicory (page 270); Breaded Lamb
Chops with Potato and Pepper
Gratin (page 274)*

BREADED LAMB CHOPS *with* POTATO *and* PEPPER GRATIN

{ *Costolette d'Agnello Impanate* }

CUOSTI RI CRASTAGNEDDU 'MPANATI

Throughout Sicily, it's popular to encrust meat with breadcrumbs. Thinly pounded veal and beef are staple dishes in homes around the island. One of my favorite aromas in the kitchen is the toasty smell of meat and breadcrumbs being seared in olive oil. I like to lightly drizzle the chops with a balsamic glaze or 'nzogghiu parsley-mint sauce (page 43). Do not overdo the drizzle, or the crispy crust will become soggy.

Serves 4

¹/₂ cup olive oil

¹/₄ cup balsamic vinegar

1 tablespoon dried Sicilian oregano

8 lamb chops

2 large eggs, beaten

2 cups fine breadcrumbs (page 42)

Vegetable oil

Potato and Pepper Gratin (recipe below)

1 In a glass or stainless steel bowl, mix the olive oil, vinegar, and oregano. Add the lamb chops, turn to coat, and cover. Marinate in the refrigerator for 2 hours or up to 8 hours.

2 Remove the lamb from the marinade, and discard the marinade. Use a meat mallet to pound out the lamb: Hold the bone in one hand and the mallet in the other, and give two light hits on each side so the meat is ¹/₂ inch thick. Do not pound out too much.

3 Place the beaten egg in a shallow bowl and the breadcrumbs in a separate bowl. Dip a chop in the egg, let excess drip off, then dredge in the breadcrumbs to coat. Repeat with the remaining chops.

4 Heat the vegetable oil in a cast-iron pan or a heavy-bottomed sauté pan over medium heat until hot. In batches, add the chops to the pan, making sure they are well spaced so that they fry rather than steam. Cook for about 2 minutes on one side, then flip each chop over by holding the bone. Cook until the breadcrumbs are toasty brown in color and the lamb reaches desired doneness, 4 to 6 minutes. Transfer to paper towels to drain excess oil. Serve with the Potato and Pepper Gratin.

Potato and Pepper Gratin

Serves 4

4 red bell peppers

2 tablespoons olive oil

2 tablespoons salt

6 Yukon gold potatoes, peeled and held in water

Ground black pepper

1 teaspoon dried Sicilian oregano

1 cup grated pecorino *primo sale* cheese

1 tab unsalted butter

6 tablespoons coarse breadcrumbs (page 42)

1 Preheat the oven to 400°F. Rub the peppers with the olive oil and 1 tablespoon of the salt. Place in a baking pan and bake for about 30 minutes, until the peppers have turned brown in patches. Let the peppers cool in a bowl covered with plastic wrap for about 10 minutes. Strain the liquid in the bottom of the roasting pan. Reduce the oven temperature to 350°F.

2 When the peppers are cool, peel off the skins and gently tear each pepper with your hands into four segments. Keep a bowl of water at your side while you peel and tear the peppers, because the seeds will get stuck to your hands during the process. (To remove seeds from a piece of pepper, dunk your hands in the clean water. Hold the top of the pepper piece with one hand and slide your pointer and middle finger tightly down each side of the pepper. Do not dunk the pepper in the water because that removes too much of the flavor acquired through the roasting process.) When all four peppers are peeled, seeded, and torn, place them in a bowl. Pour half of the cooking liquid over the peppers and reserve the remaining liquid.

3 Thinly slice the potatoes on a mandolin about $1/8$ inch thick. Do not submerge the sliced potatoes in water as the natural starches that are necessary to hold the potato together during the cooking process will wash away. In a mixing bowl, toss the sliced potatoes with $1/2$ cup of the reserved roasted pepper liquid, the remaining 1 tablespoon salt, black pepper to taste, and the oregano.

4 Grease a deep 8-inch square casserole dish with the butter and dust with half of the breadcrumbs. Layer one-third of the potatoes on the bottom of the casserole, spreading the slices out flat so that they fill the entire bottom. Sprinkle with about one-fourth of the cheese, followed by a layer of roasted peppers. Continue with two more layers of each ingredient. Top with more cheese and with the remaining breadcrumbs. Bake for about 30 minutes, until a paring knife easily slides through the layers of the dish. Let cool slightly before portioning; the cheese needs to set so that the layers hold firm together. Cut into squares to serve. Or, for a more decorative presentation, use a round cookie cutter to cut out rounds of the gratin.

OLIVE OIL MASHED POTATOES

{ *Purea di Patate all'Olio d'Oliva* }

PATATI SCACCIATI CU L'OGGHIU

Potatoes are a staple of the Sicilian diet, although only one golden variety is consumed. They are most often served with meat. The following recipe calls for mashing the potatoes with olive oil rather than butter as in the American version, and with Yukon gold potatoes for creaminess.

Serves 4

1 pound Yukon gold
potatoes, peeled and
cut in small chunks

Salt

$1/2$ cup extra-virgin olive oil

1 Place the potatoes in a pot and cover with cold salted water. Bring to a boil over high heat. At this point, check if the potatoes are cooked, by slipping a paring knife inside a piece of potato. If the knife slides in easily, the potatoes are cooked. If not, leave in the boiling water for a few more minutes and test again.

2 Drain the potatoes, transfer to a mixing bowl, and roughly mash with a fork. Drizzle in the olive oil and continue to mash until incorporated together. Add salt to taste and mix well. This can be prepared in advance and heated when it's time to serve.

SEARED PORK TENDERLOIN *with* A SICILIAN CHOCOLATE SAUCE

{ *Maiale con Salsa di Cioccolato* }

MAIALI CU CIOCCOLATU

This dish is made with pork from the black pigs of the Nebrodi Mountains (see page 56). To replicate the intensity of the meat from black pigs, look for pasture-raised meat, as opposed to conventional factory-raised pork.

The sauce, which is an adaptation of a very old recipe from the southeastern corner of Sicily, consists of bitter chocolate from Modica (see page 318), red wine, Marsala, honey, and herbs. The taste is nuanced, layering the warm flavors of cocoa with the acidity of the wine and the brightness of the herbs. While chocolate from Modica is available in limited quantities in the United States (see Sources, page 326), you can substitute any high-quality dark chocolate that doesn't contain milk.

Serves 4

4 long, thin slices guanciale or pancetta

1 pound pork tenderloin, cut into 4 equal pieces

4 garlic cloves, lightly crushed with your fist

2 sprigs fresh marjoram

2 bay leaves

1 cinnamon stick

1 whole fresh spicy red pepper

¹/₄ cup full-bodied red wine

¹/₄ cup dry Marsala

¹/₄ cup Meat Broth (page 146)

¹/₂ ounce bitter chocolate from Modica, grated

¹/₄ cup unsalted butter

¹/₃ cup chestnut flower honey or another dark honey

Salt, if needed

¹/₂ cup pistachios, roughly chopped

1 Wrap a slice of guanciale around each piece of pork and use a toothpick to secure the slice in place. Heat a heavy-bottomed sauté pan—large enough to hold all 4 pieces of meat with space between them—over high heat. When the pan is hot, add the meat and sear on all sides. Reduce the heat to medium and cook for about 8 minutes. Add the garlic, marjoram, bay leaves, cinnamon stick, and spicy pepper. Reduce the heat, cover, and cook for another 2 minutes, until an instant-read thermometer inserted into the center of the pork reaches 145°F, or desired temperature is reached.

2 Transfer the meat, garlic, herbs, and spices to a plate. To the same sauté pan, add the red wine and Marsala and simmer over medium heat until reduced by one-third, scraping the bottom of the pan with a wooden spoon to release the flavor of any stuck pieces of meat. Add the broth and simmer for 10 minutes, until reduced by half. Add the chocolate, butter, and honey. Stir well and let cook for another minute. Taste to determine if the sauce needs salt.

5 Strain the sauce through a fine-meshed strainer. Place the pork pieces in the sauce, and sprinkle with the chopped pistachios before serving.

CHICKEN GRATIN

{ Gallina al Gratin }

GADDINA GRATINATA

This chicken dish is simple to prepare and in a way it makes two dishes out of one. First you make a chicken broth, which you can later use as a base for any number of other dishes such as soup, risotto, or stew. Then you remove the chicken pieces and bake them in the oven with a breadcrumb crust. The simmered meat is especially tender and succulent, contrasting with the crispy crust outside.

The dish is an adaptation of an old recipe from the province of Caltanissetta, and was documented in Giuseppe Coria's encyclopedic Sicilian recipe book, Profumi di Sicilia. In the version described by Coria only chicken thighs are used, but I like to use a whole quartered chicken. I serve the gratin with a vegetable medley, varying based on the time of year. In the spring it's great with Twice-Cooked Fava Beans (page 218), while in the summer it's delicious with Peperonata (page 255) or roasted eggplant. In the fall the dish works nicely with roasted mushrooms, and in the winter I pair it with roasted cauliflower.

Serves 4

1 quartered whole chicken from making Chicken Broth (page 147; reserve broth for another use)

2 tablespoons extra-virgin olive oil

Grated zest of ½ organic lemon

Juice of 2 lemons

1 tablespoon dried Sicilian oregano

1 cup grated aged pecorino cheese

1 cup fine breadcrumbs (page 42)

Salt and ground black pepper

1 Take the quartered chicken pieces out of the broth they were boiled in and remove the skin. In a small bowl, combine the olive oil, lemon zest, lemon juice, and oregano. Rub the marinade on the chicken pieces.

Cover and marinate in the refrigerator for at least 1 hour or as long as overnight.

2 Preheat the oven to 400°F.

3 In a mixing bowl, combine the cheese with the breadcrumbs, adding salt and black pepper to taste. Pat the chicken dry with paper towels, then dredge each piece of chicken in the breadcrumb mixture to form a crust around the meat.

4 Place the chicken pieces in a baking pan and bake for about 20 minutes, until the breadcrumbs turn golden brown. Serve immediately.

The Other Meats

Horse and donkey meat have a place historically on the Sicilian table, and today these animals make up about 3 percent of all cultivated livestock. The flavor of horse meat is somewhere between that of beef and game. It is low in fat but very rich in iron, often recommended by doctors on the island for those who are anemic. In the province of Catania, horse meat is cured and made into a prosciutto.

Donkey meat is rarer than horse meat. Due to the fact that most donkeys are raised for their milk, very few are selected for their meat. However, the delicacy can be found in select restaurants or meat shops. Donkey meat is grilled or slow-cooked in a stew. When in Catania, look for horse-meat sandwiches, which are sold as street food.

Other meats consumed in Sicily include those that are hunted in the wild, such as wild boar, duck, porcupine, and goose.

MAMMA ADELE'S BRAISED GOAT

{ *Capretto al Forno di Mamma Adele* }

CAPRETTU 'NFURNATU RI MAMMA ADELE

This luscious goat dish is an old family recipe of Fabio Sireci, proprietor and third-generation winemaker of Feudo Montoni (see pages 10–11). At Christmas and Easter, the local shepherd gifts the Sireci family a suckling baby goat, which fed off the milk of its mother goat, who grazed on the array of wild herbs and grasses on the lands of the family's winery. So, for the holiday dinner, Fabio's mother, Adele, is able to prepare a succulent meal of the goat braised in tomatoes, along with stewed peas and potatoes.

Mamma Adele cooks from her heart, like most Sicilian matriarchs, without paying attention to the exact amounts of onions and tomatoes, nor to the temperature of the oven. Regarding the cooking time of the dish, she says "é prontu quan' é prontu"—"the meat is ready when it's cooked." As for the exact amounts of the ingredients, well, they simply need to feel right. The aromas, texture, and visual appearance of the dish speak to her, indicating when the dish is ready to serve. I did my best to translate the broad directions of her intuitive cooking here. Ultimately, this is a very simple dish, but if rushed, or prepared without care, the end result will surely not be the same as Mamma Adele's.

To cook the goat, and to create the perfect sughetto *(or sauce-like coating) around the slow-cooked meat, Mamma Adele uses chopped peeled tomatoes and a cup of Feudo Montoni's most prized red wine, Vrucara, which is vinified from a unique clone of Nero d'Avola grapes specific to the winery that dates back to the fifteenth century. The vines that grow the grapes for Vrucara are around ninety years old, and are scattered around the field in an indistinct manner. The flavor profile of the wine, like that of the meat of the goat, is an expression of the land, which is constantly enriched with a steady flow of care and undivided attention from Fabio. With the exception of the salt and pepper, all the ingredients in this recipe, when cooked at Montoni, are produced and grown on the land, reinforcing the Sireci family's bond with the uncontaminated nature that surrounds them, and making it a perfect holiday dish to celebrate life and love.*

You can source the goat from your butcher, although you probably will need to order it in advance. The segments used for this recipe can be from any part of the animal. Since each piece contains the bone, ask your butcher to cut it for you with a meat cleaver. When ordering the goat, ask for a small young goat, as the meat will be more tender. When I prepare this in Sicily, I use a whole baby goat (cut into pieces the size of a fist), as it cooks very quickly and is tender. Note that the same dish can be prepared with lamb and is equally delicious.

Serves 6

Goat

5 Yukon gold potatoes

10 pounds bone-in goat meat, cut into 3- to 4-inch segments

3 yellow onions, cut in ¹/₄-inch-thick slices

¹/₂ cup extra-virgin olive oil

1 cup Nero d'Avola red wine, preferably Vrucara

3 cups canned peeled plum tomatoes, chopped

4 or 5 intact sprigs fresh rosemary

4 or 5 bay leaves

2 teaspoons salt, plus more to taste

1 teaspoon ground black pepper

Peas

¹/₂ onion, finely chopped

2 tablespoons olive oil

2¹/₂ pounds fresh peas (about 1 pound shelled), or 1 pound frozen peas

3 cups Vegetable Broth (page 147)

Salt

1 FOR THE GOAT: Preheat the oven to 350°F. Cut the potatoes in half lengthwise and then into ¼-inch-thick half-moon slices.

2 Wash the goat pieces in a strainer. Distribute them in two deep baking pans, about 10 by 20 inches each. Add the onions, potatoes, olive oil, wine, tomatoes, rosemary, bay leaves, salt, and pepper and mix thoroughly so that the meat is well coated with all the ingredients.

3 Bake for about 2 hours, stirring the meat several times so that all sides of the cubes are moistened by the wine, oil, and tomatoes. The cooking time will vary depending on the tenderness of the goat. The larger the goat, the tougher the meat, and therefore a longer cooking time. To test if the meat is done, remove a piece from the pan and press a fork against it. The meat cube should hold its shape, but should be soft and moist.

4 MEANWHILE, FOR THE PEAS: In a sauté pan, combine the onion, olive oil, and a few tablespoons of water and cook over low heat until the onion is translucent. Add the peas, broth, and a pinch of salt. Cook until the broth is absorbed into the peas and the peas lose their bright green color, about 30 minutes. Taste for salt and add more accordingly. Serve the peas alongside the goat and potatoes.

SICILIAN BEEF STEW

{ Stracotto di Manzo alla Siciliana }

STRACOTTU RI MANZU

This dish is perfect for the early spring, when fresh peas and carrots are in season, but the air is still laden with a chill, a temperature that calls for a pot of meltingly tender braised meat. A stracotto (which translates to "extra cooked") is a dish in which the meat is so soft that it can be cut with a fork. This style of cooking meat requires a cut with more fat and less connective tissue, such as beef short ribs or beef tail.

Serves 4

2 cups full-bodied red wine	1 cup finely chopped onions
1 cinnamon stick	¹⁄₂ cup finely chopped celery
6 whole cloves	¹⁄₄ cup tomato paste
3 bay leaves	5 cups Meat Broth (page 146)
1 teaspoon whole black peppercorns	Salt
3 sprigs fresh parsley and/or thyme	¹⁄₂ pound Yukon gold potatoes, cut into bite-size pieces
2 pounds short ribs, bones removed and cut into 2-inch chunks	2 large carrots, cut into bite-size pieces
2 tablespoons lard or vegetable oil	1 cup shelled green peas

1 In a glass or stainless steel bowl, combine the wine, cinnamon stick, cloves, bay leaves, peppercorns, and parsley sprigs. Add the short ribs, turning to coat. Cover and marinate in the refrigerator overnight or up to 10 hours.

2 The next day, remove the meat from the marinade (reserve the marinade). Let the meat sit at room temperature for about 1 hour before cooking. Strain the marinade through a strainer, reserving both the liquid and the spices and herbs. Wrap the solids in a piece of cheesecloth and set aside.

3 Heat the lard in a heavy-bottomed stockpot over high heat. Pat the short rib pieces dry. When the lard is melted and hot, reduce the heat to medium and, in batches, add the short ribs. Do not crowd the pot or the meat will not sear, but rather, it will steam, defeating the purpose of searing. It's important to sear all sides of the meat in order to lock in the juice and flavor. As you sear the short ribs, transfer them to a bowl.

4 Add the onions, celery, and ¹⁄₂ cup water to the pot. Reduce the heat to medium and cook until the onion is translucent and the water evaporates. Return the meat to the pot and raise the heat to high. Add the tomato paste and stir vigorously with a wooden spoon. Add the reserved marinade and deglaze the pot, using your wooden spoon to scrape up any meat bits or tomato paste stuck to the bottom. Add the broth, along with the cheesecloth holding the spices and herbs. If the broth does not cover all of the meat in the pot, add some water. After the liquid comes to a boil, reduce the heat to low. Cover the pot and cook over low heat for 2 hours, until the meat is soft. (Alternatively, you can transfer the pot, if it is ovenproof, to a preheated 350°F oven and bake.) About halfway into the cooking, add salt to taste.

5 Meanwhile, blanch the potatoes, carrots, and peas separately in a large pot of salted boiling water. Do not fully cook the potatoes or carrots, just blanch them lightly: the potatoes for about 8 minutes, the carrots for about 8 minutes, and the peas for about 2 minutes.

6 After the meat has cooked for 2 hours, add the blanched potatoes and carrots to the pot and cook until they are tender, 30 to 40 minutes. At this point, the meat should be very soft. Add the blanched peas and stir for a few more minutes. Serve immediately.

BRASED *and* GLAZED LAMB SHANKS

{ *Agnello Brasato e Glassato* }

AGGLASSATU

The word for the sauce in this dish, glassato, *comes from the French verb* glacer, *meaning "to ice." As soon as the sauce cools off, it condenses, forming a noticeable glaze that resembles an icing. In Sicilian dialect, the sauce can also be referred to as* agglassatu *or* glassatu. *This dish is typically prepared with large cuts of meat, and I like to use the shank, because its meat doesn't tend to dry out during the braising process and the bone adds additional flavor. Traditionally the meat is consumed as a main course and the sauce is used to dress pasta as a first course, most commonly* maltagliati *pasta (see page 197). But you can serve the meat and sauce together as a main course, perhaps with just polenta or crusty bread on the side.*

Serves 4

2 tablespoons lard or olive oil

4 lamb shanks (about $^1/_3$ pound each)

4 onions, finely chopped

1 cup white wine

6 cups Meat Broth (page 146)

1 cup fresh parsley, stems removed and finely chopped

4 garlic cloves, crushed

Salt and ground black pepper

1 pound Yukon potatoes, peeled and cut into 2-inch cubes

1 cup grated aged pecorino cheese

$^1/_2$ cup cubed caciocavallo cheese

1 Heat the lard in a large stockpot over medium heat. Two at a time, add the lamb shanks and cook to brown well on all sides. Remove the meat from the pot temporarily.

2 Add the onions and $^1/_2$ cup water. Using a wooden spoon, stir the onions, scraping the bits of meat stuck to the bottom of the pot. When the water evaporates, continue to cook and stir the onions as they start to brown.

3 Return the meat to the pot, along with the wine. When the wine evaporates, add the broth, parsley, garlic, and some salt and pepper. Keep in mind that salty cheese will be added later, so do not fully salt the sauce. Lower the heat, cover the pot, and cook for about $1^1/_2$ hours. Occasionally remove the lid and stir to ensure that the onions are not sticking to the bottom.

4 Add the potatoes and cook for another 45 minutes, at which point the meat and potatoes should be tender and cooked through. Remove the meat and keep warm. Pass the braising liquid and potatoes through a food mill, crushing the potatoes. (The meat and sauce can be prepared in advance up to this point and held for a few hours covered in the refrigerator.)

5 When ready to serve, return the sauce and meat to the pot and heat through over medium heat. Add the pecorino and caciocavallo. When the cheese melts, taste for salt, adding more accordingly. Serve immediately.

STUFFED BEEF ROLL

{ *Falsomagro* }

BRUCIULUNI

Falsomagro is a rolled beef log that is prepared throughout Sicily, most commonly on Christmas Day. In some areas it is called by other names. In Bagheria, for instance, it's known as bruciuluni. *As to be expected, the stuffing ingredients differ from city to city, and from family to family. In this version, mortadella, ground beef, and pecorino are rolled up in butterflied eye round steak. Some cooks will add sausage, salame, pancetta, caciocavallo cheese, or cured lard to their stuffing. The meat is secured with butcher's twine like a roast, and cooked in a tomato-based sauce. As with the* brasato *(page 281), traditionally the sauce is tossed with pasta and served as a first course prior to serving the meat on its own.*

The name falsomagro *("false thin") is a coy reference to the surprise of the finished dish: A lean piece of meat conceals a hearty and rich filling stuffed inside; the richness is apparent only when the roll is sliced at the table.*

Serves 8

Beef roll

4 large eggs

3 pounds beef eye round, butterflied into one long piece measuring about 10 by 13 inches

1 cup fine breadcrumbs (page 42)

1 cup grated aged pecorino cheese

1 pound ground beef or pork

1 tablespoon Garlic Paste (page 40)

¼ pound mortadella, thinly sliced

1 cup shelled peas

Sauce

2 tablespoons lard or olive oil

Salt

2 cups Soffritto (page 40)

1 cup red wine

1 cup tomato paste

4 cups Tomato Pulp (homemade, page 70, or store-bought)

3 cups Meat Broth (page 146)

Ground black pepper

2 carrots, sliced

2 cups shelled peas

1 FOR THE BEEF ROLL: Add 2 of the eggs to a small pot filled with cold water and bring to a boil over high heat. Cook for 5 minutes, until the eggs are medium hard-boiled. Drain and cover with cold water. When cool enough to handle, remove the shells and cut into ¼-inch-thick slices. Set aside.

2 Lay the beef on a work surface. Using the flat side of a meat mallet, pound on both sides to even out the thickness of the meat to about ⅓ inch thick. Be careful not to puncture the flesh.

3 Lightly beat the remaining 2 eggs in a medium bowl. Add the breadcrumbs, pecorino, ground meat, and garlic paste and mix well. Spread the mixture on top of the piece of beef. Arrange the boiled egg slices, mortadella, and peas on top. Roll the meat carefully and tie the roll with butcher's twine, as you would a roast.

4 TO COOK THE BEEF ROLL AND MAKE THE SAUCE: Preheat the oven to 350°F. In a large ovenproof stockpot or casserole, heat the lard over high heat. Sprinkle the beef roll with some salt. Add to the pot and cook, turning to brown on all sides. Add the soffritto, wine, tomato paste, and tomato pulp, being careful not to splash any of the wine on the stovetop. Use a wooden spoon to release any stuck meat pieces or juices on the bottom of the pan. Cover the pot and bake in the oven for 1 hour, turning the meat every so often so that it cooks uniformly. Add the meat broth, pepper, and carrots and, soon after, add the peas. Bake for 1 hour longer. To test if the meat is tender, poke a fork inside the meat roll: If it goes in without resistance, it is ready. Remove the string with kitchen scissors.

5 To serve, cut the meat roll into 1-inch-thick slices and place on a bed of the sauce on a large platter.

Chapter 10

FRUITS & DESSERTS

J UST STEPS FROM MY HOUSE IN SANT'ANNA, a pasticceria supplies the townspeople with a quintessential assemblage of Sicilian cookies, pastries, and cakes. Starting at dawn, the owners heat up their ovens, filling the narrow village streets with a flirtatious perfume, a warm mélange of toasty and sugary aromas.

During my childhood summers in Sant'Anna, my mother assigned me the task of procuring sweets from the pastry shop whenever we would visit the house of a relative. What a wonderful job it was! In my young mind, the very thought of an aunt, uncle, or cousin correlated with another trip to that marvelous store. A glimpse at the glass counter was parallel to looking through a kaleidoscope, where a palate of vibrant colors swirled in front of my eyes.

Like most pastry shops, the one in Sant'Anna divides the counter between dry cookies and pastries. Almond cookies decorated with candied orange peel sit side by side with rustic *reginelle* (crumbly cookies covered in toasted sesame seeds), sponge cakes layered with ricotta cream and glazed with green marzipan, and tiny pies filled with pastry cream and topped with miniature strawberries. My mother used to fill my money pouch with the exact amount of Italian *lira* needed for the cookies, but the shop owners used to gift me an extra treat to munch on every time.

Beyond my grandmother's typical Sicilian home-style sweets, such as *sfinci* (page 302) and almond *cubbaita* (page 297), the pastry shop in Sant'Anna was my first introduction to the array of textures, ingredients, and flavors included in typical Sicilian desserts. Over the last six years, during my research trips, desserts were always the highlight. I visited pastry, gelato, and granita shops all around the region, from Capello in Palermo to Cerniglia in San Giuseppe Jato to Subba in Lipari to Bam Bar in Taormina, and many, many more. Each time, I arrived in my professional garb, notepad in hand, ready to conduct interviews, but within moments, the sweet aromas rendered me a child again, as if I were standing at the banquette of Sant'Anna's pastry shop.

The Most Decadent Breakfast

During my childhood summers in Sant'Anna, mornings commenced with the toasty scent of semolina bread baking in the wood-burning oven of the *panificio* and permeating the narrow village streets. Straight out of bed, I used to venture to pick up a few loaves, ripping off and devouring the crusty ends with haste. Before walking home, I often stopped at the town's main café, Bar Roma, for a brioche roll filled with their homemade granita. I relished in the sensation of biting into that warm, sweet bread and then feeling cold lemony ice on my teeth. As the ice melted, it would drip down my fingers and I would try to eat the treat quickly, usually leaving my entire face covered with a sticky sweet film.

Brioche is a soft, egg-based bread that is typically eaten for breakfast. During summer months, it's popular to overstuff a brioche with gelato or granita. A slit is cut into one side of a brioche, which is then smeared with gelato or granita, using a paddle. If not for breakfast, these treats are also enjoyed as a snack in the afternoon or as a late-night treat. Sicilians can be found strolling down the piazza with a gelato-stuffed brioche in hand. I can't think of a better start or finish to a hot summer day.

CONFECTIONS FROM THE CLOISTERS

Convents are mainly to thank for the elaborate dessert tradition of the island. Before the advent of pastry shops in the nineteenth century, the majority of sweets were produced by cloistered nuns who coveted the recipes, keeping them top secret. Initially, desserts prepared in convents were not sold to the public, but rather were gifted to bishops, dukes, counts, and others who helped support the mission of the sisters. Sweets such as *frutta di Martorana* (fruit-shaped marzipan), *ova murina* (spiced almond crêpes stuffed with milk custard), and cannoli were all born in the realm of the monastery. Nuns were usually the unmarried second daughters of noble families and often were accompanied by servants. Sometimes servants taught the nuns dessert recipes, while other times individual nuns devised their own personal creations.

Established in 1299, by the noble Chiaramonte family, the Cistercian monastery of Santo Spirito in Agrigento is one of Sicily's last remaining cloistered monasteries, where nine devout nuns live in service to God. To support themselves and maintain their large monastic structure, the nuns sell pastries, ranging from multiple types of cookies prepared from local almonds, hazelnuts, and candied fruit to their famous sweet pistachio couscous, the recipe for which is believed to have been created by a North African servant centuries ago. They also operate a small bed and breakfast on the property. When visiting their shop, make sure not to miss a visit inside the chapel, which is adorned with stunning stucco engravings that date back to the early 1700s.

CITRUS-GLAZED FIGS

{ *Fichi Cotti nel Succo di Arancia e Limone* }

FICHI ABBAGNATI

Figs have a long history in Sicily, having been part of the fruit realm as far back as antiquity. In fact, Greek mythology considered the fig a sacred fruit and the exportation of figs was banned. It was considered sacrilegious to steal a fig off a tree, an offense worthy of unleashing the wrath of the gods. At the time, Aristotle, along with other Greek writers, also documented that fig tree juice was used to produce cheese, a technique being revitalized today to produce goat's milk cheese in Sicily (see page 62). While Plato wrote that figs had the power to make people smart, the Roman naturalist Pliny was convinced that figs make young people strong, aid the elderly, and reduce wrinkles. Thus, for multiple reasons, figs were considered the super-fruit of antiquity.

There are multiple varieties that range in color from black to dark purple to a light green. Figs tend to be very delicate and must be handled with care. If storing them for over a day, keep them held in the refrigerator in an airtight container so that they don't absorb the odors of other foods.

In addition to fresh, figs are often dried in Sicily, either on the tree or, similar to tomatoes, cut in half and dried under the sun. Dried figs are used in winter dishes, especially in desserts. For example, buccellato *(page 308) is prepared with a filling predominately comprised of dried figs as well as other dried fruits and nuts.*

This recipe is a simple yet delicious way to enjoy fresh figs when they are in season. Use any variety of fig you prefer and do not peel them. They are delicious served over a bowl of vanilla gelato.

Serves 4

1 cup fresh lemon juice	$1/2$ cup sugar
$1^1/2$ cups fresh orange juice	1 pound fresh figs

1 Combine the lemon juice, orange juice, sugar, and figs in a saucepan. If the juice does not cover the figs, add enough water to cover. Bring to a simmer over medium heat. Reduce the heat and simmer for 10 minutes, until the figs are soft to touch and the liquid has reduced to a glaze.

2 With a slotted spoon, transfer the figs to an airtight container and cover. Transfer the cooking liquid to a small container and cover. Refrigerate until chilled, or for up to 3 days. When ready to serve, pour the glaze on top of the figs.

CHRISTMAS GIFTS

My first taste of Sicily's intense citrus fruits took place one Christmas season during my childhood. I woke up to find a box with my name on it under the tree. I ripped it open, only to find another box inside, then another and another, until finally, I discovered an envelope with plane tickets to Palermo. "Pack your bags," bellowed my father, John, "because you and I are leaving for Sicily in three hours." Upon arrival, he drove straight to Maria's house to surprise the family, Christmas presents in tow and a glow of happiness in his eyes. Their house was filled with navel oranges, citrons, and mandarins, all fruits from their property. For one week, we filled our stomachs with these gems and even spent some time helping to pick the fruit on their farm. Up until today, every time I even scratch my nail against the skin of a fragrant Sicilian orange, I remember that special trip at my father's side.

Oranges and lemons are a major symbol of Sicily today, but citrus was first imported from Asia a thousand years ago. The many types of citrus that grow in Sicily today are crossbreeds and international varieties. When purchasing oranges at markets around the island, look for *biondo, basiliano, vaniglie,* and blood oranges (varieties include *tarocco, moro,* and *sanguinelle,* all of which have a red-streaked pulp). *Biondo* is a variety that grows in the town of Scillato, a mountainous village also known for its pristine mineral water. The trees that grow on this fertile land produce some of the sweetest oranges with a well-balanced acidity. *Brasiliano* is a parent category for a few varieties of navel oranges, all of which have a bold tartness and make a delicious juice. *Vaniglie* are less acidic, more delicate and floral, with sweet notes of vanilla, hence the name. Although sweet, they have a low sugar content and are one of the few fruits that are a good option for diabetics.

As for lemons, multiple varieties exist as well that mature all throughout the year in Sicily. On the eastern side of Sicily, a green variety (not to be confused with a lime), is known as *verdello*. Another variety is the *lumia,* which is somewhat reminiscent of a Meyer lemon due to its highly floral-smelling rind. The citron fruit, known in Italian as *cedro,* is another quintessential citrus found in Sicily and harvested during the Christmas season. While citrons resemble lemons in tartness, their white pith can be as much as 2 inches thick. It is lightly sweet and has a unique texture that is both firm and spongy at the same time. Citrons are often candied to make *cedrata,* a filling used in cookies and cakes.

PISTACHIO ICE CREAM

{ Gelato di Pistachio }

GELATO RI FASTUCHI

Pistachios grow in small quantities around Sicily, but the most popular are those grown on the western slopes of Mount Etna, in the town of Bronte, where the pistachio trees thrive in the volcanic soil. The trees produce nuts every other year and require little work other than pruning the branches. Between the end of August and the beginning of September, most town residents can be found harvesting pistachios, which are key to the area's economy.

Emerald green in color with streaks of deep red, the pistachios are longer and thinner, with a sharper, fresher taste than California varieties. However, production of Bronte pistachios is limited, making the nuts expensive, even in Sicily. Therefore, to satisfy demand among Sicilians, less expensive varieties are regularly imported from California and the Middle East and sold in the shell for snacking.

To experience the taste of pistachios from Mount Etna, when in Sicily during the month of September, you can experience a weeklong harvest celebration in Bronte. Tastings are prepared by local restaurants and pastry shops that include sweet and savory pistachio-based specialties, such as cookies, gelato, cake, meats crusted with pistachios, and more, all set to the backdrop of music and folk dance.

When preparing this recipe, make sure to use pistachios that are raw and unsalted. For the most delicate gelato, with a bright green color, you will need to remove the thin skin that forms an outer layer on the nut, which is easily done with the fingers after blanching the nuts in boiling water for a minute or two. In select specialty Italian stores (see Sources, page 326), you can also find pure unsweetened pistachio paste from Sicily, an ideal substitute (but use only 1 cup of paste in this recipe, as it is highly intense in flavor and very concentrated).

Serves 8

2½ cups shelled pistachios (blanching is optional)

4 cups milk

5 large egg yolks

1 cup sugar

1 In a food processor fitted with a sharp blade, finely puree the pistachios with a few tablespoons of the milk to form a creamy, well-blended puree.

2 In a heavy-bottomed pot, bring the remaining milk to a boil. Remove from the heat and add the pistachio puree. Let the mixture sit for about 1 hour, so that the flavor fully infuses the milk.

3 In a small bowl, whisk the egg yolks with the sugar until the sugar dissolves and the yolks are creamy looking and light yellow in color.

4 If you prefer a smooth gelato, strain the milk mixture through a fine-mesh strainer to remove the pistachio pieces. Bring the milk mixture to a simmer. Add the yolk mixture very slowly, whisking until fully incorporated.

5 Cook the mixture over low heat (do not let it come to a boil), stirring constantly with a wooden spoon, until the liquid thickens to the consistency of a custard, about 8 minutes. Cover and place in the refrigerator until the custard is thoroughly chilled.

6 Transfer the custard to an ice-cream maker and follow the manufacturer's directions to churn into ice cream. Serve immediately or store in the freezer for up to 2 days. If kept longer in the freezer, ice crystals will form on the surface of the gelato and change the texture from creamy to grainy.

A FRUIT WORTH ITS THORNS

Although the prickly pear is a native of Central America, today it is considered a symbol of Sicily. Grown wild and also cultivated throughout the island, this cactus plant can reach heights of up to fifteen feet and live for as long as fifty years. In June, prickly pear buds open up into bright yellow flowers, which transform into mature fruits called *agostani* by August. However, following a centuries-old tradition, these cactus fruit are plucked to make way for new flowers and second fruits—known as *i bastardoni* ("the big bastards")—that emerge between October and December. Larger and meatier than the *agostani*, the *bastardoni* boast an intense sweetness and concentrated flavor that make them worth the wait.

In fact, as demonstrated in the scene in Giuseppe Tornatore's film *Cinema Paradiso* when the two lovers enjoyed salad eaten directly out of prickly pear blades, the entirety of the prickly pear bush can be consumed. The blades can be baked, or breaded and pan-fried, while the flowers, which possess diuretic properties, are sold dried and as a tisane. The flesh of the fruit, which can be found in three varieties, is used for making jams, liqueurs, syrups, juice, granita, and a savory spiced conserve known as mostarda.

THE FINER POINTS OF ICE

Introduced to Sicily in the ninth century by Muslim conquerors, sugar is a staple ingredient in the island's frozen desserts. Muslim Sicilians of that era prepared *sherbat,* a precursor to today's sorbet, which was made from water-based fruit, herb, spice, and flower infusions mixed with sugar. Sorbet is still a popular frozen dessert not only in Sicily but in all of Italy. It has a thick consistency and is eaten with a spoon, as with ice cream, although it is devoid of milk.

Granita, on the other hand, which is particular to Sicily, is also prepared with water and fruit or flower infusions but has a more icy and liquid texture. At home it can be make by shaving nearly frozen blocks of flavored, sweetened water with a fork, but in bars and pastry shops, granita is usually made in an ice cream machine. (This latter technique results in a texture nearly indistinguishable from that of sorbet.) Granita melts quickly, as its water content is high, and therefore it is often consumed as a frozen beverage, rather than as a spoon dessert.

Before refrigeration was widespread in the region, mountaintop caves were used to preserve ice during the winter, which was then sold in blocks during the warmer months. Granita makers stirred flavored, sweetened water in metal vats, which they placed inside a wooden vessel. Between the two containers, they inserted a mixture of ice and salt.

Last but not least, gelato is Italy's version of ice cream. It contains milk and/or cream. It is thick in texture, much silkier and smoother than American ice cream. The first "Italian" gelato shop, called Café Procope, was founded in Paris by a Sicilian cook, Francesco Procopio dei Coltelli, who relocated to France in the sixteenth century. He is often credited with inventing modern-day gelato, although it is uncertain if milk was already being used to prepare frozen desserts in Sicily prior to the inauguration of his famous Parisian café.

Although gelato can be found at any local Sicilian bar, it is sometimes purchased from manufacturers or prepared with processed ingredients in an industrial style. However, look out for ice cream shops, known as *gelaterie,* that prepare artisan-quality gelato using fresh, high-quality ingredients. These gelatos contain slightly less fat than industrial ice cream and much less air, making them denser and thicker. The main ingredient in an artisan gelato is fresh cows' milk, although a small quantity of milk powder is sometimes used as a stabilizer.

ALMOND *or* LEMON ICE

{ *Granita di Mandorla o Granita di Limone* }

GRANITA RI MENNULI O GRANITA RI LIMUNA

One evening in July 2012, my mother and I were invited to a tasting dinner in Sciacca. Arriving over an hour early, we decided to watch the sunset from the port-side café bar. Overflowing with local residents, this old-fashioned coffee bar, with its cracked tiles, collage of press clippings, and faux wood wall panels, is known for serving one the best granitas in all of Italy.

After seating ourselves at an outdoor white plastic table, I proceeded to the bar. There sat the eighty-two-year-old owner, Aurelio Licata, behind a polished stainless steel counter. When he brought our order outside, I asked him why his granita is so famous. What exactly is his secret? As he curled his fingers around the edges of his white mustache, Aurelio mumbled something and walked back inside the café. I assumed that I had offended him. Moments after, he arrived with a wood crate full of lemons, banging it down on the flimsy table. Then, he ran his fingernail over the aromatic rind of one of the lemons, and placed the fruit under my nose. He bellowed, "These are real Sicilian lemons," and added: "This is my only secret."

Below I've listed the ingredients for almond and lemon granita, both of which are prepared in the same fashion. In western Sicily, lemon granita is the most popular, although in Palermo I've enjoyed some fantastic mulberry granita when the berries are in season in midsummer. If visiting the island during that period, make sure not to miss the taste of mulberry granita. In eastern Sicily, along with seasonal flavors including lemon, granita is commonly flavored with nut milks or with floral essences.

Serves 4

Lemon granita	*Almond granita*
2³/₄ cups water	1¹/₂ cups water
1 cup sugar	³/₄ cup sugar
2³/₄ cups fresh lemon juice	4 cups unsweetened fresh almond milk

1 Combine the water and sugar in a small saucepan and bring to a boil over medium-low heat. As soon as the water boils and the sugar is dissolved, remove the pan from the stovetop. Let the sugar syrup cool down.

2 Mix the sugar syrup with the almond milk or lemon juice and transfer to a shallow freezer-safe container, around 8 inches square. Cover the container and put it in the freezer. After 30 minutes, use a spoon to mix the partially frozen granita, so that the ice crystals begin to break up. Every hour, mix the granita again until it transforms into a frozen yet flaky mass, about 8 hours. (Alternatively, churn the liquid in an ice-cream maker according to the manufacturer's directions. This method, used in most shops around Sicily, yields a smoother sorbet-like texture, rather than the flakiness achieved with the hand method.)

3 Serve immediately or hold in the freezer for up to 1 week.

FEASTING UNDER THE TREES

Mulberries are sweet, juicy fruits that are low in acidity when fully ripe, and have an intense flavor unrivaled among other berries. Mulberries grow on trees, not on bushes—don't confuse the black variety with blackberries. They were first introduced to Sicily in the tenth century, when silkworms were cultivated on their trees. Today three varieties of mulberry are cultivated here: white, red, and black. The white sometimes possess lavender or pink hues when ripe. The black variety is used to make a highly prized granita, available only in midsummer when the berries are in season.

After a visit to Sicily in the 1960s, my grandmother brought back young mulberry trees—one of each type—to her farm in Goshen, New York, where they flourished on her property. I used to lie underneath them with Grandma and eat mulberries for hours. The berries of the white and red varieties have a thin stem, which I hold between my thumb and pointer finger, pulling the ripe fruit into my mouth with my front teeth. When I started my garden at Montoni, I found one of each mulberry tree variety here, too. In early to midsummer when the fruits are mature, I like to relax underneath the trees, getting my hands and face (and clothes) stained with the juice the berries exude. It's as if Grandma were sitting next to me.

ALMOND SEMIFREDDO

{ Parfait di Mandorle }

PARFE' RI MENNULE

This is a classic Sicilian frozen dessert, often prepared at home. My cousin Giusy recited the recipe to me years ago, as she served it at a midsummer dinner in her home, and I've been making it ever since. She drizzles the semifreddo with warm chocolate sauce before serving it. It's best to toast the almonds on the stovetop. I've found that it's all too easy to burn them in the oven.

Serves 8

2 cups blanched almonds	**1 teaspoon vanilla extract**
1½ cups sugar	**1 quart heavy cream**
4 large egg yolks	**1 cup warm chocolate sauce (optional)**

1 In a heavy-bottomed skillet, arrange the almonds in one layer. Cover and cook over medium heat, moving the pan in circles around the burner, until the almonds turn light golden brown, about 2 minutes. Immediately transfer to a heatproof plate and let cool, then finely chop.

2 In the skillet, combine the chopped toasted almonds, ½ cup of the sugar, and a few drops of water. Cook over medium-low heat, stirring the almonds briskly with a wooden spoon, until the melted sugar coats the almonds and turns slightly brown, about 5 minutes. Transfer to a heatproof plate and let cool. If the almonds stick together at this point, break them up with a fork or very gently pulse them in a food processor for no more than 2 seconds.

3 In a large bowl, using an electric hand mixer, beat the egg yolks with the remaining 1 cup sugar until the yolks lighten in color, 3 to 4 minutes. If using a whisk, this process might take a few minutes more. Add the vanilla and stir to incorporate.

4 In another bowl, with an electric hand mixer, whip the heavy cream to semi-stiff medium peaks.

5 Add half of the caramelized almonds to the yolk mixture, then slowly fold in the whipped cream with a rubber spatula, being careful not to overmix. Transfer the mixture to an 8-inch square glass baking dish and immediately transfer to the freezer. After about 1 hour, top with the remaining caramelized almonds and cover the pan with plastic wrap. Freeze overnight before serving.

6 To serve, cut the semifreddo with a knife into individual pieces, and using a rubber spatula, remove each piece from the pan and transfer to a plate. Drizzle with the chocolate sauce, if you like, just before serving.

ALMOND HONEY BRITTLE

{ *Torrone di Mandorle e Miele* }

CUBBAITA

This sweet is prepared during the Christmas season in Sicily with almonds, sesame seeds, pistachios, or some combination of the three. Some home cooks use caramelized sugar instead of honey, but I tend to stay true to my family recipe: My grandmother made it only with almonds and honey, as pictured on page 301 and detailed here.

While relatively simple to prepare, the brittle requires fortitude from the cook. Stirring the almonds in the pan with the reduced honey and rolling the hot mixture into a log tests the forearms. Then, after the honey solidifies and the almonds are tightly packed in the rock-like structure, slicing the brittle takes additional force. Each time I make her brittle, I remember how strong my grandmother was, despite her petite figure.

Makes 1 pound brittle

³/₄ pound blanched almonds	**1¹/₂ cups wildflower honey**
Grated zest of 1 organic orange	

1 In a heavy-bottomed skillet, arrange the almonds in one layer. Cover and cook over medium heat, moving the pan in circles around the burner, until the almonds turn light brown, about 2 minutes. Immediately transfer to a heatproof plate and let cool. If they turn darker brown, they tend to taste bitter. Mix the almonds with the orange zest.

2 Meanwhile, heat a heavy-bottomed pan over very low heat. Add the honey and heat, stirring constantly, until it starts to form bubbles. Add the toasted almonds and cook, stirring constantly, until the honey reduces significantly and resembles the consistency of melted wax as it thickens around the almonds, about 5 minutes.

3 Moisten your work surface (either a marble or wood surface will work well) with water; this helps keep the brittle from sticking. Scoop the almond-honey mixture with a wet spatula onto the damp work surface, being careful not to touch the hot mixture. Using the wet spatula, flatten the mixture, forming it into a long flat log with a thickness of no more than ³/₄ inch.

4 When the brittle has cooled enough that you can touch it, use your hands—moistened with some water—to better form the brittle into a log with rounded edges. Transfer to a baking sheet lined with parchment paper. Use a very sharp chef's knife to cut the brittle into bite-size morsels. Once fully cooled, the brittle can be placed in airtight containers and stored for up to 1 month at room temperature.

The recipe calls for skinned (blanched) almonds. If you can't find them, purchase almonds with their skins on and blanch them for less than 1 minute in boiling water. Drain and cool, and the skins will slip off easily; just use the tips of your fingers to remove them.

FRUITS OF THE IMAGINATION

According to legend, *frutta di Martorana* (marzipan fruit) originated during Norman rule, in the year 1143. Cloistered nuns of Palermo's Martorana monastery (housed in the church of Santa Maria dell'Ammiraglio) were preparing for the visit of an archbishop, but their courtyard was scarce of fruit. To embellish the garden, they created miniature fruit sculptures, prepared with a mixture of egg whites, sugar, and finely ground almonds, and hung them from the trees. The archbishop so appreciated the nuns' creativity that he requested that they send a basket of the sweets to King Roger II's court as a gift. For centuries, the recipe for *la frutta di Martorana* remained secret. It wasn't until the late 1800s that pastry shops began to produce their versions of the nuns' specialty.

Today, you can find the sweets all over Sicily. In addition to the traditional fruit shapes, bakers mold the almond mixture into vegetable, fish, and other creative shapes. Traditionally, Sicilians prepare *la frutta di Martorana* for All Souls' Day on November 2, when it is given to children, who are told that the fruit is a gift from their deceased ancestors.

Around the island today there are several recipes for the dough, which is known as *pasta reale* ("royal paste") or *marzapane* (marzipan). Pastry shops usually add flour, almond extract, and a large quantity of sugar to the mixture, making the *frutta martorana* harder, sweeter, and less enjoyable. When homemade, the almonds are more pronounced. In some areas, such as in the city of Marsala, the dough is comprised solely of ground almonds, water, and sugar. It is then cooked briefly, over a low flame, and must be stirred constantly with a wooden spoon until the water evaporates and the dough thickens. When cooked, the sugar melts, and the end result is a dough that is smooth with a pronounced almond taste.

No matter the exact ingredients used to make the *pasta reale,* a few days are required to craft these delicacies. The first day, the almonds are blanched, peeled, and ground into a fine paste, which is mixed with the other ingredients to form the dough. As mentioned above, some recipes call for the almond mixture to be cooked at this stage. Using little clay molds, the dough is shaped and then placed on racks to dry. The next day, the dried shapes are painted by hand with vegetable dye and then left to dry for another day. On the third day, the sweets are glazed and left to dry once again before they are ready to eat.

Beyond *la frutta di Martorana*, *pasta reale* is the base of other sweets around Sicily. In Catania, for instance, bakers mold a dough of almond paste and green food coloring in the shape of green olives for the Feast of Saint Agata. For Easter, in many parts of the island, lamb figurines in all sizes are sculpted using *pasta reale.*

RUSTIC ALMOND COOKIES

{ *Biscotti di Mandorle* }

BISCOTTI RI MENNULE

In pastry shops around the island, almond cookies are ubiquitous. They are commonly found topped with a piece of candied cherry or orange, or with a blanched skinned almond. (In lieu of a garnish, the cookies can be sprinkled with powdered sugar.) This version is a more rustic, hand-formed cookie, which I learned from my friend's aunt (zia) Melina. Rather than use blanched almonds or almond flour, which is more typical for pastry shop versions, Zia Melina prepares her biscotti with raw skin-on almonds—from her own trees (she also adds some bitter almonds).

Not only are Zia Melina's cookies delicious, but they possess a pleasant crunchiness and are wonderful dipped in a cup of warm milk for breakfast. For a gluten-free guest, Zia Melina made the same recipe, omitting the flour. The cookies spread out on the baking tray. Instead of the crunchiness, they were soft and chewy, but equally delicious.

Makes about 2 dozen cookies

1³/₄ cups sugar

4 large eggs, beaten

1 cup all-purpose flour

¹/₂ teaspoon ground cinnamon

1 pound raw almonds (skin-on), finely chopped in a food processor

1 Preheat the oven to 350°F. Line two baking sheets with parchment paper.

2 In a large mixing bowl, whisk the sugar and eggs until the sugar dissolves. Add the flour, cinnamon, and almonds and mix the ingredients together with a rubber spatula.

3 Using your hands, shape about 1 tablespoon of the dough into a round shape, no more than 2 inches in diameter. Place on the baking sheets, making sure to leave a few inches between the rounds. Bake for about 30 minutes, until the cookies are firm on the outside yet still soft inside. Transfer to a wire rack and let cool. The cookies can be prepared up to 2 days in advance and kept in an airtight container.

THE COOKIE CABINET

We Sicilians tend to have a bit of a sweet tooth, hence the fact that cookies, cannoli, chocolates, nut bars, and other sweet bites are not only eaten as dessert, but also as a snack between meals, usually followed by an espresso, often at a café (called a bar in Italian) or pasticceria. I love the fact that holidays and festivals are associated with specific sweets, which of course vary in execution from town to town.

Cassatelle

A must-try Sicilian pastry, *cassatelle* are dough pockets typically shaped like half moons. Throughout the island, they are prepared in multiple styles during the Easter season. In pastry shops and coffee bars of Castellamare del Golfo, in the province of Trapani, *cassatelle di ricotta* are stuffed with ricotta cream, and then fried. In the province of Palermo, these sweets are stuffed with a chickpea cream that is laced with cinnamon, chocolate, and *zuccata*. In Ragusa, tuma cheese (see page 80) is added to the ricotta cream, and in multiple other towns, dried fruits and nuts are used. Slightly more nuanced are the *cassatelle di Agira,* typical of the province of Enna, which are stuffed with cocoa, chopped almonds, chickpea flour, sugar, cinnamon, and dried lemon zest. The filling of these morsels is soft and moist, with a predominant taste of almonds.

Crispeddi di Riso

On the eastern side of Sicily, for Saint Joseph's Day, these fried rice fritters are prepared more commonly than *sfinci*. Their name, *crispeddi,* derives from the fact that they possess a crispy texture when fried. The rice is mixed with cinnamon and orange zest.

Cucchiteddi

Cucchiteddi are almond-based cookies that hail from the town of Sciacca and are prepared from a mixture of sugar, lemon zest, ground almonds, and flour. They are stuffed with candied Sicilian squash preserves (or *zuccata;* see page 313) and topped with a thin layer of sweet icing.

Cuddrireddri di Delia

The production of these fried cookies is so rare that Slow Food includes them in their roster of protected food products. The origin of these cookies dates back to the thirteenth century in the town of Delia. The ingredients are simple (consisting of semola flour, eggs, sugar, lard, red wine, cinnamon, and orange peel), but the crown shape of the cookies is elaborately formed with a series of traditional tools before being delicately fried in extra-virgin olive oil. Such tools are coveted by bakers and families in Delia because there are only a few artisans left who know how to construct them.

Le Genovesi

Hailing from the former cloistered San Carlo convent of Erice, *le Genovesi* are round treats consisting of a shell of sweet dough stuffed with pastry cream. They are best enjoyed warm, straight from the oven. Pastry master Maria Grammatico spent her childhood as an apprentice in the convent, and these bites are now produced in her kitchen daily.

'Mpanatigghi

These unique half-moon-shaped cookies—prepared exclusively in Modica—are stuffed with a paste made from chocolate, ground beef, almonds, walnuts, cinnamon, and cloves. Introduced by the Spanish in the sixteenth century, *'mpanatigghi* trace their lineage to Spanish empanadas.

Nacatuli Eoliani

These decorative cookies are prepared on the Aeolian Islands during the Christmas season. Wrapped in a very thin layer of pastry crust, they are stuffed with a mixture of sweetened almond paste, mandarin liqueur, orange zest, and cinnamon.

Pignolata

This sweet treat consists of mounds of bite-sized morsels of fried dough that are cooked with honey. This specialty is commonly prepared by home cooks for the holidays.

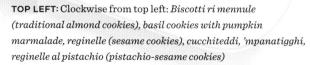

TOP LEFT: Clockwise from top left: *Biscotti ri mennule (traditional almond cookies), basil cookies with pumpkin marmalade, reginelle (sesame cookies), cucchiteddi, 'mpanatigghi, reginelle al pistachio (pistachio-sesame cookies)*
TOP RIGHT: *Pignolata*
BOTTOM RIGHT: *Nacatuli eoliani*
BOTTOM LEFT: *Almond Honey Brittle (page 297)*

DOUGHNUTS

{ Frittelle }

SFINCI

A nineteenth-century historian, Michele Amari, claimed that sfinci *were first prepared in Sicily during Muslim rule. Culinary historian Pino disagreed, arguing that* sfinci *are a derivation of a sweet prepared by the ancient pagan inhabitants. Either way, these irresistible treats have been a part of Sicilian cuisine for centuries.*

My grandmother prepared ricotta-based sfinci *every year on March 19 for Saint Joseph's Day, and any time she wanted to surprise my mother and me with a treat. She would roll the fried doughnuts in honey, or toss them with sugar mixed with a touch of cinnamon. In summer months, when ricotta is out of season in Sicily, my cousin Maria prepares her* sfinci *with mashed potato. Take your pick from the two variations here: The ricotta* sfinci *are creamy and richer, while the potato* sfinci *are light and airy.*

Each version makes 3 to 4 dozen doughnuts

Batter for ricotta-based doughnuts

6 large eggs

¹/₂ cup sugar

1¹/₂ pounds fresh ricotta

2 cups plus 2 tablespoons all-purpose flour

4 teaspoons baking soda

1 teaspoon vanilla extract

Batter for potato-based doughnuts

2 Yukon gold potatoes, peeled and cut in half

1 cup milk

3 large eggs

3¹/₂ tablespoons unsalted butter, at room temperature

Batter for potato-based doughnuts, continued

1 tablespoon active dry yeast, dissolved in 1 tablespoon lukewarm water

1 teaspoon vanilla extract

1 pound (about 3²/₃ cups) all-purpose flour

1 teaspoon baking powder

For frying

Vegetable oil, for frying

¹/₂ cup wildflower honey, or 1 teaspoon ground cinnamon mixed with 1 cup granulated sugar

1 FOR THE RICOTTA BATTER: Beat the eggs with the sugar in a stand mixer until the mixture turns a pale yellow. Add the ricotta, followed by the flour, baking soda, and vanilla, mixing until well incorporated. Hold the batter in the refrigerator for up to 1 day until ready to fry.

2 FOR THE POTATO BATTER: Put the potatoes in a pot and cover with cold water. Bring to a boil over high heat and cook until the potatoes are soft but not mushy. Transfer the potatoes to a plate lined with paper towels and let dry. Pass them through a ricer or food mill and into a mixing bowl, turning the potato into a soft airy pulp. Add the milk, eggs, butter, yeast, and vanilla and whisk well to incorporate all of the ingredients. Slowly add the flour, mixing so that it doesn't form lumps. Stir in the baking powder. Cover and let the batter rise in the refrigerator for 1 hour.

3 TO FRY EITHER BATTER: Heat a few inches of oil in a heavy, large pan. I like to use a cast-iron pot. Heat over medium-high heat until the oil reaches 375°F. If you do not have a deep-fry thermometer, check by placing a dollop of batter in the oil. If it starts to sizzle lightly and rise to the top, the temperature is probably right. If the dough browns quickly, the oil is too hot.

4 Fill a tablespoon with dough and hold the spoon in your hand over the oil. Using the thumb of your other hand, push the dough into the hot oil. Repeat, frying the dough in a batch of 6 to 8 doughnuts for 2 to 3 minutes, or until golden brown and fluffy. Place the doughnuts on a plate lined with paper towels to drain. Repeat with the remaining batter.

5 Place the warm doughnuts in a large mixing bowl. Add the honey or the cinnamon sugar and toss to coat. Serve immediately.

THE SHAPE OF SURPRISE

The cannolo is a much-loved Sicilian treat (the plural is *cannoli*) known the world over. The word comes from the Latin *canna* ("cane" or "reed"); the small tubular shell may have originally been fried around a piece of wood reed. Today, the term *cannolo* is used in the Sicilian culinary realm for many little tube-shaped shells stuffed with sweet or savory fillings. Traditional dishes include a fried tuma cheese stuffed with ragù. Chefs in the island's upscale restaurants commonly use the form in inventive ways, wrapping a variety of sweet or savory foods in the tubular shape and using the word *cannolo* as part of the dish's title. So don't be confused if you see a cannolo listed in the appetizer or pasta section of a menu.

There are several legends as to the origins of the cannolo. One of the most romanticized stories is that the tubular sweet was first prepared by women in the harem of Caltanissetta during Muslim rule of Sicily as a dessert for their emir. Another legend places the origins in a convent of the same village, which was believed to have housed Muslim converts to Christianity when the Normans conquered Sicily.

However, the dessert might have come about even before Muslim rule, as an official Roman text mentions a Sicilian sweet made from a "tubus farinarius, dulcissimo, edulio ex lacte factus," meaning a tube-shaped sweet dough with a stew prepared from milk.

Restaurant chefs around Sicily prepare cannoli in a variety of shapes, in thin tubes, in layers, and in cones. Pastry shops sell them filled with ricotta cream laced with candied fruit and chocolate, or with pastry cream in pistachio, chocolate, or other creative flavors.

It's only in a few pastry shops around the island, including those in Piana Degli Albanesi—an Arbëreshë village—and surrounding towns, that cannoli are filled to order with ricotta cream. Pastry shops there will explain that this is the only way to ensure the freshness and crispiness of the shell, which otherwise gets soggy when filled in advance with moist ricotta.

LAYERED CANNOLI

{ *Cannoli a Millefoglie* }

This dessert is a composition made of layers of flat crispy cannoli shells and clouds of sweet ricotta cream, topped with a crumble of pistachio and chocolate—which I've dubbed a pistachio couscous. The taste is of the always delicious Sicilian cannolo, but the presentation is new. It has become a favorite in my Sicilian restaurant, where I created it because I found that guests would order a cannolo to share only to see the shell shatter into too many small pieces when they tried to cut it in half. This rendition allows diners to more elegantly take one layer at a time if they wish.

This is the only recipe in this cookbook that I created from scratch, making it a Sicilian-inspired dessert, more than a traditional recipe (although a Sicilian pastry maker did give me the cannoli dough recipe). I made this the exception because I believe that this version is actually much simpler for the home cook to prepare. Frying the cannoli shells as strips is much easier than the traditional rolled tube shapes. You can prepare either long flat rectangle pieces (as pictured), or cut the dough into randomly shaped chips.

The candied orange peel and pistachio "couscous" are additions to the dessert that are optional but that add more Sicilian flavor. The Sicilian pistachio paste is available in the United States (see Sources, page 326), and gives the pistachio-chocolate medley an extra burst of nutty goodness. I also like to serve the cannolo with a scoop of pistachio gelato (page 291), but it's spectacular on its own, too.

Note that you need to let the cannoli dough rest in the fridge overnight, so be sure to make the dough the day before you plan on assembling the cannoli.

Serves 8

Cannoli dough

1 pound all-purpose flour

1½ cups sugar

2 cups red wine

10 large eggs

1 cup lard or softened butter

½ teaspoon salt

Vegetable oil, for frying

Ricotta cream

12 ounces fresh ricotta

½ cup confectioners' sugar

½ cup Soft Candied Orange Peel, finely chopped (recipe on page 306 or see Sources, page 326)

1 cup semisweet chocolate chips, chilled

Pistachio "couscous"

1½ cups shelled pistachios

½ cup semisweet chocolate chips

2 tablespoons pistachio paste, preferably from Sicily, plus more if needed

2 tablespoons Candied Squash Preserves (page 313) or Mandarin Marmalade (page 65)

1 FOR THE CANNOLI DOUGH: Combine the flour, sugar, wine, eggs, lard (or butter), and salt in a stand mixer fitted with a paddle. Mix for about 8 minutes, until the dough forms into a ball. Wrap the dough in plastic wrap and let rest overnight in the refrigerator.

2 FOR THE RICOTTA CREAM: In a mixing bowl, whisk together the ricotta and confectioners' sugar. Add the candied orange, folding it into the ricotta-sugar mixture with a rubber spatula. Add the chocolate chips, folding them gently into the ricotta with the spatula. (The chocolate bits should be cold, rather than room temperature, so that they don't melt away into the ricotta). Place the ricotta cream in a pastry bag and hold in the refrigerator until ready to use. It can be prepared up to 1 day in advance.

continued ↓

3 To roll out the dough, sprinkle a work surface with flour. Divide the cannoli dough into six equal-sized pieces. Using a rolling pin, begin to stretch out one piece, sprinkling with a touch of flour if the dough sticks to the work surface. Roll the dough until very thin: Hold it up to the light and you should be able to see through the dough. Repeat with the remaining pieces of dough. Cut the dough sheets into about ten rectangles, about 2 inches wide and 5 inches long.

4 To fry the cannoli shells, pour a few inches of vegetable oil into a large heavy pan. I like to use a cast-iron pot. Heat over medium-high heat until the oil reaches 325°F. If you don't have a deep-fry thermometer, you can test whether the oil is hot enough by dropping a small bit of dough into the oil. If it starts to sizzle lightly and rise to the top, it is probably the right temperature. If the dough turns brown quickly, the oil is too hot. Working in batches without crowding the pieces, fry the rectangles of dough until golden brown, about 5 minutes, turning them upside down in the middle of the cooking process. Transfer to a plate lined with paper towels to drain.

5 FOR THE PISTACHIO "COUSCOUS": Pulse the pistachios in a food processor until well chopped. Add the chocolate chips, pistachio paste, and squash preserves or mandarin marmalade. Blend until all of the ingredients are incorporated. The couscous should be crumbly and slightly moist. If it's too dry, you can add a touch of the orange-scented syrup from the candied orange peel. The pistachio couscous will last, covered, in the refrigerator for up to 1 week; bring it to room temperature before using.

7 To assemble the cannoli, on individual dessert plates, place a small dollop of ricotta cream and top with a piece of cannolo shell. Add a layer of ricotta cream, covering the surface of the shell. (If you prefer, you can pipe the ricotta cream on top of the shells using a pastry bag, which will create a more uniform look for the dessert). Top with a sprinkle of the pistachio couscous. Alternate more layers of the shell with the ricotta cream and the pistachio couscous. I suggest layering no more than 4 pieces of the shell to ensure that the dessert does not topple. Serve immediately.

Soft Candied Orange Peel

Candied orange peel is used both as an ingredient in several Sicilian desserts (such as a topping for almond cookies or as a garnish for cassata), or it can be eaten as a snack, especially when first dipped in melted chocolate and then cooled in the refrigerator.

Makes 1 cup

2 large organic navel oranges   4 cups sugar

1 Wash the oranges in warm water and cut them in half horizontally. Using a grapefruit spoon, remove the pulp from the orange (don't remove the white pith) and set the pulp aside for another use (perhaps to make marmalade). Place the orange peels with the pith attached in a stockpot and cover with cold water. Bring to a boil, then drain. Repeat this step twice.

2 Place the triple-blanched orange peels in a pot and add the sugar and 4 cups water. If the liquid does not cover the orange peels, add equal parts of water and sugar until it does. Bring to a boil and immediately reduce the heat to low. Cook the orange peels for about $1\frac{1}{2}$ hours, until the peels appear translucent and a paring knife slips easily into the thickest part of the peel. Turn off the heat and let the orange peels cool in the syrup.

3 When cool, remove the peels from the syrup and, using a sharp chef's knife, cut the peels into $\frac{1}{8}$-inch-wide strips. Store the strips in some of the syrup; they'll keep in the fridge for up to 1 month. Reserve the remainder of the orange-scented syrup for the pistachio "couscous" or to drizzle on top of other desserts.

CHRISTMAS RING CAKE

{ Buccellato }

CUCCIDDATU

All over Sicily in the late summer, figs can be found tied together in bunches and hanging from a string to dry in the sun. As they lose their moisture, the sugars concentrate, enhancing the flavors. With the absence of fresh fruit in the winter, these preserved figs bring the flavors of summer to the table. They are featured in Christmas cookies, known as cucciddati, *and in this classic crown-shaped tart, which is stuffed with the dried figs, along with raisins and lots of nuts. As to be expected, variations on this dessert abound, but most stuffings include almonds, candied Sicilian squash, and chocolate bits.*

Makes 1 ring cake

Pastry dough

4 cups all-purpose flour

1½ tablespoons baking powder

½ cup lard, or softened butter

½ cup sugar

½ teaspoon salt

¼ cup milk

1 tablespoon Marsala

1 teaspoon vanilla extract

2 large eggs

Filling

1 cup Marsala

¾ pound dried Calimyrna figs, stems removed

1 cup golden raisins

Filling, continued

1 cup blanched almonds, skins removed

½ cup walnuts

½ cup shelled pistachios

½ cup pine nuts

½ cup *vino cotto* (see page 37)

1 tablespoon grated orange zest

1 tablespoon Mandarin Marmalade (page 65 or see Sources, page 326)

1 teaspoon ground cinnamon

¼ teaspoon ground cloves

1 large egg, beaten

1 FOR THE PASTRY DOUGH: Stir together the flour and baking powder in a medium bowl. Combine the lard, sugar, and salt in a food processor and pulse just a few times to combine them. Add the milk, Marsala, and vanilla to the food processor and mix well. Add the flour mixture, little by little, pulsing after each addition. With the machine still running, add the eggs one at a time. When all ingredients have blended together to form a mass, remove the dough from the processor and form it into a ball. Cover with plastic wrap and refrigerate for at least 1 hour or up to 2 days.

2 FOR THE FILLING: In a small saucepan over high heat, bring the Marsala and 1 cup water to a boil. Remove from the heat, add the dried figs, and let soak for about 30 minutes to rehydrate.

3 Transfer the figs with a slotted spoon to the cleaned food processor and coarsely chop them. Do not turn them into a paste. Transfer to a large mixing bowl. Separately, coarsely chop the almonds, walnuts, pistachios, and pine nuts in the processor. (It's best to chop each type individually because each kind of nut breaks down at a different rate and it's important not to chop them too finely.) Add all of the chopped nuts to the chopped figs in the mixing bowl. Add the *vino cotto*, orange zest, marmalade, cinnamon, and cloves and incorporate all ingredients well with a spatula. Form the filling into a sticky ball, cover with plastic wrap, and refrigerate for about 3 hours or up to 2 days.

4 When you're ready to shape and bake the *buccellato*, remove the pastry dough from the refrigerator and bring it to room temperature, so that it's malleable and easy to work with. Place the dough between two 24-inch-long pieces of waxed paper. Using a rolling pin, roll out the dough to form a rectangle about 7 by 20 inches and set aside. To shape the filling, roll it with your hands into a 2-inch-diameter log about 18 inches in length.

5 Remove the top piece of waxed paper from the dough. Place the log of filling in the center of the pastry dough and wrap the sides of the pastry around the filling, using the remaining piece of waxed paper to help wrap the dough. Seal together the two edges of the dough with your fingers. Remove the bottom piece of wax paper, rotate the log so it's seam side down, and repair any holes in the dough with your fingers.

6 Transfer the log to a large baking sheet, then gently curve the log to connect the two ends together, forming a ring. (The filling should touch.) Seal the ends of dough together with your fingers. Using the palms of your hands, smooth out the ring, so that the circle is as neat as possible and the dough is even. Place the uncovered baking sheet in the refrigerator to chill the ring for 15 minutes before adding the decorative pattern to its surface.

7 To decorate the surface of the pastry dough, use a crimper, a small set of tongs with a scalloped edge, or a fork. Pinch the dough lightly, breaking holes to form a pattern, but without touching the inner filling too much. As you work, dip the decorating tool in flour, to keep it from sticking to the dough. Try to repeat the same pattern around the entire pastry. Return the *buccellato* to the refrigerator and chill for 1 hour.

8 Preheat the oven to 380°F. Brush the pastry with the beaten egg. Bake the *buccellato* until the dough turns a solid golden brown in color, about 25 minutes. Before slicing, let the *buccellato* cool completely. It will keep for a few days at room temperature in an airtight container.

A Return to Elegance

It wasn't until the late eighteenth century that Sicily's commercial wine industry started to surge, when the British merchant, Jon Woodhouse, chose Marsala as a place to create a fortified wine similar to port and Madeira. His Marsala was well priced compared to the other fortified wines, due to the lower costs of Sicilian labor and grapes. For nearly one hundred years, the British controlled the industry, until Sicilians entered the Marsala trade after the unification of Italy in 1860.

For over a century, Marsala was a counterpart to sherry and Madeira, but by the 1950s, the wine was used mainly as a cooking wine, overshadowed by a cheaper version produced in California. By the mid-1980s, the laws for the Marsala DOC were tightened, and today the wine—made in both dry and sweet forms—is resuming its former roles as both an apéritif and a dessert wine. It's produced in multiple categories, but highly prized bottles of Marsala are labeled as *Riserva,* meaning they were refined in wood for at least four years, or as *Vergine,* denoting a minimum of five years in wood barrels.

A CAKE THAT SHINES AS THE SUN

Above all Sicilian desserts, cassata (opposite, top left) is the most ornate of cakes, decorated with delicate icing and with pieces of candied fruit on top of a layer of *pasta reale,* or almond paste (see page 298). Inside are layers of sponge cake and ricotta cream.

Cassata most likely originated during the Muslim rule of Sicily in the tenth century. In Arabic, the word *qas'ah* means a large deep bowl, the vessel in which the dessert is prepared. However, over the centuries the dessert transformed as new ingredients and cooking techniques were introduced to the island. During the Norman era, almond paste, invented in the convent of the Martorana, was added. Later the Spanish introduced chocolate, which was added to the ricotta, as well as to the sponge cake. Toward the end of the nineteenth century, a Palermitan pastry chef, Salvatore Gulì, invented the so-called *cassata Siciliana*, adding decorative pieces of candied fruit and a final cover of icing.

Made in the round form of a sun, which sets and is reborn the next day, the cake is a symbol of the death and resurrection of Christ, and thus is a staple on the Easter table. Today, the cake is commonly found throughout the island all year long, not only at Easter.

A CAKE FILLED WITH CHEESE

The town of Polizzi Generosa, which is nestled in the Madonie Mountains, is known for *lo sfoglio* (opposite, bottom left), a traditional thick-shortcrust pie with a sweet cheese filling. In the local dialect, it is called *lu sfuagghiu.* For the filling of the cake, fresh tuma cheese (page 80) is mixed with chocolate bits, cinnamon, and sugar. In addition to round cakes, individual-sized crescent-shaped *sfogliatelle* are sold and can be enjoyed while strolling through the streets of this characteristic mountain village.

Lo sfoglio was first created in the seventeenth century by the Benedictine nuns of the Convent of Santa Margherita of Polizzi Generosa in honor of their patron saint, San Benedetto. Every September, a festival for this cake unfolds in the town. In addition to tastings, the festival includes guided tours of the historical center of the village, open churches, and folklore presentations.

BREASTS OF THE VIRGIN

Minne di vergine are little cakes found in two different parts of Sicily, each on opposite sides of the island. Interestingly, the origin of this dessert, and even the translation of the name, has a different story in each area.

In Catania, around the time of the Feast of Saint Agatha on February 5, *minne di vergine* ("breasts of the virgin") honor the third-century martyr whose breasts were severed from her body after she refused to marry a Roman emperor due to her decision to devote her life to religion. Prepared with similar ingredients to a cassata, the cakes resemble little breasts, each semispherical shell of pastry stuffed with ricotta cream, covered by white icing, and decorated with a candied cherry. Nowadays they can be found all year round in pastry shops in Catania.

In Sambuca di Sicilia, the dessert has nothing to do with Saint Agatha, but is attributed to an eighteenth-century nun, Sister Virginia Casale di Rocca Menna, who was asked to prepare a dessert for a noble wedding that would entice the eaters. The name *minne di vergine* is said to hail from the nun's name. Sister Virginia's cakes (opposite, bottom right) are filled with *biancomangiare* and *zuccata* (milk custard and candied squash) as opposed to ricotta, and offered without icing or cherries, just a topping of tiny colorful sprinkles.

CHOCOLATE CAKES

Around Sicily, chocolate cakes are ubiquitous. One popular cake, *la torta setteveli,* is prepared with seven layers of chocolate cake and mousse. Chocolate and pistachio flavors are often combined (opposite, top right).

ALMOND CRÊPES FILLED *with* CUSTARD

{ *Crêpes con Biancomangiare* }

OVA MURINA

This sweet dates to the seventeenth century and the convent of Badia Grande of Sciacca. Locals say the dessert was invented by the cloistered nuns as a substitute for cannoli during the summer months when ricotta was out of season.

Biancomangiare is a milk custard used to fill the crêpes that is used as a base in many other typical Sicilian desserts as well. It is often prepared on its own to be eaten as a pudding. Zuccata is candied Sicilian long squash (see page 152), which is a conserve that adds sweetness and a chunky yet soft texture to this dessert. It is made only in certain towns of western Sicily and is unknown in many other areas of the island.

Note that you can use all-purpose flour in place of the almond flour and any other marmalade instead of the zuccata.

Serves 8

Almond crêpes

3 tablespoons
unsalted butter

1 cup almond flour

2 tablespoons unsweetened
cocoa powder

1 tablespoon espresso
powder

1 teaspoon ground cinnamon

A few pinches of sugar

Pinch of salt

2 large eggs

1¹⁄₂ cups milk, plus more
if needed

¹⁄₂ vanilla bean, seeds only

Olive oil, for the pan

Biancomangiare

³⁄₄ cup cornstarch

¹⁄₂ cup sugar

¹⁄₂ vanilla bean, cut in
half lengthwise

4 cups milk

¹⁄₂ cup *zuccata*
(recipe opposite)

1 FOR THE ALMOND CRÊPES: First brown the butter by cooking it in a small pot over medium heat until browned and fragrant; set aside.

2 In a large mixing bowl, mix the almond flour with the cocoa powder, espresso powder, cinnamon, sugar, and salt. Make a well and pour in the eggs. Beat the eggs slowly, incorporating the flour mixture that surrounds them. Be gentle, otherwise lumps of flour could form. Whisk the milk and the seeds of the vanilla bean. Slowly pour in the milk while stirring. Keep stirring the batter until small bubbles form on the surface, then stir in the browned butter. General rule of thumb: If the batter seems thicker than cream, add a little more milk.

3 Pour a little olive oil on a folded paper towel, and evenly wipe it on a 8-inch skillet. Place the skillet over medium heat. Pour in about 3 tablespoons batter. Immediately use your wrist to tilt and move the pan, spreading the batter evenly and covering the whole surface with a thin layer. Place over medium heat and cook for about 1 minute, until the crêpe is opaque around the edges. Flip and cook the other side for about 30 seconds, until the entire crêpe is cooked and starts to turn light golden brown. It's best to flip the crêpe with your fingers, because it's very delicate. Before you prepare each crêpe, wipe the skillet with the paper towel moistened with olive oil. Repeat to make about ten crêpes, until you are out of batter, stacking the cooked crêpes on a plate. (The crêpes can be prepared in advance and stored in the refrigerator.) To reheat, place the crêpes on a baking sheet, without overlapping. Place the sheet in a preheated 350°F oven for about 5 minutes, just until the crêpes are heated through.

4 FOR THE *BIANCOMANGIARE*: In a saucepan over low heat, mix the cornstarch, sugar, and vanilla bean. Add the milk little by little, whisking so that lumps do not form. When the mixture is has thickened and pulls away from the side of the saucepan, about 5 minutes, it is complete. Remove the vanilla bean pod. Make sure the *biancomangiare* is ready when it's time to serve the crêpes, as it congeals quickly and is difficult to reheat without forming lumps.

5 TO ASSEMBLE THE CRÊPES: In a mixing bowl, combine the *zuccata* and *biancomangiare*. Place 3 tablespoons of the filling in the center of a crêpe and roll the crêpe into a cylinder. Repeat with the remaining crêpes and filling. Serve immediately.

Candied Squash Preserves ZUCCATA

If you have leftover zuccata *after filling the crêpes, you can use it to stuff inside almond cookies (page 299) or for pistachio "couscous" (page 305), among other creative uses in Sicilian-inspired desserts.*

Makes at least 1 cup

1 long Sicilian squash (at least 1 pound; see page 152)	Sugar as necessary (about 2 cups)

1 Peel the squash and remove the seeds from the squash using a spoon, and cut it into ¹/₂-inch-wide strips about 1 inch long. Place the squash pieces in a large pot, cover with cold water, and bring the water to a boil. Immediately transfer the squash with a slotted spoon to a strainer to drain. When dry, weigh the squash and measure out an equal amount of sugar.

2 In a heavy-bottomed saucepan over medium heat, cook the squash with one-third of the measured sugar, while stirring, until the sugar dissolves, about 5 minutes. Transfer to a bowl, cover, and refrigerate overnight. The next day, combine the squash and the remainder of the measured sugar in a saucepan. Cook over low heat, while stirring, until it turns into a thick paste, about 20 minutes. Let cool, transfer to an airtight container, and refrigerate until ready to use or up to 10 days.

CAROB CUSTARD

{ Crema di Carruba }

CREMA RI CARRUBBI

This carob custard created by Accursio Capraro has a nutty flavor and is rich and smooth. I tasted it served with a sugar brûlée, caramelized pears, and a hazelnut crumble, but it's delicious served on its own, too.

My grandmother used to chew on whole pods of dried carob, reminiscing about her childhood in Sicily. She always told me that carob was the poor man's version of chocolate. Yet, while there are similar notes in both the cocoa bean and the carob pod, I find the flavor of carob to be more nuanced and intense. The carob tree can be found all around the Mediterranean basin. In Sicily's cuisine today, carob flour is used to produce desserts and marmalades. The flour of carob seeds is used as a thickener, but is also an ingredient in some gluten-free breads and pastries. Syrup made from carob pods is used to make candy, liqueurs, beverages, gelato, and other desserts, such as this custard. Carob syrup can be found in specialty Italian stores (see Sources, page 326).

To serve the custard with caramelized pears, cook de-seeded segments of firm pears in a mixture of water and white wine (in equal parts) for 2 to 3 minutes. Make sure that the pears are still firm but slightly cooked when removing from the poaching liquid with a slotted spoon. Test that they are ready by inserting a knife in the center of a pear segment; it should slide through. Cook some sugar over medium heat until it melts in a heavy-bottomed pan. Add the pears and let the sugar turn light brown and coat the pears. Remove the pears from the pan and let cool slightly.

Serves 6

1¹⁄₄ cups heavy cream

4 large egg yolks

1 cup milk

¹⁄₄ cup carob syrup

¹⁄₃ cup sugar

1 Preheat the oven to 180°F. In a large bowl, combine all the ingredients and beat well with a whisk until the sugar is thoroughly dissolved.

2 Pour the mixture into six 4-ounce ceramic or aluminum molds. Place the molds into a large deep baking dish. Pour 1¹⁄₂ inches room-temperature water into the baking dish, being careful not to splash the puddings.

3 Carefully transfer the baking dish to the oven and bake for 30 minutes, until the custard sets. To check for doneness, remove one mold and gently move it back and forth. If it is set, the custard will not be wobbly. Let cool on a rack until ready to serve. You can make this custard up to a day ahead; store it in the refrigerator, covered, until ready to serve.

The Miracle of Saint Lucia

On December 13, for the feast day of Saint Lucia, Sicilians pay tribute to a miracle believed to have been performed by the saint during a famine in 1582, when mysterious ships of grain delivered wheat to the people of Sicily. Out of starvation, the hungry ate the wheat without taking time to grind it into flour. To this day Sicilians eat nothing made with wheat flour on December 13 to honor Saint Lucia's miracle. Instead, they eat cooked wheat grains called *cuccia*, in both sweet and savory versions. In some families, the cooked wheat berries are mixed with almonds and honey and combined with *biancomangiare* (milk custard; recipe on page 312), as pictured.

CLOCKWISE FROM TOP RIGHT: *Almond Crêpes Filled with Custard (page 312);* biancomangiare *milk custard (see page 312) with* vino cotto *(page 37) and cooked grain for Santa Lucia (see the sidebar opposite); Carob Custard (opposite)*

WATERMELON PUDDING

{ *Gelo di Anguria* }

GELU RI MULUNI

When summer arrives and watermelon is in season, pastry shops around the island offer up a refreshing sweet pudding, known as gelo, in small cups and as a filling in pies, topped with chocolate bits and pistachios. Most popularly it is served for the holiday of Ferragosto on August 15. Traditionally, the gelo was shaped into ceramic molds with characteristic shapes. Variations of this gelo are made with other juices, liquors, and flavorings such as coffee, cloves, vanilla, and candied fruits.

While watermelon holds the most sway in Sicily, other melons are popular too. The yellow cartucciaru melons from Paceco, in the province of Trapani, as well as the green purceddu melons from Alcamo, in the province of Palermo, are included in Slow Food's presidium. Both have unique flavor profiles and are worth seeking out when in Sicily. The former is cultivated starting in June, while the latter starts its season in August.

To make the watermelon juice, remove the seeds and rind from a watermelon and cut the flesh into large chunks. Thoroughly puree the chunks in a blender or food processor or pass the watermelon pieces through a food mill. Strain through a fine-mesh strainer to eliminate any fibers or remaining chunks. You'll need about 2 pounds of watermelon pieces to make 4 cups of juice.

1 In a heavy-bottomed saucepan, mix the watermelon juice with 1/2 cup of the sugar. Heat over low heat, stirring, until the sugar dissolves. Taste for sweetness and add up to 1/4 cup more sugar according to taste.

2 Add the cornstarch and cook, whisking frequently, for about 10 minutes, until the pudding thickens. At first, the cornstarch will alter the color of the juice and make it appear opaque and lackluster, but when the pudding is fully cooked, it will regain a shiny texture. Taste the pudding at this point to make sure that it is smooth. If somewhat gritty in texture, keep whisking for another minute or two until all of the cornstarch is fully dissolved in the watermelon juice. Add the cinnamon and flower water and whisk again to incorporate well. Let the pudding cool to room temperature, then add the chocolate bits. Stir gently so that the chocolate does not melt and turn the pudding cloudy.

3 Pour the mixture into four 12-ounce ceramic, glass, or aluminum ramekins. Sprinkle the pudding with the finely chopped pistachios. Chill in the refrigerator for about 1 hour before serving or up to 24 hours. You can serve the puddings in the ramekins, or the puddings can be easily unmolded and served on plates.

Serves 4

4 cups watermelon juice

1/2 cup to 3/4 cup sugar

2/3 cup cornstarch

1/2 teaspoon ground cinnamon

1 tablespoon flower water, such as jasmine, rose, or orange flower

1/4 cup shelled pistachios, finely chopped

1/4 cup semisweet chocolate bits, chilled

MEXICO BY WAY OF MODICA

The chocolate of Modica is a unique Aztec-style sweet, first introduced to both Sicily and Spain in the sixteenth century by Spanish conquerors. This Baroque city became a center of chocolate production because the city's aristocrats could afford the expensive cocoa beans, which were considered a luxury.

Quite different from the typical creamy milk chocolate, Modica's iconic chocolate is characterized by a grainy, rough, and crumbly sensation on the palate. This texture is a result of a simpler and some might say more natural production process: The cocoa bean paste is only heated to 104°F, which is too low a temperature to melt the sugar or to allow it to amalgamate with the cocoa. The chocolate is also devoid of butter, any added cocoa butter, milk, or other type of fat. However, it comes in several flavors. Traditionally, the chocolate was only laced with cinnamon or vanilla, but nowadays chocolate factories also produce bars flavored with spicy chile, carob, salt, orange, and coffee. My favorites remain the two classic flavors, though.

Another chocolate specialty of Modica is an old Aztec warm drink, known as *xocolàtl*, which translates to "bitter water" and is made from cocoa beans. To prepare this drink, the cocoa beans are first ground on a ridged stone (called a *metate*), which extrudes the cocoa butter to obtain a grainy paste. Then, the paste is mixed with hot water and poured back and forth between two vessels, which helps mix the cocoa paste with the water. A foam usually forms on the top layer and often the drink is flavored with spices or honey. While much different from the usual hot chocolate consumed today, this beverage, which comes closer to how the Aztecs themselves enjoyed chocolate, warms one's body in cold months and is full of antioxidants. It's probably for this reason that Spanish warriors traditionally consumed it to fortify their health.

THE FRUIT QUEEN

When my mother, Josephine, made her first trip as an adult to the Old Country, in 1980, the extended family celebrated her return with feasts at every home. What sticks in her mind most from that late spring visit are the abundant platters of fruit served at the end of each meal: white mulberries, plump sweet cherries, highly fragrant strawberries, fuzzy apricots, and loquats (which resemble apricots in size, color, and shape but have a thinner skin, larger pit, a soft juicy flesh, and a pronounced acidity, even when ripe). She was so impressed, not only with the highly concentrated flavors, but with the fact that all of the fruits were grown on our cousins' farmlands on the outskirts of the village. Relatives dubbed her "the fruit queen" as she stuffed her bags with seeds to plant back at home in the States.

Indeed, the rich soil and steady sun have made the island a fruit-lover's paradise, and Sicilians have special ways of enjoying these gems. After a long summer *pranzo* (lunch), my family will enjoy slices of peeled peaches soaking in homemade wine, which I love to devour before enjoying a little afternoon nap on a hot August day. During the hot months, Sicilians often prepare *macedonia,* in which bite-sized morsels of seasonal fruits are marinated with lemon juice and sugar, then chilled before serving. At a restaurant in Modica, I've tasted an elegant version of this rustic dish that included jasmine flowers, berries, and chunks of peaches and melon in a fruit soup. To the surprise of the waitstaff, on my last visit, I couldn't resist devouring two portions of this aromatic, refreshing dessert.

The best way to learn about the different types of fruit is to taste your way around them. You will be surprised by the selection available in markets from Palermo to Sciacca, from Siracusa to Catania. (Note, however, that some of the rarest and choicest varieties can be found only on family farms. When staying at an *agriturismo,* ask the owners what

fruits are in season and they're sure to offer a taste.) I often suggest that travelers to Sicily should carry around paper napkins and a small Swiss Army knife (as "the fruit queen" does). Purchase fruits and eat them while sitting on a bench in a town square or in a public garden under the shade of an old palm tree. What better way to enjoy both the scenery and the typical flavors of Sicily?

LEMON LIQUEUR

{ *Limoncello* }

LIMONCELLO

On the outskirts of the town of Salemi, in a tiny laboratory barely larger than most New York City kitchens, Rosalba Calia produces nearly 100,000 bottles of amaro (a liqueur made from bitter herbs), along with limoncello each year. Her husband started the business nearly ten years ago, but passed away soon after. In his honor, and as a sign of her continued love for him, Rosalba continues to make liqueurs.

Her limoncello, a true artisan product, is made with the zest from organic lemons, which she peels one by one with a potato peeler. It's essential to peel only the yellow part of the peel (the zest) and avoid the white pith, which is bitter and would impart an unpleasant flavor to the limoncello.

Limoncello and other sweet after-dinner drinks— made from oranges, cinnamon, carob, and rose, among other flavors—are traditionally served after a big meal to help the digestion. Since the high alcohol content prohibits the liquid from freezing, bottles of limoncello and other liqueurs are often held in the freezer, which not only ensures they will be refreshing, but also tends to slightly thicken the liquid.

Makes about 2 quarts

Peeled zest of 8 organic lemons

1 quart pure 100-proof grain alcohol

2½ cups sugar

1 Place the lemon zest in a large glass container, add the pure alcohol, cover, and let sit in a dark pantry for 15 days.

2 In a medium saucepan, combine 1 quart water and the sugar, bring to boil, and boil until the sugar dissolves. Let the sugar syrup cool.

3 Strain the alcohol through a fine-mesh sieve and discard the zest. Return to the glass container and add the sugar syrup. Let the liqueur sit for nearly 1 week in the dark pantry before serving. It will stay flavorful for up to 1 year.

WHEN IN SICILY

Pasticcerie * Pastry Shops

Following is a list of some of my favorite pastry shops and which desserts to taste when visiting them.

PROVINCE of PALERMO

Pasticceria Cappello
Via Colonna Rotta 68,
Palermo
tel. 091489601
Chocolate cake *setteveli* (see page 311) and *frutta di Martorana* (see page 298)

Pasticceria Cerniglia
Via Palermo,
173 San Giuseppe Jato
tel. 0918572352
Cannoli as well as cassata and other famous Sicilian cakes

Piccanti Tentazioni
Via Giorgio Kastriota 34,
Piana degli Albanesi
tel. 3280625838
Cannoli

PROVINCE of TRAPANI

Euro Bar
Via G. Garibaldi 11/13,
Dattilo
tel. 0923861434
Famous cannoli

Gelateria Ciolla
Piazza Regina 1,
Mazara del Vallo
tel. 0923908424
Excellent gelato

Pasticceria Maria Grammatico
Via Vittorio Emanuele 14, Erice
tel. 0923869390
Le Genovesi cookies (see page 300)

PROVINCE of AGRIGENTO

Bar Roma
Via Vittorio Emanuele 2,
Sant'Anna di Caltabellotta
tel. 0925952769
This is the gelato and lemon granita that I grew up on in my ancestral village. Ask for owners Sicilia and Benedetto.

Bar La Bella Pasticceria e Gelateria
Via A. De Gasperi 23, Sciacca
tel. 092521524
Cucciddati cookies (see page 308)

EuroCaffè
Via A. Ognibene 114, Menfi
tel. 092574015
Almond-based pastries

Monastero di Santo Spirito (Cloistered Monastery)
Cortile Santo Spirito 9,
Agrigento
tel. 3287370299
Couscous di pistacchio, almond and pistachio biscotti

Pasticceria di Rosalia
Via Sant'Antonino 1,
Sant'Anna di Caltabellotta
tel. 0925952256
This wonderful pastry shop in my ancestral village prepares typical cookies and cream-based sweets.

PROVINCE of CALTANISSETTA

Filomena Alaimo
Viale Luigi La Verde 85, Delia
tel 0922 826825
Famous *Cuddrireddri di Delia* cookies (see page 300)

PROVINCE of ENNA

La Bottega Delle Cassatelle Di Maione Graziella
Via V. Emanuele, 196, Agira
tel. 0935594035
Cassatelle di Agira cookies (see page 300)

PROVINCE of RAGUSA

Antica Dolceria Bonajuto
Corso Umberto I 159, Modica
tel. 0932941225
'Mpanatigghi cookies (see page 300) & artisanal chocolate of Modica (see page 318)

PROVINCE of SIRACUSA

Agatino Finocchiario
Piazza Umberto I 35/36,
Avola
tel. 0931814047
Almond-based sweets

PROVINCE of CATANIA

Savia
Via Etnea 300, Catania
tel. 095322335
Almond based-desserts and torrone

PROVINCE of MESSINA

Bam Bar
Via Giovanni di Giovanni 45,
Taormina
tel. 094224355
Unforgettable granita

Irrera 1910
Piazza Cairoli 12, Messina
tel. 090673823
Granita, almond sweets, and *pignolata* (see page 300)

Subba
Via Vittorio Emanuele 92,
Lipari
tel. 0909811352
Unique pumpkin-basil cookies and granita

Ristoranti & Pizzerie
* Restaurants & Pizzerie

Sicily is full of wonderful places to eat, from family-run trattorie to Michelin-starred restaurants. This is a brief list of restaurants that I visit often, but for an extended list, refer to my website: www.melissamuller.it

I suggest calling the restaurants in advance regarding the days they are closed, which can vary.

Accursio
Via C. Grimaldi 414, Modica
tel. 0932941689
Upscale food in a relaxed atmosphere

Antica Filanda
Contrada Raviola, Caprileone
tel. 0941919704
Typical cuisine of the Nebrodi Mountains

Don Camillo
Via delle Maestranze, 96, Siracusa
tel. 093167133
A landmark upscale but unpretentious restaurant owned by Chef Giovanni Guarnieri in Ortigia, Siracusa's historical center

Hosteria del Vicolo
Vicolo Sammaritano 10, Sciacca
tel. 092523071
Upscale food—especially seafood dishes—in a relaxed atmosphere

Il Bavaglino
Via B. Saputo 20, Terrasini
tel. 0918682285
An elegant restaurant with a beautiful sea view

La Capinera
Via Nazionale 177, Spisone, Taormina
tel. 0942626247
Upscale and elegant restaurant at the seaside underneath Taormina

Osteria Ballaro'
Via Calascibetta 25, Palermo
tel. 091326488
A casual trattoria in the heart of Palermo

Pizzeria Mistral
Via Bordonaro 30, Palermo
tel. 0916372285
Pizzeria

Signum
Via Scalo 15, Salina
tel. 0909844222
Resort restaurant, led by a young chef Martina Caruso

Tiramisu
Via Cappuccini 1, Taormina
tel. 094224803
Casual restaurant and pizzeria

Festivals

Festivals and feast days are a major part of Sicilian culture. In all Sicilian towns and cities, religious festivals are celebrated to honor patron saints. During such festivals, inhabitants participate in or bear witness to processions, fireworks, and cultural activities, such as theater, musical concerts and dance. Major Catholic holidays are also celebrated, with regional variations throughout the island.

Such festivals have an importance in traditional Sicilian cuisine that cannot be understated. There are countless dishes prepared only on feast days. In addition, secular food and wine celebrations, known as *sagre*, are organized around the harvest of typical foods. The festivals listed here offer ways to taste the island's delicacies in convivial environments, often abounding with traditional Sicilian music and folklore. When planning a trip, I suggest verifying the exact festival dates for that year.

JANUARY

Festival of the Black Pigs of Nebrodi, Longi (Messina)
Annually from January 4 to 6

FEBRUARY

Festival for the Flowering of the Almond Trees, Agrigento
Annually

MARCH

Blood Orange Festival, Centuripe (Enna)
Annually

APRIL

'Mpurnatu Festival, Campobello di Licata (Palermo)
Annually in mid-April (in celebration of a traditional pasta dish called *'mpurnatu*, prepared only in this town, with ziti, a ground beef ragù, cauliflower, hard-boiled egg, and grated pecorino cheese, topped with breadcrumbs)

Orange Festival, Scillato (Palermo)
Annually

MAY

Sambuca di Sicilia Festival, Sambuca di Sicilia (Agrigento)
Annually in mid-May

JUNE

Caper Festival, Pollara (Salina)
Annually in the beginning of June

AUGUST

Busiate Festival, Salemi (Trapani)
Annually, in celebration of the unique handmade *busiate* pasta (see page 206)

Onion Festival, Giarratana (Ragusa)
Annually in mid-August

Verdello Lemon Festival, Roccalumera (Messina)
Annually

Sagra della Manna, Pollina (Palermo)
Annually, in celebration of manna, the sap of the ash tree (see page 36)

SEPTEMBER

Wine Festivals (around the island)
Milo (Catania): last week of August and first week of September
Viagrande (Catania): mid-September
Pedalino frazione di Cosimo (Ragusa): end of September
Piedimonte Etneo (Catania): end of September

Couscous Festival, San Vito Lo Capo (Trapani)
Annually in mid- to late September

Pistachio Festival, Bronte (Mount Etna/Catania)
Annually in late September

OCTOBER

Honey Festival, Sortino (Siracusa)
Annually in the beginning of October

Walnut Festival, Motta Camastra (Messina)
Annually in mid-October

L'Ottobrata, Zafferana Etnea (Mount Etna/Catania)
Annually, every Sunday in October, in celebration of wine, chestnuts, mushrooms, and honey grown and crafted on the slopes of the volcano

NOVEMBER

Chestnut Festival, San Salvatore di Fitalia (Messina)
Annually

Feast of Saint Martin (throughout the island)
Annually on November 11, in celebration of the first tasting of the year's wine, often accompanied by *sfinci* (doughnuts)

Olive Harvest Festival, Pollina (Palermo)
Annually on the second Sunday in November

DECEMBER

Feast of Saint Lucia (throughout the island)
Annually on December 13, often celebrated with *arancine* in Palermo and savory or sweet cooked wheat berries (*cuccia*; see page 314)

SOURCES

The following sources offer high-quality products from Sicily or great substitutes when you want to capture Sicilian flavor without access to the same ingredients you would find there.

AMAZON.COM

Many of the following items are easy to find in your local Italian market, but Amazon is an excellent online source. You can also find a ravioli cutter here.

- Carob syrup
- Chickpea flour
- Pistachio paste (including unsweetened)
- Remilled semola flour
- Rennet for making cheese (including vegetable rennet)
- Saba (Northern Italian grape must reduction)
- Sicilian anelletti pasta
- Sun-dried tomato paste

BUONITALIA.COM

The Italian specialty foods store in Chelsea Market now offers online service; however, the store has a wider selection of Sicilian ingredients (including a large selection of dried legumes and other packaged Sicilian specialities) than what is available online.

- Candied Italian fruit to garnish Sicilian cakes and cookies
- Marmalades (various types)
- Sicilian almond milk
- Sicilian capers, packed in sea salt
- Sicilian honey (various types)
- Sicilian oregano
- Sicilian sun-dried tomatoes
- Squid-ink from Sicily
- Tuna bottarga

CUCUZZASQUASH.COM

Although many farmers' markets and specialty grocery stores now sell Sicilian squash and their tender leaves in the summer months, this website offers an online source for procuring them.

- Sicilian long squash (*cucuzza*), fresh and seeds

DI PALO'S

200 Grand St, New York, NY 10013, USA
+1 212-226-1033

This family-owned historical store in New York's Little Italy neighborhood was first opened over a century ago by the ancestors of the current owners. Known for its wide range of high-quality Italian cheeses and salumi, the shop also carries several specialty gourmet items. This has been my go-to shop in New York since my childhood. I especially appreciated that the owners offer a taste of the products to their customers, making the experience very personal. When in New York City, don't miss a visit to their shop.

- A good selection of Sicilian cheeses
- Italian salumi (Sicilian salumi are not imported to the United States)

EATALY.COM

This mecca (with stores in New York, Chicago, and Boston) carries a wide variety of Sicilian (and other regional Italian) ingredients; visit the stores for fresh pasta, unique condiments, and hard-to-find Sicilian produce like cardoons.

- Chocolate from Modica
- Preserved tuna, packaged in Sicily
- Sicilian almonds
- Sicilian green and black olives, jarred in olive oil
- Pistachios from Bronte, both whole and chopped
- Sardines from Sicily, packed in salt and canned
- Sicilian sea salt
- Dried legumes from Italy (including grass peas, chickpeas, lentils)

GUSTIAMO.COM

This online shop offers high-quality hand-selected ingredients from Italy. In addition to hard to find Sicilian flours, Gustiamo also sells ready-to-use tomato sauce from Sicily.

Remilled semola flour

Tumminia flour

Tumminia flour pasta

Ventresca
(bluefin tuna belly)

NDUJAARTISANS.COM

'Nduja (spicy Calabrian pork spread) and other pork products made in the Midwest with antibiotic and hormone-free Berkshire Pork.

'Nduja Spicy Salame

SEEDS FROM ITALY (WWW.GROWITALIAN.COM)

This online shop offers Italian heritage seeds for wild and cultivated fruits and vegetables. In addition to seeds for two essential Sicilian ingredients—wild fennel and cucuzza (Sicilian squash)—this shop also carries Sicilian purple cauliflower seeds and Sicilian garlic seeds.

Sicilian long squash
(*cucuzza*) seeds

Sicilian finocchietto (wild fennel) seeds

ZABARS.COM

This online shop for the legendary Upper West Side, New York, store carries some unique products including a hand-rolled Tunisian couscous.

Les Moulins Mahjoub
M'hamsa (hand-rolled)
Couscous

Saba (Northern Italian grape must reduction)

ACKNOWLEDGMENTS

During childhood summers spent in my grandmother's native town, Sant'Anna, I started gathering traditional recipes, unknowingly commencing research, in order to share my love of Sicily. I am forever grateful to my parents, John and Josephine, who so generously gave me the greatest gift imaginable when bringing me to Sicily year after year.

My heart would like to thank Feudo Montoni, a land that symbolizes everything I love about life, nature, and Sicily itself. Thank you to the entire family at Feudo Montoni, which has allowed me to finally take part in life in a Sicilian rural environment. Particular thanks to Fabio Sireci and his Mamma Adele, to Zia Franca and her husband, Zio Lino Belliotti, and to Giusy Scaccia.

Fabio Sireci

Thank you to the entire town of Sant'Anna and all of those family and friends who always welcomed me and inspired my love of Sicily. The spark that first ignited my love of food was kindled in the kitchen of my cousin Maria's home. *Grazie* to my cousins: Maria, Accursio, Enza, Nino, Paolo, Giusy, Marilena, Angelica, and Carola. Childhood moments were relived with my best friend, Maria Grazia, when she cooked on multiple occasions for the photo shoots. I'd like to thank the mayor of Caltabellotta, Paolo Segreto, and the mayor of Sant'Anna, Gaspare Sala, for their support of this project.

While there are many professors at Columbia University I credit my learning to, I owe so much to journalism professor Samuel Freedman. In his Book Writing Seminar, this book transformed from an idea into reality. But Sam's contribution to this book didn't stop there, as he followed its trajectory from proposal stage to fruition. Sam introduced me to

cookbook agent Carole Bidnick, to whom I'm indebted for believing in this project from the very start. If not for Carole's expertise, guidance, and deep-rooted familiarity with the publishing industry, this book would not have seen the light of day.

I'm very grateful to the editor of this book, Christopher Steighner, who respected the magnitude of this project from the very beginning and who granted me a platform to represent the splendor of Sicily. Sincere thanks to Aliza Fogelson, who jumped in at the eleventh hour to bring this book to fruition, and to Rizzoli's publisher, Charles Miers. Thank you to the photography team and stylists who shot a slew of photos on multiple trips to New York and Sicily, and to the designer, Toni Tajima, who dedicated so much time to make this book shine.

When gathering tablecloths, plates, and utensils to use for the photographs, I felt touched by being able to use some of my grandma's and her mother's hand-crocheted linens and old china. In addition, stunningly beautiful linens were generously supplied by the Italian company Arichini. Vietri too was so generous to lend their exquisite Italian dishes and serving platters.

On an island where secrecy in personal affairs is considered a virtue, I discovered no such reticence when it came to researching Sicily's food. Everyone from farmers and home cooks to Michelin-starred chefs eagerly shared their stories—and recipes—with me. These recipes are the backbone of this book, juxtaposing old traditions with new ideas, yet as a whole representing Sicilian food today. Thus, the amount of research that went into this book is immense and the number of people who played a role in that research is very long. Particular appreciation goes to: Alfio Garozzo, Mariarita, Christina, and to the Sisters of the Cloistered Monastery of Santo Spirito.

And to all those who read or cook from this book, my hope is that this work inspires you to truly explore Sicily and to taste your *own* way around this magnificent island.

INDEX

(Page references in *italics* refer to illustrations.)